Editorial project:
2022 © **booq** publishing, S.L.
c/ Domènech, 7-9, 2º 1ª
08012 Barcelona, Spain
T: +34 93 268 80 88
www.booqpublishing.com

ISBN: 978-84-9936-690-6

Editorial coordinator:
Claudia Martínez Alonso

Art director:
Mireia Casanovas Soley

Editor:
Francesc Zamora Mola

Layout:
Francesc Zamora Mola
Cristina Simó Perales

Translation:
© **booq** publishing, S.L.

Printing in Spain

MISTY LANDSCAPE, EUGENE, OREGON. © PHILIP SPERANZA

IT, NATURE

Deep green, hundred-foot-tall Douglas firs play hide and seek with white winter mists. Volcanic mountain tops change from white snow caps to earth-brown twice a year. These short and long views of changing natural phenomena shape the boundaries of Architecture in the Pacific Northwest. Its architecture reflects an exploration, not only of a new land but also of a new relationship with the land both physically and metaphorically. During most of the 19th century, It represented the extreme western "edge" of Western civilization.

The architecture of the Pacific Northwest is shaped by both the natural environment and the collective values of its people in a place of frontier mentality. The notion of Thoreau's individual "living off the land" has now given way to collective sustainability, but the underlying values remain essentially the same. From residential architecture to urban planning, traditions of isolation, economic access, and racial exclusion, these cities confront the modernist notion of humans and nature with urgent solutions for humanity as part of nature as one.

This book shares current innovations in single-family, multi-family, accessory dwelling, and commercial building types, organized by over twenty active architectural practices in the Pacific Northwest. It reveals how these architects respond to thinking of the residents they serve, including challenges of affordability, equity, energy conservation, and technological connectivity.

MY, RESPONSIBILITY

Nature affects the individual experience of architecture in the Pacific Northwest most directly in the form of a temperate maritime climate of cold, damp winters and dry, hot summers. Buildings are often executed in local timber, with large areas of high-level glazing used to bring in the diffused winter daylight. Nature is also directly celebrated, with framed views of the landscape and its wild inhabitants, from the creatures of the prairie and forest at Hacker Architects' Columbia Gorge Discovery Center & Historical Museum to eagles and osprey at Maya Lynn's Bird Blind. But its greatest impacts on architecture are often pragmatic and subtle, such as passive environmental controls and wildfire and earthquake resilience.

Most buildings in the Pacific Northwest are located in cities or along rivers or sounds. These locations often offer long orienting views to iconic mountains such as Mount Rainier from downtown Seattle, the North Shore Mountains in central Van-

couver, and Mount Hood from urban Portland. The inhabitants of these cities and many smaller ones across the region are constantly reminded of the close proximity and bucolic call of the wilderness.

Smaller, inland cities such as Bend, Pullman, and Boise, have more days of sunlight and are rapidly growing centers for remote work and retirement. Coastal towns along iconic Highway 101, such as Bandon, Yachats, and Cannon Beach, are smaller and serve as winter retreats and summer resorts, as do the more remote enclaves of the San Juans and Vancouver Island.

Remoteness from the East Coast centers of theory and architectural experimentation has created an unpretentious modern vernacular consisting of wood, shed roofs, and glass. Construction methods borrow from California modernism, but with much more thought given to rain and daylight. Summer and winter present sharply contrasting sunlight, rainfall, and wind conditions that present rich opportunities for passive environmental design. The phenomena of subtly changing daylight are deliberately explored, for example, in Steven Holl's well-known St. Ignatius Chapel in Seattle.

Asian influence can be seen in the way nature is architecturally celebrated, through devices such as rain gardens, curated landscapes, and the melting of the boundary between inside and out seen at The Shire built landscape by John Yeon and the work of Seattle's Olson Kundig. In urban districts, such as Portland's historically African American Albina neighborhood, porches are not merely rain shelters, however, but also a key means of connecting home and the street, family and community.

The lumber industry has affected the development of entire northwest towns. But conflicts between imported cultural traditions and contemporary natural challenges are now exemplified by wood-burning and air pollution in rural towns, further exacerbated over the last decade by increasingly fierce wildfires. Movements to ban fossil fuels and reduce energy usage through passive environmental design are burgeoning across the region. Sustainable design strategies embrace technological advances in metals, plastics, and other materials such as thermally discontinuous metal doors and windows, and high-efficiency unplasticized poly-vinyl chloride windows, produced by Innotech of Vancouver, British Columbia. Innovations in mass wood construction are also being advanced as the lumber industry pivots to smaller, faster-grown timber for use in engineered wood technologies such as cross-laminated timber.

WATZEK HOUSE WITH MOUNT HOOD IN THE BACKGROUND.
© JOHN YEON ARCHIVES

CONTRADICTIONS IN GROWTH. SEATTLE, WASHINGTON. © IVAN KOSTIC

OUR, RESPONSIBILITY

The 1999 Seattle World Trade Organization protests demanding workers' rights, sustainable economies, and environmental and social issues, marked one of the great public demonstrations for Green rights in the history of North America. The economic region of Cascadia, as the Pacific Northwest is described by urbanist Richard Florida, grew exponentially during and after WWII as a strategic center for aerospace and defense (Boeing and Raytheon), computing (Microsoft and Intel), and more recently sportswear (Nike, Columbia, Adidas North America, and REI), e-commerce (Amazon) and the filmmaking (Vancouver, British Columbia). The prosperity this has generated, coupled with cries in places like Seattle to protect the 80% single-family zoning of legal housing land use and urban growth boundaries in Oregon and geographic limits in Seattle and Vancouver, has created a housing availability and affordability crisis. While other North American West Coast cities sprawl, measures like Oregon's House Bill 2001 effectively making single-family illegal represent a necessary acknowledgment that a typological break toward more sustainable higher density is vital.

Most Pacific Northwest cities have liberal policies supporting social welfare systems, but the overwhelmingly white culture has a history of segregation and displacement of Black, Indigenous and People of color. It is now a major destination for migratory Latinos escaping unaffordable Californian cities and is host to some of the fiercest racial justice protests of 2021. The result has been an urgent call for innovative affordable housing design, acknowledgment of racist "redlining" that denied mortgages to minorities, and active support of minority-owned business activities.

At the leading edge of confronting global climate change, the region is facing unprecedented local environmental challenges in the form of wildfires and air pollution. Cities that historically had the lowest national air quality indexes for pollen because of the region's long-established grass seed industry are now enacting policies banning fossil fuels and incentives for green and sustainable building construction. Public transit systems continue to grow to support regional infrastructure efficiency. The region wants to make a statement to the world at large that the time to change individual and cultural habits has come.

THEIR (ARCHITECTS), RESPONSIBILITIES

The Pacific Northwest's most progressive architectural practices combine innovative wood construction with community-engaged affordable housing. The reduction of energy costs over the building's life and the integration of performative passive house strategies such as rainscreens, efficient doors and windows, enhanced insulation, and careful solar orientation have all become strategies not just for high-end living but the broader spectrum of housing types.

The works featured in this book include sustainable single-family housing, multi-family, and mixed-use developments supporting social equity and cultural diversity; also accessory dwelling units making affordable housing available without increasing infrastructure costs or enlarging cities. The practices included range from established firms working at the scale of urban design to newcomers speculating on alternative ways to approach problems that have eluded solutions by traditional methods. The practices embrace new technologies to enhance the human experience in balance with local climates and landscapes. Emerging sustainable design processes are increasingly using computing analytics to reduce energy and carbon use, utilizing daylighting and weather analysis, and coupling simulation and computer fabrication with Building Information Modeling (BIM) software. Mobile apps and embedded sensor technologies inform heating and cooling habits, connect remote work activities, and apprise people to open windows and doors. Pacific Northwest cities are leaders in making geospatial information systems for planning, mass transit, and everyday use accessible to the public. Meanwhile, online services like Seattle-based Walk Score, Bike Score, and Transit Score use index algorithms to allow responsible behaviors. Social community services empower social equity movements, while online homestay services allow flexible housing types despite slow-changing zoning codes. The region's name "Silicon Forest" reflects technological innovation with green values, specifically ever finer-grained differences of space and time that connect people to nature.

Pacific Northwest architects and their works illustrated in this book vary widely, but four characteristics emerge: 1) Pragmatism, emphasizing affordability, building, economics, and practical methods; 2) Data-driven Design, based on user and climate-informed design processes and integration; 3) Sustainability, focusing on green, holistic, low-carbon, and mass timber solutions; and 4) Responsibility, stressing the importance of community, social collaboration, and radical action.

Philip Speranza, Registered Architect OR, NY, and CA.

DIESE, NATUR

Tiefgrüne Douglasien, die Hunderte von Metern hoch sind, spielen Verstecken mit dem Winternebel. Die vulkanischen Berggipfel wechseln zweimal im Jahr von weiß zu erdigem Braun. Diese kurzen und langen Einblicke in die sich verändernden Naturphänomene prägen die Grenzen der Architektur im pazifischen Nordwesten. Ihre Architektur spiegelt nicht nur die Erkundung eines neuen Landes wider, sondern auch eine neue Beziehung zu diesem Land, sowohl physisch als auch metaphorisch. Während des größten Teils des 19. Jahrhunderts war sie der westliche Rand der westlichen Zivilisation.

Die Architektur des pazifischen Nordwestens ist sowohl von der natürlichen Umgebung als auch von den kollektiven Werten der Menschen in einem Gebiet mit Grenzlandmentalität geprägt. Thoreaus individuelle Vorstellung vom „Leben auf dem Land" ist der kollektiven Nachhaltigkeit gewichen, aber die zugrunde liegenden Werte sind im Wesentlichen dieselben geblieben. Von der Wohnarchitektur bis hin zur Stadtplanung, den Traditionen der Isolation, dem wirtschaftlichen Zugang und der rassischen Ausgrenzung konfrontieren diese Städte die modernistische Vorstellung von Mensch und Natur mit dringenden Lösungen, damit die Menschheit Teil der Natur als Ganzes wird.

In diesem Buch werden die aktuellen Innovationen von mehr als zwanzig Architekturbüros aus dem pazifischen Nordwesten in den Bereichen Einfamilienhäuser, Mehrfamilienhäuser, Nebengebäude und Gewerbebauten vorgestellt. Sie zeigt, wie diese Architekten auf die Vorstellungen der Bewohner reagieren, denen sie dienen, einschließlich der Herausforderungen der Erschwinglichkeit, der Gerechtigkeit, der Energieeinsparung und der technologischen Konnektivität.

MEINE, VERANTWORTUNG

Die Natur beeinflusst die individuelle Erfahrung der Architektur im pazifischen Nordwesten am unmittelbarsten in Form eines gemäßigten maritimen Klimas mit kalten, nassen Wintern und heißen, trockenen Sommern. Die Gebäude sind oft aus einheimischem Holz gebaut, und große Glasflächen lassen diffuses Winterlicht herein.

Die Natur wird auch direkt genossen, mit gerahmten Ansichten der Landschaft und ihrer wilden Bewohner, von den Prärie- und Waldtieren im Columbia Gorge Discovery Center & Historical Museum von Hacker Architects bis zu den Adlern und Fischadlern in Maya Lynn's Bird Blind. Die größte Auswirkung auf die Architektur haben sie jedoch oft auf pragmatische und subtile Weise, z. B. durch passive Umweltkontrollen und Widerstandsfähigkeit gegen Waldbrände und Erdbeben.

Die meisten Gebäude im pazifischen Nordwesten befinden sich in Städten, an Flüssen oder in Meeresgebieten. Von diesen Standorten aus bietet sich oft ein weitreichender Blick auf ikonische Berge wie den Mount Rainier in der Innenstadt von Seattle, die North Shore Mountains in der Innenstadt von Vancouver und den Mount Hood in der Stadt Portland. Die

Bewohner dieser und vieler kleinerer Städte in der Region werden ständig an die Nähe und den bukolischen Ruf der Wildnis erinnert.

Kleinere Städte im Landesinneren, wie Bend, Pullman und Boise, haben mehr Sonnentage und sind schnell wachsende Arbeits- und Alterszentren. Kleinere Küstenstädte entlang des berühmten Highway 101 wie Bandon, Yachats und Cannon Beach dienen als Winter- und Sommerfrische, ebenso wie die abgelegeneren Enklaven der San Juans und Vancouver Island. Die Abgeschiedenheit von den Zentren der Architekturtheorie und -experiment an der Ostküste hat eine moderne, unprätentiöse Bauweise aus Holz, Dächern und Glas hervorgebracht. Die Bauweise ist vom kalifornischen Modernismus inspiriert, aber mit viel mehr Aufmerksamkeit für Regen und Tageslicht. Sommer und Winter bieten einen starken Kontrast zwischen Sonneneinstrahlung, Regen und Wind, was eine großartige Gelegenheit für eine passive Umweltgestaltung darstellt. Die Phänomene des sich subtil verändernden Tageslichts werden zum Beispiel in Steven Holls bekannter St. Ignatius Chapel in Seattle bewusst erforscht.

Der asiatische Einfluss zeigt sich in der Art und Weise, wie die Natur architektonisch zelebriert wird, z. B. durch Regengärten, Landschaftsprojekte und die Verwischung der Grenze zwischen drinnen und draußen, wie sie in der von John Yeon in The Shire und von Olson Kundig in Seattle gebauten Landschaft zu sehen ist. In Stadtvierteln wie dem historisch afroamerikanischen Albina-Viertel in Portland sind Veranden nicht nur ein Schutz vor Regen, sondern auch ein wichtiges Mittel, um Haus und Straße, Familie und Gemeinschaft miteinander zu verbinden.

Die Holzfällerindustrie hat die Entwicklung ganzer Städte im Nordwesten beeinflusst. Doch die Konflikte zwischen importierten kulturellen Traditionen und den natürlichen Herausforderungen der Gegenwart zeigen sich heute beispielhaft in der Holzverbrennung und der Luftverschmutzung in ländlichen Dörfern, die im letzten Jahrzehnt durch immer heftigere Waldbrände noch verschärft wurde. Überall in der Region gibt es Bestrebungen, fossile Brennstoffe zu verbannen und den Energieverbrauch durch passives Umweltdesign zu senken. Nachhaltige Designstrategien umfassen technologische Fortschritte bei Metallen, Kunststoffen und anderen Materialien, wie z. B. thermisch diskontinuierliche Metalltüren und -fenster und hocheffiziente Fenster aus weichmacherfreiem Polyvinylchlorid, die von Innotech in Vancouver, British Columbia, hergestellt werden. Die Innovationen im Holzbau schreiten ebenfalls voran, da sich die Holzindustrie auf kleinere, schneller wachsende Hölzer für den Einsatz in technischen Technologien, wie z. B. Brettsperrholz, verlegt.

UNSERE, VERANTWORTUNG

Die Proteste in Seattle 1999 gegen die Welthandelsorganisation, bei denen die Rechte der Arbeitnehmer, eine nachhaltige Wirtschaft sowie ökologische und soziale Belange gefordert wurden, waren eine der größten öffentlichen Demonstrationen für grüne Rechte in der Geschichte Nordamerikas. Die Wirtschaftsregion Cascadia, wie sie der Stadtplaner Richard Florida im pazifischen Nordwesten beschreibt, wuchs während und nach dem Zweiten Weltkrieg exponentiell als strategisches Zentrum für Luft- und Raumfahrt und Verteidigung (Boeing und Raytheon), Computertechnik (Microsoft und Intel) und in jüngerer Zeit für Sportbekleidung (Nike, Columbia, Adidas North America und REI), E-Commerce (Amazon) und Filmherstellung (Vancouver, British Columbia). Der daraus resultierende Wohlstand hat in Verbindung mit dem Ruf in Orten wie Seattle, 80 % der legalen Landnutzung für Einfamilienhäuser zu schützen, sowie mit den städtischen Wachstumsgrenzen in Oregon und den geografischen Grenzen in Seattle und Vancouver zu einer Krise der Verfügbarkeit und Erschwinglichkeit von Wohnraum geführt. Während andere Städte an der amerikanischen Westküste expandieren, stellen Maßnahmen wie Oregons House Bill 2001, die Einfamilienhäuser illegal macht, eine notwendige Anerkennung der Tatsache dar, dass ein typologischer Bruch hin zu einer größeren nachhaltigen Dichte unerlässlich ist.

Die meisten Städte im pazifischen Nordwesten haben eine liberale Politik, die Wohlfahrtssysteme unterstützt, aber die überwiegend weiße Kultur hat eine Geschichte der Segregation und Verdrängung von Schwarzen, Ureinwohnern und Farbigen. Sie ist heute ein wichtiges Ziel für Latinos, die aus den unbezahlbaren kalifornischen Städten fliehen, und ist Schauplatz einiger der heftigsten Proteste gegen Rassismus im Jahr 2021. Das Ergebnis war ein dringender Ruf nach innovativer Gestaltung von erschwinglichem Wohnraum, die Anerkennung rassistischer „roter Linien", die Minderheiten Hypotheken verweigerten, und die aktive Unterstützung des Unternehmertums von Minderheiten.

Die Region steht an vorderster Front im Kampf gegen den globalen Klimawandel und sieht sich gleichzeitig mit noch nie dagewesenen lokalen Umweltproblemen wie Waldbränden und Luftverschmutzung konfrontiert. Städte, die in der Vergangenheit aufgrund der etablierten Grassamenindustrie in der Region die niedrigsten nationalen Luftqualitätswerte für Pollen aufwiesen, erlassen nun Maßnahmen, die fossile Brennstoffe verbieten und Anreize für den Bau grüner und nachhaltiger Gebäude schaffen. Die öffentlichen Verkehrssysteme werden weiter ausgebaut, um die Effizienz der regionalen Infrastruktur zu unterstützen. Die Region möchte der ganzen Welt zeigen, dass es an der Zeit ist, individuelle und kulturelle Gewohnheiten zu ändern.

IHRE (ARCHITEKTEN), VERANTWORTLICHKEITEN

Die fortschrittlichsten Architekturbüros des pazifischen Nordwestens kombinieren innovative Holzbauweise mit erschwinglichem Wohnraum für die Allgemeinheit. Die Senkung der Energiekosten über die gesamte Lebensdauer des Gebäudes und die Integration von Passivhaus-Strategien wie Regenschutz, effiziente Türen und Fenster, verbesserte Isolierung und sorgfältige Sonnenausrichtung sind zu Strategien nicht nur für den gehobenen Wohnungsbau, sondern für das breiteste Spektrum von Wohnformen geworden.

Die in diesem Buch versammelten Arbeiten der Architekten umfassen nachhaltige Einfamilienhäuser, Mehrfamilienhäuser und gemischt genutzte Gebäude, die neue Strategien zur Förderung von sozialer Gerechtigkeit und kultureller Vielfalt vorstellen, sowie zusätzliche Wohneinheiten, die das Wohnen erschwinglich machen, ohne die Infrastrukturkosten zu erhöhen oder die Städte zu vergrößern. Die teilnehmenden Studios reichen von etablierten Firmen, die auf der Ebene der Stadtplanung arbeiten, bis hin zu Newcomern, die über alternative Wege zur Lösung von Problemen nachdenken, die sich den traditionellen Methoden entzogen haben.

Architekten setzen neue Technologien ein, um die menschliche Erfahrung im Einklang mit dem lokalen Klima und der Landschaft zu verbessern. Neue nachhaltige Entwurfsprozesse nutzen zunehmend Computeranalysen zur Senkung des Energie- und Kohlenstoffverbrauchs, verwenden Tageslicht- und Wetteranalysen und koppeln Computersimulation und Fertigung mit Software zur Gebäudedatenmodellierung (BIM). Mobile Apps und eingebettete Sensortechnologien melden die Heiz- und Kühlgewohnheiten, stellen die Verbindung zu den Arbeitsplätzen her und informieren die Menschen, wenn sie Fenster und Türen öffnen sollen. Die Städte im pazifischen Nordwesten sind Vorreiter bei der Bereitstellung von Geoinformationssystemen für die Öffentlichkeit in den Bereichen Planung, öffentlicher Verkehr und Alltagsnutzung. Online-Dienste wie „Walk Score", „Bike Score" und „Transit Score" aus Seattle nutzen Indexalgorithmen, um verantwortungsbewusstes Verhalten zu fördern. Sozialdienste auf Gemeindeebene stärken auch die Bewegungen für soziale Gerechtigkeit, während über das Internet verfügbare Wohnungsdienstleistungen trotz langsamer Änderungen der Bauvorschriften flexible Wohnformen ermöglichen. Der Name der Region, „Silicon Forest", spiegelt technologische Innovation mit ökologischen Werten wider, insbesondere die immer feineren räumlichen und zeitlichen Unterschiede, die den Menschen mit der Natur verbinden.

Die in diesem Buch vorgestellten Architekten aus dem pazifischen Nordwesten und ihre Werke sind sehr unterschiedlich, aber vier gemeinsame Merkmale zeichnen sich ab: 1) Pragmatismus, der den Schwerpunkt auf Erschwinglichkeit, Bauweise, Wirtschaftlichkeit und praktische Methoden legt; 2) datengesteuertes Design, das sich auf nutzer- und klimainformierte Design- und Integrationsprozesse stützt; 3) Nachhaltigkeit, die sich auf grüne, ganzheitliche, kohlenstoffarme und massive Holzlösungen konzentriert; und 4) Verantwortung, die die Bedeutung von Gemeinschaft, sozialer Zusammenarbeit und radikalem Handeln betont.

Philip Speranza, eingetragener Architekt OR, NY und CA.

ELLE, NATURE

Des sapins de Douglas d'un vert profond, hauts de plusieurs centaines de mètres, jouent à cache-cache avec les brumes hivernales. Les sommets des montagnes volcaniques passent du blanc au brun terreux deux fois par an. Ces aperçus, courts et longs, de phénomènes naturels changeants façonnent les limites de l'architecture dans le nord-ouest du Pacifique. Leur architecture reflète l'exploration, non seulement d'une nouvelle terre, mais aussi d'une nouvelle relation à la terre, tant physiquement que métaphoriquement. Pendant la majeure partie du XIXe siècle, elle a représenté l'extrémité occidentale de la civilisation occidentale.

L'architecture du nord-ouest du Pacifique est façonnée à la fois par l'environnement naturel et par les valeurs collectives de ses habitants à l'esprit frontalier. La notion individuelle de « vivre de la terre » de Thoreau a cédé la place à la durabilité collective, mais les valeurs sous-jacentes restent essentiellement les mêmes. De l'architecture résidentielle à l'urbanisme, en passant par les traditions d'isolement, l'accès économique et l'exclusion raciale, ces villes confrontent la notion moderniste de l'homme et de la nature à des solutions urgentes pour que l'humanité fasse partie de la nature dans son ensemble.

Ce livre présente les innovations actuelles en matière de bâtiments unifamiliaux, multifamiliaux, de logements accessoires et de bâtiments commerciaux organisés par plus de vingt cabinets d'architectes actifs dans le nord-ouest du Pacifique. Il révèle comment ces architectes répondent à la pensée des résidents qu'ils servent, y compris les défis de l'abordabilité, de l'équité, de la conservation de l'énergie et de la connectivité technologique.

MA, RESPONSABILITÉ

La nature affecte l'expérience individuelle de l'architecture dans le nord-ouest du Pacifique de la manière la plus directe sous la forme d'un climat maritime tempéré avec des hivers froids et humides et des étés chauds et secs. Les bâtiments sont souvent construits en bois local et de grandes surfaces vitrées sont utilisées pour laisser entrer la lumière diffuse de l'hiver.

La nature est également appréciée directement, avec des vues encadrées du paysage et de ses habitants sauvages, des créatures de la prairie et des bois du Columbia Gorge Discovery Center & Historical Museum de Hacker Architects aux aigles et aux balbuzards de Maya Lynn's Bird Blind. Mais leur plus grand impact sur l'architecture est souvent pragmatique et subtil, comme les contrôles environnementaux passifs et la résistance aux incendies et aux tremblements de terre.

La plupart des bâtiments du nord-ouest du Pacifique sont situés dans des villes ou le long de rivières ou de zones sonores. Ces lieux offrent souvent des vues à long terme sur des montagnes emblématiques telles que le mont Rainier depuis le centre-ville de Seattle, les North Shore Mountains dans le centre-ville de Vancouver et le mont Hood depuis la ville de Portland. Les habitants de ces villes et de nombreuses autres villes plus petites de la région se souviennent constamment de la proximité et de l'appel bucolique de la nature sauvage.

Les petites villes de l'intérieur, telles que Bend, Pullman et Boise, bénéficient d'un plus grand nombre de jours d'ensoleillement et sont des centres de travail et de retraite à distance en plein essor. Les villes côtières situées le long de l'emblématique route 101, telles que Bandon, Yachats et Cannon Beach, sont plus petites et servent de retraites hivernales et de stations estivales, tout comme les enclaves plus éloignées des San Juans et de l'île de Vancouver.

L'éloignement des centres de théorie et d'expérimentation architecturales de la côte est a donné naissance à un vernaculaire moderne et sans prétention fait de bois, de toits et de verre. Les méthodes de construction sont inspirées du modernisme californien, mais avec beaucoup plus d'attention à la pluie et à la lumière du jour. L'été et l'hiver présentent un fort contraste entre les conditions d'ensoleillement, de pluie et de vent, ce qui offre une grande possibilité de conception environnementale passive. Les phénomènes de changement subtil de la lumière du jour sont délibérément explorés, par exemple, dans la célèbre chapelle St. Ignatius de Steven Holl à Seattle.

L'influence asiatique se manifeste dans la manière dont la nature est célébrée sur le plan architectural, par des dispositifs tels que les jardins de pluie, les projets paysagers et l'effacement de la frontière entre l'intérieur et l'extérieur, que l'on retrouve dans le paysage construit de The Shire par John Yeon et à Seattle par Olson Kundig. Dans les quartiers urbains, comme le quartier historiquement afro-américain d'Albina à Portland, les porches ne sont pas seulement des abris contre la pluie, mais aussi un moyen essentiel de relier la maison et la rue, la famille et la communauté.

L'industrie forestière a affecté le développement de villes entières dans le Nord-Ouest. Mais les conflits entre les traditions culturelles importées et les défis naturels contemporains sont désormais illustrés par la combustion du bois et la pollution de l'air dans les villages ruraux, exacerbées au cours de la dernière décennie par des feux de forêt de plus en plus violents. Des mouvements visant à bannir les combustibles fossiles et à réduire la consommation d'énergie grâce à une conception environnementale passive voient le jour dans toute la région. Les stratégies de conception durable englobent les avancées technologiques dans le domaine des métaux, des plastiques et d'autres matériaux, comme les portes et fenêtres métalliques à rupture thermique et les fenêtres en polychlorure de vinyle non plastifié à haut rendement produites par Innotech de Vancouver, en Colombie-Britannique. Les innovations dans la construction en bois progressent également, car l'industrie du bois s'oriente vers des bois plus petits et à croissance plus rapide pour les technologies d'ingénierie, comme le bois lamellé-croisé.

NOTRE, RESPONSABILITÉ

Les manifestations de 1999 à Seattle contre l'Organisation mondiale du commerce, qui réclamaient des droits pour les travailleurs, des économies durables et des questions environnementales et sociales, ont constitué l'une des plus grandes manifestations publiques pour les droits écologiques de l'histoire de l'Amérique du Nord. La région économique de Cascadia, décrite par l'urbaniste Richard Florida dans le nord-ouest du Pacifique, a connu une croissance exponentielle pendant et après la Seconde Guerre mondiale en tant que centre stratégique pour l'aérospatiale et la défense (Boeing et Raytheon), l'informatique (Microsoft et Intel) et, plus récemment, les vêtements de sport (Nike, Columbia, Adidas North America et REI), le commerce électronique (Amazon) et le cinéma (Vancouver, Colombie-Britannique). La prospérité qu'elle a engendrée, associée aux appels lancés dans des endroits comme Seattle pour protéger le zonage unifamilial de 80 % de l'utilisation légale des terres pour le logement et les limites de croissance urbaine en Oregon et les limites géographiques à Seattle et Vancouver, a créé une crise de la disponibilité et de l'accessibilité des logements. À l'heure où d'autres villes de la côte ouest américaine se développent, des mesures telles que le House Bill 2001 de l'Oregon, qui rend illégal le logement unifamilial, représentent une reconnaissance nécessaire qu'une rupture typologique vers une plus grande densité durable est vitale.

La plupart des villes du nord-ouest du Pacifique ont des politiques libérales qui soutiennent les systèmes d'aide sociale, mais la culture majoritairement blanche a une histoire de ségrégation et de déplacement des Noirs, des populations autochtones et des personnes de couleur. Elle est désormais une destination majeure pour les Latinos qui fuient les villes californiennes inabordables et accueille certaines des manifestations de justice raciale les plus féroces de 2021. Il en résulte un appel urgent à la conception de logements abordables innovants, la reconnaissance des « lignes rouges » racistes qui empêchaient les minorités d'obtenir des prêts hypothécaires, et un soutien actif à l'esprit d'entreprise des minorités.

À l'avant-garde de la lutte contre le changement climatique mondial, la région est confrontée à des défis environnementaux locaux sans précédent, sous la forme de feux de forêt et de pollution atmosphérique. Des villes qui, historiquement, affichaient les taux de qualité de l'air les plus bas au niveau national en ce qui concerne le pollen, en raison de l'industrie des semences de gazon bien établie dans la région, adoptent aujourd'hui des politiques qui interdisent les combustibles fossiles et encouragent la construction de bâtiments verts et durables. Les systèmes de transport public continuent de se développer pour soutenir l'efficacité des infrastructures régionales. La région veut faire savoir au monde entier que le moment est venu de changer les habitudes individuelles et culturelles.

LEURS (ARCHITECTES), RESPONSABILITÉS

Les cabinets d'architectes les plus progressistes du nord-ouest du Pacifique combinent la construction en bois innovante avec des logements abordables pour la communauté. La réduction des coûts énergétiques sur la durée de vie du bâtiment et l'intégration de stratégies de type « maison passive », telles que des pare-pluie, des portes et des fenêtres efficaces, une meilleure isolation et une orientation solaire soignée, sont devenues des stratégies non seulement pour les logements haut de gamme, mais aussi pour le plus large éventail de types de logements.

Les travaux des architectes réunis dans ce livre comprennent des logements unifamiliaux durables, des développements multifamiliaux et à usage mixte qui présentent de nouvelles stratégies favorisant l'équité sociale et la diversité culturelle, ainsi que des logements accessoires qui rendent le logement abordable sans augmenter les coûts d'infrastructure ni étendre les villes. Les studios inclus vont d'entreprises bien établies travaillant à l'échelle de la conception urbaine à de nouveaux venus spéculant sur des façons alternatives d'aborder des problèmes qui ont échappé aux solutions des méthodes traditionnelles.

Les architectes dans leur ensemble adoptent les nouvelles technologies pour améliorer l'expérience humaine en équilibre avec les climats et les paysages locaux. Les nouveaux processus de conception durable font de plus en plus appel à l'analyse informatique pour réduire la consommation d'énergie et de carbone, à l'analyse de l'éclairage naturel et des conditions météorologiques, et au couplage de la simulation et de la fabrication informatiques avec les logiciels de modélisation des informations du bâtiment (BIM). Les applications mobiles et les technologies de capteurs intégrés signalent les habitudes de chauffage et de climatisation, connectent les activités professionnelles à distance et informent les gens de l'ouverture des fenêtres et des portes. Les villes du nord-ouest du Pacifique montrent la voie en rendant les systèmes d'information géospatiale accessibles au public pour la planification, les transports publics et l'utilisation quotidienne. Parallèlement, des services en ligne tels que Walk Score, Bike Score et Transit Score, basé à Seattle, utilisent des algorithmes d'indexation pour encourager les comportements responsables. Les services sociaux communautaires renforcent également les mouvements en faveur de l'équité sociale, tandis que les services de logement disponibles sur l'internet permettent des types de logement flexibles malgré la lenteur des changements dans les codes de zonage. Le nom de la région, « Silicon Forest », reflète l'innovation technologique et les valeurs écologiques, notamment les différences de plus en plus fines entre l'espace et le temps qui relient les gens à la nature.

Les architectes du Nord-Ouest du Pacifique et leurs œuvres illustrées dans ce livre varient considérablement, mais quatre caractéristiques communes se dégagent : 1) le pragmatisme, qui met l'accent sur le caractère abordable, la construction, l'économie et les méthodes pratiques ; 2) la conception axée sur les données, qui s'appuie sur des processus de conception et d'intégration éclairés par l'utilisateur et le climat ; 3) la durabilité, qui met l'accent sur des solutions écologiques, holistiques, à faible émission de carbone et sur le bois de masse ; et 4) la responsabilité, qui souligne l'importance de la communauté, de la collaboration sociale et de l'action radicale.

Philip Speranza, architecte registré OR, NY et CA.

ELLA, LA NATURALEZA

Los abetos de Douglas, de color verde intenso y cientos de metros de altura, juegan al escondite con las nieblas del invierno. Las cimas de las montañas volcánicas cambian de blanco a marrón tierra dos veces al año. Estas visiones cortas y largas de los fenómenos naturales cambiantes conforman los límites de la arquitectura en el noroeste del Pacífico. Su arquitectura refleja una exploración, no solo de una nueva tierra, sino también de una nueva relación con la tierra tanto física como metafóricamente. Durante la mayor parte del siglo XIX, representó el extremo occidental de la civilización occidental.

La arquitectura del noroeste del Pacífico está moldeada tanto por el entorno natural como por los valores colectivos de sus gentes en un lugar de mentalidad fronteriza. La noción individual de Thoreau de «vivir de la tierra» ha dado paso a la sostenibilidad colectiva, pero los valores subyacentes siguen siendo esencialmente los mismos. Desde la arquitectura residencial hasta la planificación urbana, las tradiciones de aislamiento, el acceso económico y la exclusión racial, estas ciudades confrontan la noción modernista de los seres humanos y la naturaleza con soluciones urgentes para que la humanidad forme parte de la naturaleza como un todo.

Este libro comparte las innovaciones actuales en los tipos de edificios unifamiliares, multifamiliares, viviendas accesorias y comerciales, organizados por más de veinte estudios de arquitectura activos en el noroeste del Pacífico. Revela cómo estos arquitectos responden al pensamiento de los residentes a los que sirven, incluyendo los desafíos de asequibilidad, equidad, conservación de energía y conectividad tecnológica.

MI, RESPONSABILIDAD

La naturaleza afecta a la experiencia individual de la arquitectura en el noroeste del Pacífico más directamente en forma de un clima marítimo templado de inviernos fríos y húmedos y veranos secos y calurosos. Los edificios se construyen a menudo con madera de la zona, y se utilizan grandes superficies acristaladas para que entre la luz difusa del invierno.

La naturaleza también se disfruta de forma directa, con vistas enmarcadas del paisaje y sus habitantes salvajes, desde las criaturas de la pradera y el bosque en el Columbia Gorge Discovery Center & Historical Museum de Hacker Architects hasta las águilas y águilas pescadoras en el Bird Blind de Maya Lynn. Pero su mayor impacto en la arquitectura suele ser pragmático y sutil, como los controles ambientales pasivos y la resistencia a los incendios forestales y a los terremotos.

La mayoría de los edificios del noroeste del Pacífico están situados en ciudades o a lo largo de ríos o zonas de sonidos. Estas ubicaciones suelen ofrecer largas vistas orientadas a montañas emblemáticas como el monte Rainier desde el centro de Seattle, las montañas de la costa norte en el centro de Vancouver y el monte Hood desde la zona urbana de Portland. Los habitantes de estas ciudades y de muchas otras más pequeñas de la región recuerdan constantemente la proximidad y la llamada bucólica de los espacios naturales.

Las ciudades más pequeñas del interior, como Bend, Pullman y Boise, tienen más días de luz solar y son centros de trabajo y jubilación a distancia en rápido crecimiento. Las ciudades costeras situadas a lo largo de la emblemática autopista 101, como Bandon, Yachats y Cannon Beach, son más pequeñas y sirven de refugio invernal y de centro turístico de verano, al igual que los enclaves más remotos de los San Juans y la isla de Vancouver.

La lejanía de los centros teóricos y de experimentación arquitectónica de la costa este ha creado una lengua vernácula moderna y sin pretensiones, compuesta por madera, tejados y vidrio. Los métodos de construcción se inspiran en el modernismo californiano, pero con mucha más atención a la lluvia y la luz del día. El verano y el invierno presentan un fuerte contraste entre la luz solar, la lluvia y las condiciones de viento, lo que supone una gran oportunidad para el diseño ambiental pasivo. Los fenómenos de cambio sutil de la luz del día se exploran deliberadamente, por ejemplo, en la conocida capilla de San Ignacio de Steven Holl en Seattle.

La influencia asiática se aprecia en el modo en que se celebra arquitectónicamente la naturaleza, a través de dispositivos como los jardines de lluvia, los proyectos paisajísticos y la fusión del límite entre el interior y el exterior que se observa en el paisaje construido en The Shire por John Yeon y en el de Seattle por Olson Kundig. En los distritos urbanos, como el barrio históricamente afroamericano de Albina, en Portland, los porches no son meros refugios contra la lluvia, sino también un medio clave para conectar el hogar y la calle, la familia y la comunidad.

La industria maderera ha afectado al desarrollo de pueblos enteros del noroeste. Pero los conflictos entre las tradiciones culturales importadas y los desafíos naturales contemporáneos se ejemplifican ahora con la quema de madera y la contaminación atmosférica en los pueblos rurales, agravada en la última década por los incendios forestales cada vez más feroces. En toda la región están surgiendo movimientos para prohibir los combustibles fósiles y reducir el uso de la energía mediante el diseño ambiental pasivo. Las estrategias de diseño sostenible abarcan los avances tecnológicos en metales, plásticos y otros materiales, como las puertas y ventanas metálicas térmicamente discontinuas y las ventanas de cloruro de polivinilo no plastificado de alta eficiencia, producidas por Innotech, de Vancouver (Columbia Británica). Las innovaciones en la construcción de madera también están avanzando a medida que la industria maderera se orienta hacia una de tamaño más pequeño y de crecimiento más rápido para su uso en tecnologías de ingeniería, como la madera laminada cruzada.

NUESTRA, RESPONSABILIDAD

Las protestas de 1999 en Seattle contra la Organización Mundial del Comercio en demanda de los derechos de los trabajadores, economías sostenibles y cuestiones medioambientales y sociales, marcaron una de las grandes manifestaciones públicas por los derechos de los verdes en la historia de Norteamérica. La región económica de Cascadia, como describe el urbanista Richard Florida al noroeste del Pacífico, creció exponencialmente durante y después de la Segunda Guerra Mundial como centro estratégico para la industria aeroespacial y de defensa (Boeing y Raytheon), la informática (Microsoft e Intel) y, más recientemente, la ropa deportiva (Nike, Columbia, Adidas North America y REI), el comercio electrónico (Amazon) y la realización de películas (Vancouver, Columbia Británica). La prosperidad que esto ha generado, unida a los gritos en lugares como Seattle para proteger la zonificación unifamiliar del 80% del uso legal del suelo para viviendas y los límites de crecimiento urbano en Oregón y los límites geográficos en Seattle y Vancouver, ha creado una crisis de disponibilidad y asequibilidad de la vivienda. Mientras que otras ciudades de la costa oeste norteamericana se expanden, medidas como el proyecto de ley 2001 de la Cámara de Representantes de Oregón, que hace ilegal la vivienda unifamiliar, representan un reconocimiento necesario de que es vital una ruptura tipológica hacia una mayor densidad sostenible.

La mayoría de las ciudades del noroeste del Pacífico tienen políticas liberales de apoyo a los sistemas de bienestar social, pero la cultura abrumadoramente blanca tiene una historia de segregación y desplazamiento de negros, indígenas y personas de color. Ahora es un destino importante para los latinos que huyen de las inasequibles ciudades californianas y acoge algunas de las más feroces protestas por la justicia racial de 2021. El resultado ha sido un llamamiento urgente a un diseño innovador de viviendas asequibles, el reconocimiento de las «líneas rojas» racistas que negaban las hipotecas a las minorías y el apoyo activo a las actividades empresariales de las minorías.

A la vanguardia de la lucha contra el cambio climático global, la región se enfrenta a retos medioambientales locales sin precedentes en forma de incendios forestales y contaminación atmosférica. Ciudades que históricamente tenían los índices nacionales más bajos de calidad del aire por el polen, debido a la industria de semillas de hierba establecida en la región, están ahora promulgando políticas que prohíben los combustibles fósiles e incentivan la construcción de edificios verdes y sostenibles. Los sistemas de transporte público siguen creciendo para apoyar la eficiencia de las infraestructuras regionales. La región quiere hacer una declaración al mundo en general de que ha llegado el momento de cambiar los hábitos individuales y culturales.

SUS (ARQUITECTOS), RESPONSABILIDADES

Los estudios de arquitectura más progresistas del noroeste del Pacífico combinan la construcción innovadora en madera con la vivienda asequible para la comunidad. La reducción de los costes energéticos a lo largo de la vida del edificio y la integración de estrategias propias del concepto de Casas Pasiva, como pantallas contra la lluvia, puertas y ventanas eficientes, aislamiento mejorado y una cuidadosa orientación solar, se han convertido en estrategias no solo para la vivienda de alto nivel, sino para el más amplio espectro de tipos de vivienda.

El trabajo de los arquitectos que se recogen en este libro incluye viviendas unifamiliares sostenibles, desarrollos multifamiliares y de uso mixto que presentan nuevas estrategias que apoyan la equidad social y la diversidad cultural, y unidades de vivienda accesorias que hacen que la vivienda sea asequible sin aumentar los costes de infraestructura o ampliar las ciudades. Los estudios incluidos van desde empresas consolidadas que trabajan a escala del diseño urbano hasta los recién llegados que especulan con formas alternativas de abordar problemas que han eludido las soluciones de los métodos tradicionales.

El conjunto de los arquitectos adoptan las nuevas tecnologías para mejorar la experiencia humana en equilibrio con los climas y paisajes locales. Los nuevos procesos de diseño sostenible recurren cada vez más a la analítica informática para reducir el consumo de energía y carbono, utilizando la iluminación natural y el análisis meteorológico, y acoplando la simulación y la fabricación por ordenador con el software de modelado de información de edificios (BIM). Las aplicaciones móviles y las tecnologías de sensores integrados informan sobre los hábitos de calefacción y refrigeración, conectan las actividades laborales a distancia e informan a las personas para que abran las ventanas y las puertas. Las ciudades del noroeste del Pacífico son líderes en hacer accesibles al público los sistemas de información geo espacial para la planificación, el transporte público y el uso cotidiano. Mientras tanto, servicios en línea como Walk Score, Bike Score y Transit Score, con sede en Seattle, utilizan algoritmos de índices para potenciar comportamientos responsables. Los servicios sociales comunitarios también están potenciando los movimientos de equidad social, mientras que los servicios de alojamiento disponibles en internet permiten tipos de vivienda flexibles a pesar de los lentos cambios en los códigos de zonificación. El nombre de la región, «Silicon Forest», refleja la innovación tecnológica con valores ecológicos, concretamente las diferencias cada vez más finas de espacio y tiempo que conectan a las personas con la naturaleza.

Los arquitectos del noroeste del Pacífico y sus obras ilustradas en este libro varían mucho, pero surgen cuatro características comunes: 1) Pragmatismo, que hace hincapié en la asequibilidad, la construcción, la economía y los métodos prácticos; 2) Diseño basado en datos, que se basa en procesos de diseño e integración informados por el usuario y el clima; 3) Sostenibilidad, que se centra en soluciones ecológicas, holísticas, con bajas emisiones de carbono y de madera en masa; y 4) Responsabilidad, que subraya la importancia de la comunidad, la colaboración social y la acción radical.

Philip Speranza, arquitecto registrado en OR, NY y CA.

SPERANZA
ARCHITECTURE + URBAN DESIGN

Architecture and Interior Design:
Philip Speranza, Principal
Architect, Stephen P. Maher,
Matthew Nyweide; Gilberto
Villalobos, Taylor Baek
Structural Engineer:
John Norrena/Johnson
Broderick Engineering
General Contractor:
Tim Stephens/Frontier Builders
Photographers: © Anthony
Holmes, Philip Speranza

Awards:
• 2018 American Institute of
Architects Southwest Oregon
Chapter Honor Award
• 2016 American Institute of
Architects Southwest Oregon
Colleague's Choice Award
• 2016 American Institute
of Architects Southwest
Oregon Single-Family
Residence Award

Architecture and Interior Design:
Philip Speranza, Principal
Architect; Stephen P. Maher,
Garrett Leaver, Daniel Matallana-
Mejiea, Gillian Hevey, Alden Carr
(Landscape Design)
Owner:
Deborah Seidman
Structural Engineer:
Robert Murray/
Murray Engineering PC
Civil Engineering:
Rod Morrison/LRC Group
Ecologist:
Michael Nowicki/
Ecological Solutions
General Contractor:
Kathryn and Mike Whitman/
Quatrefoil Inc
Photographer:
© Philip Speranza

Architecture and Interior Design:
Philip Speranza, Principal
Architect; Ryan Kiesler, Julia
Frost, Kayla Zander, Alden
Carr (landscape design), Allen
Suwardi, Kevin So
Structural Engineer:
Steve Shegedin/
Ang Engineering Group
Photographers:
© Ryan Kiesler, Philip Speranza

Awards:
• 2018 American Institute of
Architects Southwest Oregon,
Citation Award

Architecture and Interior Design:
Philip Speranza, Principal
Architect; Stephen Maher
Architect, Garrett Leaver, Ryan
Kiesler, Valeria Masciotti, Austen
Daich, Gianna Prather, Daniel
Matallana-Mejia, Allen Suwardi,
Betty Lou Poston, Ben Gardner,
Alden Carr
Landscape Architect:
Ignacio López Busón, Maurcio
Villarreal/PLACE Landscape
Architecture
Structural Engineer:
Mike Munzing/
Munzing Engineering
Civil Engineering: Anna Backus/
KPFF Consulting Engineering
Energy Consultant: Mike Hatten/
Solarc Energy Group
Renderings:
© Speranza Architecture
+ Urban Design

Speranza Architecture + Urban Design (SA+UD) aims to bring people closer to the changing natural and social phenomena around them. We believe in the integration of new everyday technologies in both the design process for us and built projects for inhabitants. The firm's data-driven design processes are applied across all scales and building typologies. Data acquisition workflows are used to produce human-scaled site analyses of social and natural phenomena through custom SA+UD sensor arrays that measure sound, light, temperature, and humidity to inform the environmental control of both private, indoor and communal, outdoor spaces. SA+UD was awarded four of nine South West Oregon American Institute of Architects Chapter Awards in 2018 and recently received an Oregon Energy Trust Net-Zero Award. SA+UD has done pro-bono work for both the City of Eugene and for the Kesey Farm Project. In addition to serving as the firm's lead designer, principal Philip Speranza also serves on the editorial board of The Journal of Urban Design.

Speranza Architecture + Urban Design (SA+UD) hat sich zum Ziel gesetzt, den Menschen die sich verändernden natürlichen und sozialen Phänomene ihrer Umgebung näher zu bringen. Wir glauben an die Integration neuer Alltagstechnologien sowohl im Designprozess für uns selbst als auch in den gebauten Projekten für die Bewohner. Die datengesteuerten Designprozesse des Unternehmens werden in allen Maßstäben und Gebäudetypologien angewendet. Datenerfassungs-Workflows werden verwendet, um Standortanalysen sozialer und natürlicher Phänomene im menschlichen Maßstab durch benutzerdefinierte SA+UD-Sensorarrays zu erstellen, die Schall, Licht, Temperatur und Feuchtigkeit messen, um die Umgebungskontrolle von privaten Innen- und Gemeinschaftsräumen im Freien zu informieren. SA+UD erhielt 2018 vier von neun Auszeichnungen des American Institute of Architects of Southwest Oregon und wurde kürzlich mit dem Oregon Energy Trust Net-Zero Award ausgezeichnet. SA+UD hat sowohl für die Stadt Eugene als auch für das Kesey Farm Project gemeinnützige Arbeiten durchgeführt. Philip Speranza ist nicht nur der Hauptdesigner des Unternehmens, sondern auch Mitglied des Redaktionsausschusses des Journal of Urban Design.

Speranza Architecture + Urban Design (SA+UD) vise à rapprocher les gens des phénomènes naturels et sociaux changeants qui les entourent. Nous croyons en l'intégration des nouvelles technologies du quotidien, tant dans le processus de conception pour nous-mêmes que dans les projets construits pour les habitants. Les processus de conception fondés sur les données utilisés par l'entreprise s'appliquent à toutes les échelles et typologies de bâtiments. Les flux de travail d'acquisition de données produisent des analyses de site à l'échelle humaine des phénomènes sociaux et naturels grâce à des capteurs SA+UD personnalisés qui mesurent le son, la lumière, la température et l'humidité pour la surveillance environnementale des espaces extérieurs privés, intérieurs et communautaires. SA+UD a reçu quatre des neuf prix décernés par l'American Institute of Architects of Southwest Oregon en 2018, et récemment un prix Net-Zero de l'Oregon Energy Trust. SA+UD a réalisé des travaux à but non lucratif pour la ville d'Eugene et le Kesey Farm Project. En plus d'être le directeur de l'entreprise, Philip Speranza est également membre du comité de rédaction du Journal of Urban Design.

Speranza Architecture + Urban Design (SA+UD) tiene como objetivo acercar las personas a los cambiantes fenómenos naturales y sociales que les rodean. Creemos en la integración de las nuevas tecnologías cotidianas tanto en el proceso de diseño para nosotros como en los proyectos construidos para los habitantes. Los procesos de diseño basados en datos que usa la empresa se aplican a todas las escalas y tipologías de edificios. Los flujos de trabajo de adquisición de datos generan análisis de lugares a escala humana de fenómenos sociales y naturales a través de sensores SA+UD personalizados que miden el sonido, la luz, la temperatura y la humedad para el control ambiental de espacios exteriores privados, interiores y comunitarios. SA+UD recibió cuatro de los nueve premios del Instituto Americano de Arquitectos del Suroeste de Oregón en 2018, y recientemente un premio Oregon Energy Trust Net-Zero. SA+UD ha realizado trabajos sin animo de lucro tanto para la ciudad de Eugene como para el Kesey Farm Project. Además de ser el diseñador principal de la empresa, Philip Speranza también forma parte del consejo editorial de The Journal of Urban Design.

PUSH PULL HOUSE

Veneta, Oregon, United States // Lot area: 5.58 acres; building area: 1,500 sq ft

The design of this caretaker's residence relates pragmatic habitation with a psychological connection to the natural world. Four squares are assembled and pierced via corner windows. Nature is pushed into the spaces, while the inhabitants feel pulled out toward nature. Changing views through the winter mist and summer shadows is contrasted with the inner stability of the square spaces. Each space rises to a window, bringing in light from all sides. These apertures are operated remotely for passive cooling during the summer months, while radiant slab heating and a wood stove heat the spaces in winter. Other sustainable features include eight-inch-thick insulated walls, metal roofs, and locally-harvested Douglas fir cabinetry. Building information modeling and solar gain analyses achieved a construction cost of $172/sq ft, greatly reducing energy use and allowing below-market-rate rental.

La conception de cette résidence de gardien associe une habitation pragmatique à un lien psychologique avec le monde naturel. Quatre carrés sont assemblés et perforés par des fenêtres dans les coins. La nature est poussée dans les espaces, tandis que les habitants sont attirés par la nature. Les vues changeantes à travers le brouillard d'hiver et les ombres d'été contrastent avec la stabilité intérieure des espaces carrés. Chaque espace s'élève jusqu'à une fenêtre, apportant la lumière de tous les cotés. Ces ouvertures sont actionnées à distance pour un refroidissement passif pendant les mois d'été, tandis qu'un chauffage au sol et un poêle à bois chauffent les espaces en hiver. Parmi les autres caractéristiques durables figurent des murs isolés de 20 centimètres d'épaisseur, des toits métalliques et des armoires en sapin de Douglas d'origine locale. La modélisation des informations sur le bâtiment et les analyses des gains solaires ont permis d'atteindre un coût de construction d'environ 1 720$ le mètre carré, ce qui a considérablement réduit la consommation d'énergie et a permis un loyer inférieur à celui du marché.

Der Entwurf dieses Hausmeisterhauses verbindet pragmatische Wohnlichkeit mit einer psychologischen Verbindung zur Natur. Vier Quadrate werden zusammengesetzt und in den Ecken durch Fenster perforiert. Die Natur wird in die Räume gedrängt, während die Bewohner in die Natur hineingezogen werden. Die wechselnden Ausblicke durch den Winternebel und die sommerlichen Schatten kontrastieren mit der inneren Stabilität der Platzräume. Jeder Raum steigt zu einem Fenster an und bringt Licht von allen Seiten herein. Diese Öffnungen werden ferngesteuert, um in den Sommermonaten eine passive Kühlung zu ermöglichen, während im Winter eine Fußbodenheizung und ein Holzofen die Räume beheizen. Zu den weiteren nachhaltigen Merkmalen gehören 20 cm dicke isolierte Wände, Metalldächer und Schränke aus lokalem Douglasienholz. Gebäudedatenmodellierung und Sonnenertragsanalysen erzielten Baukosten von 1.720$ pro Quadratmeter, was den Energieverbrauch erheblich reduzierte und eine Miete unter dem Marktpreis ermöglichte.

El diseño de esta residencia para vigilante relaciona la vivienda pragmática con una conexión psicológica con el mundo natural. Cuatro cuadrados están ensamblados y perforados por ventanas esquineras. La naturaleza es empujada hacia los espacios, mientras que los habitantes se sienten atraídos hacia la naturaleza. Las vistas cambiantes a través de la niebla invernal y las sombras del verano contrastan con la estabilidad interior. Cada espacio se abre a una ventana que aporta luz de todos los lados. Estas aberturas se accionan a distancia para la refrigeración pasiva durante los meses de verano, mientras que la calefacción por losa radiante y una estufa de leña calientan los espacios en invierno. Otras características sostenibles son los muros aislados de 20 cm de grosor, los tejados metálicos y los armarios de abeto Douglas de origen local. La información modelizada de la construcción y los análisis de la ganancia solar lograron un coste de construcción de unos 1720$ por metro cuadrado, lo que redujo en gran medida el uso de energía y permitió un alquiler por debajo del precio del mercado.

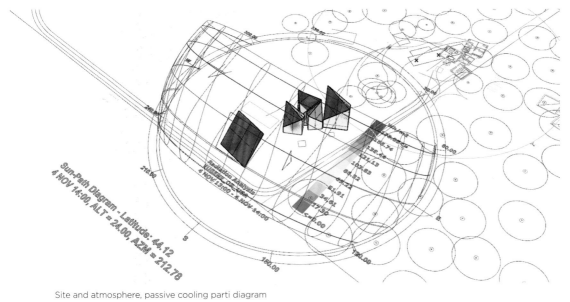

Site and atmosphere, passive cooling parti diagram

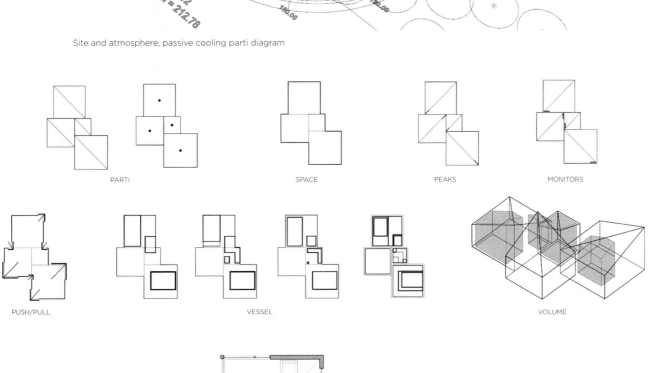

PARTI

SPACE

PEAKS

MONITORS

PUSH/PULL

VESSEL

VOLUME

1. Carport
2. Storage
3. Entry
4. Mudroom
5. Living area
6. Kitchen
7. Bedroom
8. Study
9. Bathroom

Floor plan

HUDSON HOUSE

Hide Park, New York, United States // Lot area: 5.78 acres; building area: 2,944 sq ft

The land was chosen for its northwest winter views of the Hudson River, its southwest views toward the autumn foliage of the Shaupeneak mountains, and its east views—and sounds—of a roaring waterfall. The wrap-around deck and carport around the orthogonal structure follow the natural topography. Careful digital 3D modeling and digitally fabricated models of both grade and underground rock resulted in a design that efficiently met design criteria for a one-story house on a steep rocky hillside. A small third-story volume serves as both a moon-viewing room and solar chimney, drawing cool air from deep below in the summer. High wall and roof insulation, warm tactic radiant floors, and a high-efficiency Danish wood stove warm in winter. Innovative methods using simulation and sensor analysis during design empower user control via remote window operation and heating control during inhabitation.

Le site a été choisi pour ses vues hivernales vers le nord-ouest sur le fleuve Hudson, ses vues vers le sud-ouest sur le feuillage d'automne des montagnes Shaupeneak et ses vues vers l'est, ainsi que le son d'une chute d'eau rugissante. La terrasse enveloppante et le parking autour de la structure orthogonale suivent la topographie naturelle. Une modélisation numérique 3D minutieuse et des modèles fabriqués numériquement du terrain et de la roche souterraine ont permis d'aboutir à une conception répondant efficacement aux critères de conception d'une maison de plain-pied sur une colline rocheuse escarpée. Un petit volume au troisième étage sert à la fois de chambre d'observation de la lune et de cheminée solaire, aspirant l'air frais des étages inférieurs en été. Isolation élevée des murs et du toit, planchers radiants tactiques chauds et poêle à bois danois à haut rendement gardent au chaud en hiver. Des méthodes innovantes utilisant la simulation et l'analyse de capteurs lors de la conception permettent à l'utilisateur de contrôler les fenêtres et le système de chauffage via le fonctionnement à distance.

Der Standort wurde gewählt, weil er im Winter einen Blick nach Nordwesten auf den Hudson River und nach Südwesten auf das Herbstlaub der Shaupeneak Mountains bietet und im Osten einen Blick auf einen tosenden Wasserfall ermöglicht. Das umlaufende Deck und die Parkplätze um die orthogonale Struktur folgen der natürlichen Topografie. Eine sorgfältige digitale 3D-Modellierung und digital angefertigte Modelle des Geländes und des unterirdischen Felsens führten zu einem Entwurf, der die Planungskriterien für ein einstöckiges Haus an einem steilen Felshang tatsächlich erfüllt. Ein kleiner Raum in der dritten Etage dient sowohl als Mondbeobachtungsraum als auch als Sonnenkamin, der im Sommer kühle Luft aus der Tiefe ansaugt. Hohe Wand- und Deckenisolierung, warme taktische Strahlungsböden und ein hocheffizienter dänischer Holzofen halten Sie im Winter warm. Innovative Methoden der Simulation und Sensoranalyse während der Konstruktion ermöglichen es dem Benutzer, die Fenster und das Heizsystem per Fernsteuerung zu steuern.

El terreno se eligió por sus vistas invernales al noroeste del río Hudson, sus vistas al suroeste hacia el follaje otoñal de las montañas Shaupeneak y sus vistas al este, así como el ruido, de una rugiente cascada. La cubierta envolvente y el aparcamiento alrededor de la estructura ortogonal siguen la topografía natural. El cuidadoso modelado digital en 3D y los modelos fabricados digitalmente, tanto del terreno como de la roca subterránea, dieron como resultado un diseño que cumplía eficazmente los criterios de diseño para una casa de una sola planta en una ladera rocosa empinada. Un pequeño volumen en el tercer piso sirve tanto de sala para contemplar la luna como de chimenea solar, extrayendo aire fresco de los pisos inferiores en verano. Alto aislamiento de paredes y techo, pisos radiantes tácticos cálidos y una estufa de leña danesa de alta eficiencia calientan en invierno. Los métodos innovadores utilizados en la simulación y el análisis por sensores durante el diseño permiten al usuario controlar las ventanas y el sistema de calefacción mediante el funcionamiento remoto.

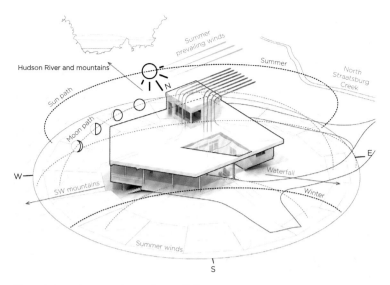

Site and atmosphere, passive cooling parti diagram

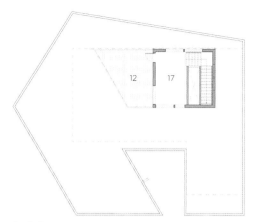

Roof plan

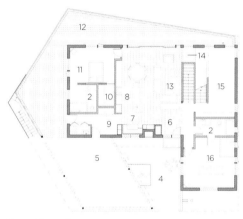

Ground floor plan

Basement floor plan

1. Ceramics Studio
2. Bathroom
3. Storage
4. Entry courtyard
5. Carport
6. Entry
7. Breakfast nook
8. Kitchen
9. Mudroom
10. Closet
11. Master bedroom
12. Deck
13. Living area
14. Reading niche
15. Studio
16. Bedroom
17. Moon room

Site plan

CARVE HOUSE

Eugene, Oregon, United States // Lot area: .135 acres; building area: 3,000 sq ft

A view of the distant Sisters Mountains and the proximity to the University of Oregon and local food stores drove this project. The steep, rocky east-facing slope suggested a four-story tower with a minimal footprint. The volume was broadly oriented to the south, carved back to the ground level, and preserving the site where it reaches the ground. A solar chimney, radiant floors, and a wood stove heat the house during the winter. Metal rain screen siding reflects the changing light conditions. This gritty, durable exterior contrasts with a warm, human-scaled interior of exposed Glulam ceilings, bleached wood floors from site clearing, and entry wood which continue to the roof deck, an "outdoor room" among the treetops. The site is naturally sheltered from the prevailing western winds, while parametric analysis was used to minimize solar gains through window apertures.

La vue sur les lointaines Sisters Mountains et la proximité de l'université de l'Oregon et des épiceries locales sont à l'origine de ce projet. La colline abrupte, rocheuse et orientée vers l'est suggérait une tour de quatre étages avec une empreinte minimale. Le volume a été orienté largement au sud, taillé jusqu'au niveau du sol et préservant le terrain. Une cheminée solaire, planchers radiants et un poêle à bois chauffent la maison pendant l'hiver. Les revêtements pare-pluie métalliques reflètent les conditions de luminosité changeantes. Cet extérieur durable et rugueux contraste avec un intérieur chaleureux et humain, avec des plafonds en bois lamellé-collé exposés, des planchers en bois blanchi provenant du défrichage du terrain, et des poutres d'entrée qui s'étendent jusqu'au toit-terrasse, une « salle en plein air » parmi les cimes des arbres. Le site est naturellement abrité des vents dominants d'ouest, tandis que l'analyse paramétrique a été utilisée pour exploiter les gains solaires à travers les ouvertures des fenêtres.

Der Blick auf die weit entfernten Sisters Mountains und die Nähe zur Universität von Oregon sowie zu den örtlichen Lebensmittelgeschäften gaben den Ausschlag für dieses Projekt. Der steile, felsige, nach Osten ausgerichtete Hang legte einen vierstöckigen Turm mit einer minimalen Grundfläche nahe. Das Volumen war breit nach Süden ausgerichtet, bis zum Bodenniveau zurückgeschnitten und bewahrte die Stelle, an der es den Boden erreicht. Ein Solarkamin, eine Fußbodenheizung und ein Holzofen heizen das Haus im Winter. Regenschutzverkleidungen aus Metall reflektieren die wechselnden Lichtverhältnisse. Dieses robuste, sandfarbene Äußere kontrastiert mit einem warmen, menschlichen Interieur mit freiliegenden Sperrholzdecken, gebleichten Holzböden aus der Rodung und Eingangshölzern, die bis zur Dachterrasse reichen, einem „Freiluftraum" inmitten der Baumkronen. Der Standort ist auf natürliche Weise vor den vorherrschenden Westwinden geschützt, während eine parametrische Analyse verwendet wurde, um die solaren Gewinne durch die Fensteröffnungen zu nutzen.

La vista de las lejanas Sisters Mountains y la proximidad a la Universidad de Oregón y a las tiendas de alimentación locales impulsaron este proyecto. La empinada y rocosa ladera orientada al este sugería una torre de cuatro pisos con una huella mínima. El volumen se orientó ampliamente hacia el sur, se talló hasta el nivel del suelo preservando el terreno. Una chimenea solar, suelos radiantes y una estufa de leña calientan la casa durante el invierno. El revestimiento metálico de protección contra la lluvia refleja la luz cambiante. Este exterior rudo y duradero contrasta con un interior cálido y humano, con techos de madera laminada expuesta, suelos de madera blanqueada procedentes del desmonte del terreno y la madera de la entrada que se prolonga hasta la cubierta del tejado, una «habitación al aire libre» entre las copas de los árboles. El emplazamiento está protegido de forma natural de los vientos predominantes del oeste, mientras que el análisis paramétrico se utilizó para aprovechar los beneficios solares a través de las aberturas de las ventanas.

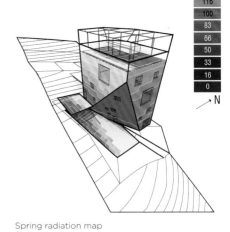

Spring radiation map

Architect, owner, and builder Philip Speranza

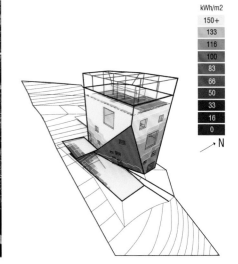

Spring radiation map

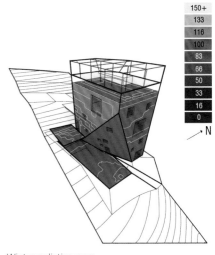

Winter radiation map

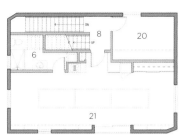

Fourth floor plan

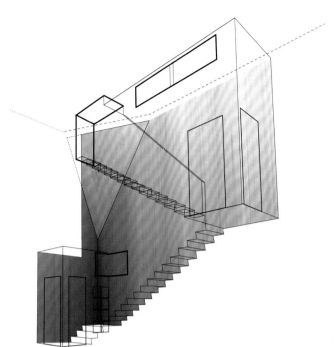

Solar chimney

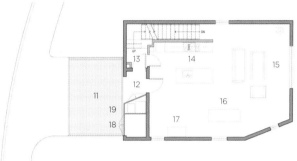

Third floor plan

Second floor plan

06.21 1:00 pm
ALTITUDE: 67.3 DEG
AZIMUTHS: 208.1
HOURLY RADIATION: 196 kW/ft2

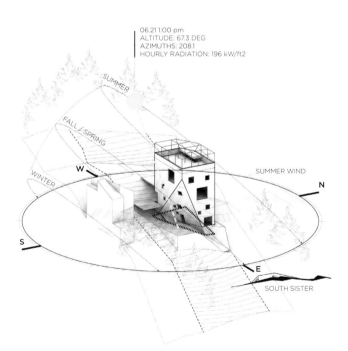

Site and Atmosphere, passive cooling parti diagram

First floor plan

1. Entry
2. Roof water
3. Living area
4. Dining area
5. Bedroom
6. Bathroom
7. Mechanical closet
8. Hallway
9. Master bathroom
10. Master bedroom
11. Bridge
12. Porch
13. Mudroom
14. Kitchen
15. Living area
16. Dining area
17. Study
18. Bike storage
19. Refuse
20. Studio
21. Office

260 FERRY STREET ADAPTIVE REUSE

Eugene, Oregon, United States // Building area: 22,300 sq ft

The adaptive reuse of a two-story board-formed concrete potato chip factory from the 1950s provides a foundation for this downtown mixed-use development part of a decade-long master plan. The site is an iconic mural of Tracktown USA, a reference to Nike's origins in town, and a gateway to downtown Eugene across the Willamette River. Innovative cross-laminate wood floors are used to create south-facing outdoor terraces and provide seismic floor bracing to save the existing concrete walls. The south terraces cantilever efficiently to let in low winter light toward iconic Spencer Butte and covered shading in the summer. The ground floor Beer Hall has covered and heated exterior areas with exposed wood and metal finishes; the second-floor offices are accessed via an interior courtyard open to the sky; and the third and fourth-floor apartments use radiant wood floors and exposed CLT ceilings.

La réutilisation adaptative d'une usine de fabrication de chips en béton de deux étages datant des années 1950 constitue la base de ce projet à usage mixte dans le centre-ville, qui fait partie d'un plan directeur de dix ans. Le site est une peinture murale emblématique de Tracktown USA, une référence aux origines de Nike dans la ville, et une passerelle vers le centre-ville d'Eugene, de l'autre côté de la rivière Willamette. Un platelage innovant en bois lamellé-croisé est utilisé pour créer des terrasses extérieures orientées vers le sud et pour fournir un contreventement sismique aux murs en béton existants. Les terrasses du côté sud sont en porte-à-faux pour laisser entrer la lumière hivernale dans l'emblématique Spencer Butte et pour fournir de l'ombre en été. La salle de brasserie du rez-de-chaussée comporte des espaces extérieurs couverts et chauffés, ainsi que des finitions en bois et en métal exposées. L'accès aux bureaux du premier étage se fait par une cour intérieure ouverte. Les appartements des troisième et quatrième étages sont équipés d'un chauffage au sol et de plafonds apparents en CLT.

Die adaptive Umnutzung einer zweistöckigen Betonknusperfabrik aus den 1950er Jahren bildet die Grundlage für dieses Projekt mit gemischter Nutzung im Stadtzentrum, das Teil eines jahrzehntelangen Masterplans ist. Der Standort ist ein ikonisches Wandgemälde von Tracktown USA, ein Verweis auf die Ursprünge von Nike in der Stadt, und ein Tor zur Innenstadt von Eugene über den Willamette River. Innovative Brettsperrholzbeläge werden zur Schaffung von nach Süden ausgerichteten Außenterrassen und zur seismischen Aussteifung zur Überbrückung der bestehenden Betonwände verwendet. Die Terrassen auf der Südseite sind auskragend, um im Winter Licht in den ikonischen Spencer Butte zu lassen und im Sommer Schatten zu spenden. Der Zugang zu den Büros im ersten Stock erfolgt über einen offenen Innenhof. Die Wohnungen im dritten und vierten Stock verfügen über eine Fußbodenheizung und sichtbare CLT-Decken.

La reutilización adaptada de una fábrica de patatas fritas de dos plantas hecha de hormigón durante la década de 1950 proporciona una base para este proyecto de uso mixto en el centro de la ciudad que forma parte de un plan maestro de una década de duración. El lugar es un mural icónico de Tracktown USA, una referencia a los orígenes de Nike en la ciudad, y una puerta de entrada al centro de Eugene a través del río Willamette. Los innovadores suelos de madera laminada cruzada se utilizan para crear terrazas exteriores orientadas al sur y proporcionan un refuerzo sísmico para salvar los muros de hormigón existentes. Las terrazas del lado sur están en voladizo para dejar pasar la luz del invierno hacia el emblemático Spencer Butte y para cubrir de sombra en verano. El Beer Hall de la planta baja cuenta con zonas exteriores cubiertas y con calefacción, y acabados de madera y metal a la vista. A las oficinas de la segunda planta se accede a través de un patio interior abierto. Los apartamentos de la tercera y cuarta planta utilizan suelos de madera radiante y techos de CLT a la vista.

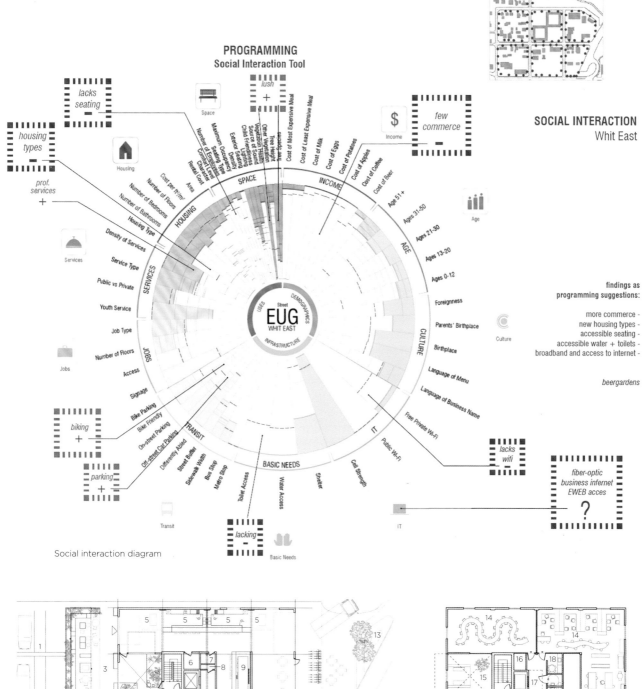

PROGRAMMING
Social Interaction Tool

lush
+

Space

lacks seating

housing types

prof. services
+

Housing

Services

few commerce

$
Income

Jobs

Transit

biking
+

parking
+

Street
EUG
WHIT EAST

USES

DEMOGRAPHICS

INFRASTRUCTURE

SPACE

INCOME

AGE

CULTURE

IT

BASIC NEEDS

HOUSING

SERVICES

JOBS

TRANSIT

Area
Rental Cost
Cost per m²/m²
Number of Floors
Number of Bedrooms
Number of Bathrooms
Housing Type
Density of Services
Service Type
Public vs Private
Youth Service
Job Type
Number of Floors
Access
Signage
Bike Parking
Bike Friendly
On-street Car Parking
Off-street Car Parking
Differently Abled
Street Buffer
Sidewalk Width
Bus Stop
Metro Stop
Toilet Access
Water Access
Shelter
Cell Strength
Public Wi-Fi
Free Private Wi-Fi
Language of Business Name
Language of Menu
Birthplace
Parents' Birthplace
Foreignness
Ages 0-12
Ages 13-20
Ages 21-30
Ages 31-50
Age 51 +
Cost of Beer
Cost of Coffee
Cost of Apples
Cost of Potatoes
Cost of Eggs
Cost of Milk
Cost of Least Expensive Meal
Cost of Most Expensive Meal
Tree Height
Other Vegetation
Source of Sound
Child Friendliness
Lighting
Seating Type
Maximum Occupancy
Number of Employees
Comfort Level
Character
Exterior Seating
Seating Density

Age

Culture

lacks wifi

IT

?

fiber-optic business infernet EWEB acces

lacking
−

Basic Needs

Social interaction diagram

findings as programming suggestions:

more commerce -
new housing types -
accessible seating -
accessible water + toilets -
broadband and access to internet -

beergardens

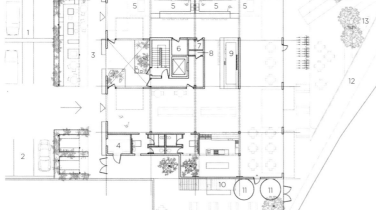

Ground floor plan (Wrap-around jungle)

Second floor plan

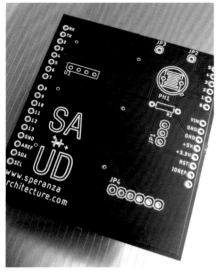

Custom sensor board

Entry courtyard

Walnut model, vicinity urban design

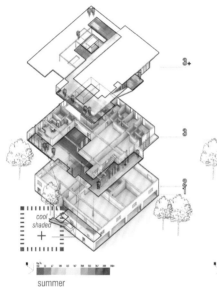

Thermal analysis

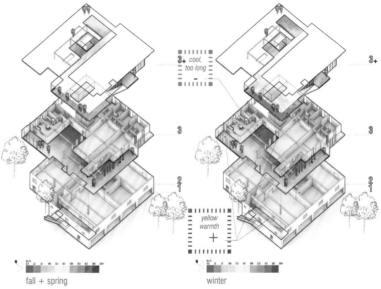

summer

fall + spring

winter

Third floor plan

Fourth floor plan

1. ADA parking
2. Parking
3. 6'-thoroughfare
4. Storage/mechanical
5. Vendor
6. Mechanical/fire
7. Kegs
8. Storage
9. Beer stand
10. Serving
11. Water cistern
12. 4'-sound barrier
13. Mound
14. Office
15. Open to above
16. Mechanical
17. Elevator lobby
18. Kitchen
19. Terrace
20. Open to below
21. Community terrace and egress
22. Dining area
23. Living area
24. Study/sleep
25. Bedroom
26. Green roof
27. Chase storage

DeForest Architects

032
∨

036
∨

040
∨

ORCAS ISLAND RETREAT

Architecture Design team:
John DeForest and Rosie Donovan
Interior Designer:
NB Design Group
Landscape Designer:
Allworth Design
Owner's Rep.:
Alison Kartiganer
General Contractor:
Krekow Jennings
Photographer:
© Tim Bies

HIGH DESERT MODERN

Architecture Design Team:
John DeForest and Ted Cameron
Interior Designer:
NB Design Group
General Contractor:
Doug Young Construction Company
Photographer:
© John Granen

TREE HOUSE

Architecture Design team:
John DeForest and Michael Knowles
Interior Designer:
Ore Studios
General Contractor:
Toth Construction
Photographer:
© Haris Kenjar

John DeForest   Brett Smith

DeForest Architects believes that the best design starts by understanding—and caring about—what matters to its clients. Many firms focus on the "what" of design; DeForest is equally interested in the who, how, and why. In addition to designing meaningful places to live and work, DA architects see themselves as personal guides to great adventures in design. DA brings experience to each project that is broad and deep. Rather than limiting themselves to a particular style, the firm approaches each project with open minds, a fresh eye, and avid curiosity. In the end, their projects look different because every client and site is different. Thanks to new technologies, DA now brings its interactive, hands-on approach to a variety of projects across the United States. From the Pacific Northwest to upstate New York, from the Sierras to Sun Valley, from Iowa heartland to the shores of Lake Michigan, DeForest brings its inventive spirit and client-inspired process to every project.

DeForest Architects ist davon überzeugt, dass die beste Gestaltung damit beginnt, dass man versteht und sich darum kümmert, was für seine Kunden wichtig ist. Viele Firmen konzentrieren sich auf das „Was" des Designs; DeForest interessiert sich gleichermaßen für das „Wer", das „Wie" und das „Warum". Neben der Gestaltung sinnvoller Lebens- und Arbeitsräume verstehen sich DA-Architekten auch als persönliche Wegweiser zu großen Designabenteuern. DA bringt in jedes Projekt eine breite und tiefe Erfahrung ein. Anstatt sich auf einen bestimmten Stil zu beschränken, geht das Unternehmen jedes Projekt mit einem offenen Geist, einem frischen Blick und einer großen Neugierde an. Schließlich sind ihre Projekte unterschiedlich, weil jeder Kunde und jeder Standort anders ist. Dank neuer Technologien bringt DA nun seinen interaktiven, praktischen Ansatz in eine Vielzahl von Projekten in den Vereinigten Staaten ein. Vom pazifischen Nordwesten bis ins Hinterland von New York, von den Sierras bis zum Sun Valley, vom Herzen Iowas bis zu den Ufern des Michigansees - DeForest bringt seinen Erfindergeist und seine vom Kunden inspirierten Prozesse in jedes Projekt ein.

DeForest Architects estime que la meilleure conception commence par la compréhension et la prise en compte de ce qui compte pour ses clients. De nombreuses entreprises se concentrent sur le « quoi » du design ; DeForest s'intéresse également au « qui », au « comment » et au « pourquoi ». En plus de concevoir des lieux où il fait bon vivre et travailler, les architectes DA se considèrent comme des guides personnels pour de grandes aventures de design. DA apporte à chaque projet une vaste et profonde expérience. Plutôt que de se limiter à un style particulier, le cabinet aborde chaque projet avec un esprit ouvert, un regard neuf et une curiosité avide. Au final, leurs projets sont différents car chaque client et chaque lieu sont différents. Grâce aux nouvelles technologies, DA apporte désormais son approche interactive et pratique à une variété de projets à travers les États-Unis. Du Pacifique Nord-Ouest au nord de l'État de New York, des Sierras à Sun Valley, du cœur de l'Iowa aux rives du lac Michigan, DeForest apporte à chaque projet son esprit inventif et son processus inspiré par le client.

DeForest Architects cree que el mejor diseño empieza por comprender y preocuparse por lo que importa a sus clientes. Muchas empresas se centran en el «qué» del diseño; DeForest se interesa igualmente por el quién, el cómo y el porqué. Además de diseñar lugares significativos para vivir y trabajar, los arquitectos de DA se ven a sí mismos como guías personales de grandes aventuras en el diseño. DA aporta a cada proyecto una experiencia amplia y profunda. En lugar de limitarse a un estilo concreto, el estudio aborda cada proyecto con la mente abierta, una mirada fresca y una ávida curiosidad. Al final, sus proyectos son diferentes porque cada cliente y cada lugar son diferentes. Gracias a las nuevas tecnologías, DA ahora trae su enfoque interactivo y práctico a una variedad de proyectos en los Estados Unidos. Desde el noroeste del Pacífico hasta el norte de Nueva York, desde las Sierras hasta Sun Valley, desde el corazón de Iowa hasta las orillas del lago Michigan, DeForest aporta su espíritu inventivo y su proceso inspirado en el cliente a cada proyecto.

ORCAS ISLAND RETREAT

Orcas Island, Washington, United States // Lot area: 20+ acres; building area: 5,280 sq ft

DeForest was charged with "restoring the soul" of this remarkable property and designing a more welcoming, sustainable main house for generations to come. Inspired by a series of "Friends and Family" workshops, the resulting design is filled with places for connection and adventure. Magnetic wall panels are placed to pin up maps and notes; niches invite collected shells and driftwood; and secret spaces, like a hidden slide and bunk beds connected via attic hatches, evoke a spirit of playfulness. Materials complement the landscape and evoke the traditional farmhouses and cabins of the islands while giving them a practical, modern spin. Site trees were milled into structural beams and board-and-batten siding. Other finishes were salvaged from snow fencing and old barns. Special details include a custom dining table with steel inlays marking the exact direction of sunrise on the solstice, the owners' childhood homes, and the place they first met.

DeForest a été chargé de « restaurer l'âme » de cette propriété remarquable et de concevoir une maison plus accueillante et durable pour les générations à venir. Inspiré d'une série d'ateliers « Amis et Famille », le design est rempli de lieux de connexion et d'aventure. Des panneaux muraux magnétiques sont placés pour épingler des cartes et des notes ; les niches invitent les coquillages et le bois flotté ; et des espaces secrets, comme un toboggan caché et des lits superposés reliés par des trappes de grenier, évoquent un esprit ludique. Les matériaux complètent le paysage et évoquent les fermes et les cabanes traditionnelles des îles tout en leur donnant une touche pratique et moderne. Les arbres du site ont été broyés en poutres structurelles et en revêtement de planches et de lattes. D'autres finitions ont été récupérées des clôtures à neige et des anciennes granges. Les détails spéciaux incluent une table personnalisée avec des incrustations d'acier marquant la direction exacte du lever du soleil au solstice, les maisons d'enfance des propriétaires et le lieu de leur première rencontre.

DeForest hat es sich zur Aufgabe gemacht, die „Seele" dieses bemerkenswerten Anwesens wiederherzustellen und ein einladendes und nachhaltiges Zuhause für kommende Generationen zu entwerfen. Inspiriert von „Friends and Family"-Workshops offenbart das Design Räume der Verbindung und des Abenteuers. Magnettafeln zum Anbringen von Karten und Notizen; Nischen mit Muscheln und Treibholz; und geheime Räume, wie eine versteckte Rutsche und Etagenbetten, die durch Luken verbunden sind, rufen einen spielerischen Geist hervor. Die Materialien ergänzen die Landschaft und erinnern an die traditionellen Cottages und Hütten der Insel, während sie einen praktischen und modernen Touch verleihen. Die gefällten Bäume wurden zu tragenden Balken und Planken- und Lattenverkleidungen. Andere Oberflächen wurden von alten Zäunen und Scheunen geborgen. Zu den besonderen Details gehören ein Tisch mit Stahleinlagen, die die genaue Richtung des Sonnenaufgangs zur Sonnenwende markieren, die Häuser, in denen die Besitzer aufgewachsen sind, und der Ort ihrer ersten Begegnung.

DeForest se encargó de «restaurar el alma» de esta notable propiedad y diseñar un hogar acogedor y sostenible para las generaciones venideras. Inspirado en unos talleres de «Amigos y familiares», el diseño revela espacios de conexión y aventura. Paneles magnéticos para fijar tarjetas y notas; nichos con conchas y madera de deriva; y espacios secretos, como un tobogán oculto y literas conectadas por escotillas, evocan un espíritu lúdico. Los materiales complementan el paisaje y evocan las casas de campo y cabañas tradicionales de la isla, a la vez que dan un toque práctico y moderno. Los árboles cortados se convirtieron en vigas estructurales y revestimientos de tablones y listones. Otros acabados fueron rescatados de vallas y graneros viejos. Detalles especiales incluyen una mesa con incrustaciones de acero que marcan la dirección exacta del amanecer en el solsticio, las casas donde los propietarios crecieron y el lugar de su primera reunión.

Upper floor plan

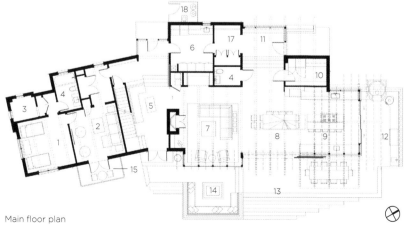

Main floor plan

1. Bedroom
2. Den
3. Storage
4. Bathroom
5. Stair hall
6. Mud room
7. Living room
8. Dining room
9. Kitchen
10. Pantry
11. Entry
12. BBQ patio
13. Patio
14. Fire pit
15. Deck
16. Master bedroom
17. Coat closet
18. Mechanical room

HIGH DESERT MODERN

Bend, Oregon, United States // Lot area: .24 acres; building area: 2,670 sq ft (not including garage)

This desert home is designed around a series of light-filled spaces that connect it to the surrounding sky and landscape. Conceived as a kind of Swiss Army knife, it expands and contracts for use by the owners, a few guests, or large gatherings. At the entry courtyard, a rolling screen and swinging gate can be used to configure the space to be cozy and private or wide open and welcoming. The partition between the living room and main suite features five sliding panels that conceal a fireplace, tv, storage, and bedroom beyond. A large, hinged wall turns a sunny sitting area into a guest bedroom. The exterior palette is designed to blend with the varied textures and subtle colors of the desert. Inside the home's clean lines and simple, light-filled volumes create a backdrop for changing collections: a row of vintage catcher's masks, salvaged industrial gears, and the trunk of an ancient lilac tree.

Cette maison du désert est conçue autour d'une série d'espaces lumineux qui la relient au ciel et au paysage environnants. Conçu comme un couteau suisse, il s'agrandit et se contracte pour être utilisé par les propriétaires, quelques invités ou de grands rassemblements. Dans la cour d'entrée, un écran roulant et un portail battant peuvent être utilisés pour configurer l'espaces de façon qu'il soit confortable et privé ou grand ouvert et accueillant. La cloison entre le salon et la suite principale comporte cinq panneaux coulissants qui cachent une cheminée, une télévision, des rangements et une chambre au-delà. Un grand mur articulé transforme un coin salon ensoleillé en chambre d'amis. La palette extérieure est conçue pour se fondre avec les textures variées et les couleurs subtiles du désert. À l'intérieur, les lignes épurées de la maison et les volumes simples et lumineux créent une toile de fond pour les collections changeantes : une rangée de masques de receveur vintage, des engrenages industriels récupérés et le tronc d'un ancien lilas.

Dieses Wüstenhaus ist um eine Reihe von lichtdurchfluteten Räumen herum gestaltet, die es mit dem umgebenden Himmel und der Landschaft verbinden. Konzipiert wie ein Schweizer Taschenmesser, dehnt und zieht es sich zusammen, um sich der Nutzung durch Hausbesitzer, wenige Gäste oder große Versammlungen anzupassen. Am Eingangshof können ein rollender Bildschirm und ein Schwingtor verwendet werden, um den Raum gemütlich und privat oder weit offen und einladend zu gestalten. Die Trennwand zwischen dem Wohnzimmer und der Master-Suite verfügt über fünf verschiebbare Paneele, die einen Kamin, einen Fernseher, einen Stauraum und ein Schlafzimmer verbergen. Eine große Pendelwand verwandelt ein Wohnzimmer in ein Gästezimmer. Die Außenpalette mischt die vielfältigen Texturen und subtilen Farben der Wüste. Im Inneren schaffen klare Linien und einfache, leichte Volumen eine Kulisse für die wechselnden Kollektionen: eine Reihe von Vintage-Empfängerhäuten, Industrieausrüstung und der Kofferraum einer antiken Luftmatratze.

Esta casa en el desierto está diseñada en torno a una serie de espacios llenos de luz que la conectan con el cielo y el paisaje circundantes. Concebida como una navaja suiza, se expande y se contrae para adaptarse al uso de los propietarios, de unos pocos invitados o de grandes reuniones. En el patio de entrada, una mampara enrollable y una puerta batiente cambian el espacio, cómodo y privado o bien abierto y acogedor. La partición entre el salón y la suite principal cuenta con cinco paneles deslizantes que ocultan una chimenea, televisión, almacenamiento y un dormitorio. Una gran pared batiente convierte una sala de estar en un dormitorio de invitados. La paleta exterior mezcla las texturas variadas y los colores sutiles del desierto. En el interior, las líneas limpias y los volúmenes simples y luminosos crean un telón de fondo para las colecciones cambiantes: una fila de máscaras de receptor vintage, engranajes industriales y el tronco de un antiguo lilo.

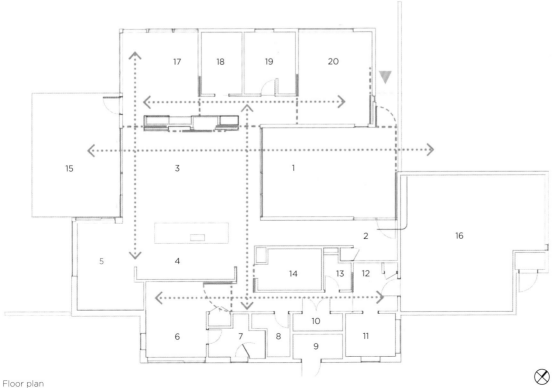

Floor plan

1. Entry courtyard
2. Entry
3. Living area
4. Kitchen/bar
5. Dining area
6. Guest bedroom
7. Guest bathroom
8. Powder room
9. Mechanical room
10. Wine cellar
11. Laundry room
12. Mud room
13. Storage
14. Pantry
15. Patio
16. Garage
17. Master bedroom
18. Master closet
19. Master bathroom
20. Office

TREE HOUSE

Burien, Washington, United States // Lot area: 1.12 acres; building area: 3,800 sq ft (not including garage)

Tree House is perched on a one-acre wooded parcel at the top of a bluff overlooking Puget Sound. Early in the design process, the clients—a graphic designer and fine artist with two children—described the pleasure they took in walking the property. In response, DA worked with them to design a home that provides different ways of experiencing the site, from rooms that are tucked into the hillside to others that float above it. For the interior, a high-contrast approach to major elements—white walls and a blackened steel moment frame, bleached hemlock floors, and walnut cabinets—appealed to the clients' love of strong graphics. A sense of delight and the unexpected was introduced through elements such as the red metal stair, fields of graphic tile, and bold colors throughout the furnishings.

Tree House est perché sur une parcelle boisée d'un acre au sommet d'une falaise surplombant Puget Sound. Au début du processus de conception, les clients, un graphiste et un artiste plasticien avec deux enfants, ont décrit leur plaisir à se promener dans la propriété. En réponse, DA a travaillé avec eux pour concevoir une maison qui offre différentes façons de découvrir le site, des pièces cachées dans la colline à d'autres qui flottent au-dessus. Pour l'intérieur, une approche très contrastée des éléments principaux – des murs blancs et un cadre de moment en acier noirci, des planchers en sapin canadien blanchi et des meubles en noyer – a fait appel à l'amour des clients pour les graphismes forts. Des éléments tels que l'escalier en métal rouge, les surfaces en mosaïque graphique et les couleurs vives de l'ameublement suscitent un sentiment d'excitation et d'inattendu.

Das Tree House thront auf einem bewaldeten Grundstück von einem Hektar an der Spitze einer Klippe mit Blick auf den Puget Sound. Zu Beginn des Designprozesses beschrieben die Kunden, ein Grafikdesigner und ein bildender Künstler mit zwei Kindern, ihre Freude daran, durch das Anwesen zu gehen. Als Reaktion darauf arbeitete DA mit ihnen zusammen, um ein Haus zu entwerfen, das verschiedene Möglichkeiten bietet, den Ort zu erleben, von Räumen, die im Hang versteckt sind, bis hin zu solchen, die darüber schweben. Für die Innenausstattung sprach eine kontrastreiche Herangehensweise an die Hauptelemente – weiße Wände und ein gebogener Rahmen aus geschwärztem Stahl, Böden aus gebleichter kanadischer Tanne und Möbel aus Walnussholz – die Liebe der Kunden zu starken Grafiken an. Elemente wie die rote Metalltreppe, grafische Mosaikoberflächen und kräftige Farben in der gesamten Einrichtung wecken ein Gefühl von Aufregung und Unerwartetem.

Tree House se alza sobre una parcela arbolada de un acre en la parte superior de un acantilado con vista a Puget Sound. Al principio del proceso de diseño, los clientes, un diseñador gráfico y una artista plástico con dos hijos, describieron el placer que les producía caminar por la propiedad. En respuesta, DA trabajó con ellos para diseñar una casa que brinde diferentes formas de experimentar el sitio, desde habitaciones que están escondidas en la ladera hasta otras que flotan sobre ella. Para el interior, un enfoque de alto contraste para los elementos principales (paredes blancas y una estructura de flexión de acero ennegrecido, suelos de abeto canadiense blanqueados y mobiliario de nogal) atrajo el amor de los clientes por los gráficos fuertes. Elementos como la escalera metalica roja, las superficies de mosaicos gráficos y colores llamativos en todo el mobiliario despiertan una sensación de emoción y de lo inesperado.

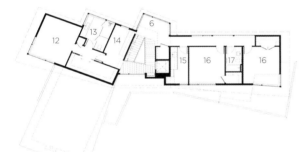

Upper floor plan

Main floor plan

1. Sunroom
2. Kitchen
3. Dining room
4. Living room
5. Deck
6. Stair hall
7. Family room
8. Mud room
9. Exercise room
10. Entry
11. Garage
12. Master bedroom
13. Master bathroom
14. Office
15. Laundry room
16. Bedroom
17. Bathroom

CLICK
ARCHITECTS

046
∨

050
∨

054
∨

TANGLETOWN RESIDENCE

Architecture Design Team:
Click Architects
Structural Engineer:
Swenson Say Faget
Builder:
Donald Baptiste/LDB Homes
Photographer:
© Will Austin Photography

CLOGSTON RESIDENCE

Architecture Design Team:
Click Architects
Structural Engineer:
Swenson Say Faget
Builder:
Donald Baptiste/LDB Homes
Photographer:
© Rafael Soldi Photography

MAPLE LEAF RESIDENCE

Architecture Design Team:
Click Architects
Structural Engineer:
Swenson Say Faget
Builder:
Donald Baptiste/LDB Homes
Photographer:
© Rafael Soldi Photography

Click Architects studio specializes in modern, innovative residential design. Founded in 2013 by architects Cheryl and Stephen Click, they are guided by their passion for excellence and love for collaboration. Each unique project is molded by careful and deliberate consideration for site specifics, programmatic desire, and the unifying idea. Their collaborative process connects clients and project team members early on to help inform design decisions, guide budget and schedule, and maintain the underlying project goals. They believe every project provides a conduit for the exploration of human experience as it relates to the built environment and the emotional response to a specific space. Staying true to their beliefs and working closely with their clients allows each project the opportunity to tell a different story. The three chosen projects focus on Seattle's urban in-fill and how they relate to the existing city fabric and the site-specific opportunities and challenges.

Click Architects hat sich auf innovative, moderne Wohnprojekte spezialisiert. Das 2013 von den Architekten Cheryl und Stephen Click gegründete Unternehmen lässt sich von seiner Leidenschaft für hervorragende Leistungen und seiner Liebe zur Zusammenarbeit leiten. Jedes einzigartige Projekt wird durch sorgfältige und bewusste Überlegungen zu den Spezifikationen des Standorts, den programmatischen Wünschen und der verbindenden Idee geprägt. Ihr gemeinschaftlicher Prozess verbindet Kunden und Projektteammitglieder von Anfang an, um die Designentscheidungen zu unterstützen, das Budget und den Zeitplan zu steuern und die grundlegenden Ziele des Prozesses zu erhalten. Sie sind der Meinung, dass jedes Projekt einen Kanal für die Erforschung der menschlichen Erfahrung in Bezug auf die gebaute Umwelt und die emotionale Reaktion auf einen bestimmten Raum darstellt. Da sie ihren Überzeugungen treu bleiben und eng mit ihren Kunden zusammenarbeiten, hat jedes Projekt die Möglichkeit, eine andere Geschichte zu erzählen. Die drei ausgewählten Projekte konzentrieren sich auf das städtische Gefüge von Seattle und darauf, wie sie sich auf bestehende Formen und ortsspezifische Möglichkeiten und Herausforderungen beziehen.

Click Architects est spécialisé dans la conception de logements modernes et innovants. Fondée en 2013 par les architectes Cheryl et Stephen Click, elle est guidée par sa passion pour l'excellence et son amour de la collaboration. Chaque projet unique est façonné par un examen attentif et délibéré des spécifications du site, du désir programmatique et de l'idée unificatrice. Leur processus de collaboration relie les clients et les membres de l'équipe de projet dès le début afin d'éclairer les décisions de conception, d'orienter le budget et le calendrier, et de maintenir les objectifs sous-jacents du processus. Ils estiment que chaque projet est un moyen d'explorer l'expérience humaine en relation avec l'environnement bâti et la réponse émotionnelle à un espace spécifique. En restant fidèles à leurs convictions et en travaillant en étroite collaboration avec leurs clients, chaque projet a l'occasion de raconter une histoire différente. Les trois projets choisis sont axés sur le tissu urbain de Seattle et sur la manière dont ils s'articulent avec les formes existantes et les possibilités et défis propres au site.

El estudio Click Architects está especializado en el diseño residencial moderno e innovador. Fundado en 2013 por los arquitectos Cheryl y Stephen Click, se guían por su pasión por la excelencia y el amor por la colaboración. Cada proyecto único es moldeado por la consideración cuidadosa y deliberada de las especificaciones del lugar, el deseo programático y la idea unificadora. Su proceso de colaboración conecta a los clientes y a los miembros del equipo del proyecto desde el principio para ayudar a informar de las decisiones de diseño, guiar el presupuesto y el calendario, y mantener los objetivos subyacentes del proceso. Creen que cada proyecto proporciona un conducto para la exploración de la experiencia humana en relación con el entorno construido y la respuesta emocional a un espacio específico. Siendo fieles a sus creencias y trabajando en estrecha colaboración con sus clientes, cada proyecto tiene la oportunidad de contar una historia diferente. Los tres proyectos elegidos se centran en el tejido urbano de Seattle y en cómo se relacionan con las formas existente y con las oportunidades y retos específicos del lugar.

TANGLETOWN RESIDENCE

Seattle, Washington, United States // Lot area: 3,997 sq ft; building area: 3,025 sq ft

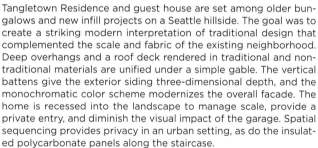

Tangletown Residence and guest house are set among older bungalows and new infill projects on a Seattle hillside. The goal was to create a striking modern interpretation of traditional design that complemented the scale and fabric of the existing neighborhood. Deep overhangs and a roof deck rendered in traditional and non-traditional materials are unified under a simple gable. The vertical battens give the exterior siding three-dimensional depth, and the monochromatic color scheme modernizes the overall facade. The home is recessed into the landscape to manage scale, provide a private entry, and diminish the visual impact of the garage. Spatial sequencing provides privacy in an urban setting, as do the insulated polycarbonate panels along the staircase.

La résidence Tangletown et la maison d'hôtes sont situées entre des bungalows plus anciens et de nouveaux projets intercalaires sur une colline de Seattle. L'objectif était de créer une interprétation moderne et frappante d'un design traditionnel qui s'intègre à l'échelle et au tissu du quartier existant. Les profonds porte-à-faux et le toit-terrasse, avec des matériaux traditionnels et non traditionnels, se rejoignent sous un simple pignon. Les lamelles verticales donnent au revêtement extérieur une profondeur tridimensionnelle, et le jeu de couleurs monochromes modernise l'ensemble de la façade. La maison est encastrée dans le paysage afin de contrôler l'échelle, de fournir une entrée privée et de réduire l'impact visuel du garage. La séquence spatiale offre une certaine intimité dans un environnement urbain, tout comme les panneaux de polycarbonate isolés le long de l'escalier.

Die Tangletown Residence und das Gästehaus befinden sich zwischen älteren Bungalows und neuen Auffüllungsprojekten an einem Hang in Seattle. Ziel war es, eine auffallend moderne Interpretation des traditionellen Designs zu schaffen, die sich in die Größe und Struktur des bestehenden Viertels einfügt. Die tiefen Überhänge und die Dachterrasse mit traditionellen und nicht-traditionellen Materialien vereinen sich unter einem einfachen Giebel. Vertikale Lamellen verleihen der Außenverkleidung eine dreidimensionale Tiefe, und die monochromatische Farbgebung modernisiert die Fassade als Ganzes. Das Haus ist in die Landschaft eingebettet, um die Größe zu kontrollieren, einen privaten Eingang zu schaffen und die optische Wirkung der Garage zu verringern. Die räumliche Abfolge bietet Privatsphäre in einer städtischen Umgebung, ebenso wie die isolierten Polycarbonatplatten entlang der Treppe.

La residencia Tangletown y la casa de invitados están situadas entre bungalows antiguos y nuevos proyectos de relleno en una ladera de Seattle. El objetivo era crear una sorprendente interpretación moderna del diseño tradicional que complementara la escala y el tejido del barrio existente. Los profundos voladizos y la cubierta del tejado, con materiales tradicionales y no tradicionales, se unen bajo un sencillo frontón. Los listones verticales dan al revestimiento exterior una profundidad tridimensional, y la combinación de colores monocromática moderniza el conjunto de la fachada. La casa está empotrada en el paisaje para controlar la escala, proporcionar una entrada privada y disminuir el impacto visual del garaje. La secuencia espacial ofrece privacidad en un entorno urbano, al igual que los paneles de policarbonato aislados a lo largo de la escalera.

South elevation

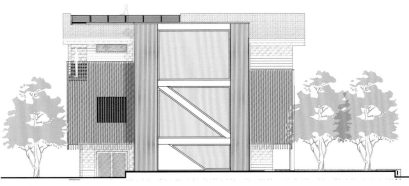

West elevation

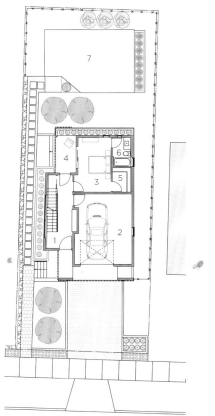

Ground floor plan

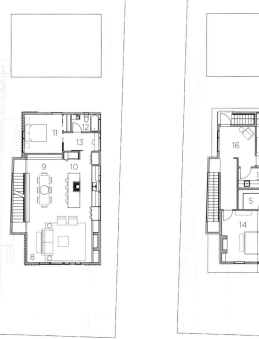

Second floor plan

Third floor plan

1. Entry
2. Garage
3. Guest suite
4. Patio
5. Closet
6. Bathroom
7. Guest house
8. Living area
9. Dining area
10. Kitchen
11. Bedroom
12. Bathroom
13. Study
14. Primary suite
15. Laundry room
16. Reading room

CLOGSTON RESIDENCE

Seattle, Washington, United States // Lot area: 6,417 sq ft; building area: 3,834 sq ft

Located in the heart of Seattle's Greenlake neighborhood, the Clogston Residence and detached studio were designed in response to site conditions and the program. The site response starts with skewing the floor plan to omit views of neighboring structures, maximize park views, and provide natural light. The space between the residence and studio creates a sheltered courtyard conditioned for outdoor activities. The main space and entry with angled volumetric ceiling planes correspond to the skewed floor plan. The cedar shingles are used at the main entry to highlight the double-height volume and large cantilever. The angled design scheme reappears at the staircase polycarbonate screen wall and the beams that bisect rooms. The detached studio, wrapped in dark-stained cedar shingles, floats above the foundation, revealing the skewed plan.

Situés au cœur du quartier Greenlake de Seattle, la résidence Clogston et le studio indépendant ont été conçus en fonction des conditions du site et du programme. La réponse au site commence par l'inclinaison du plan d'étage afin d'omettre les vues sur les structures voisines, de maximiser les vues sur le parc et de fournir de la lumière naturelle. L'espace entre la résidence et le studio crée une cour abritée et conditionnée pour les activités extérieures. L'espace principal et l'entrée, avec des plans de toiture volumétriques inclinés, correspondent au plan d'étage incliné. Des bardeaux de cèdre sont utilisés à l'entrée principale pour souligner le volume à double hauteur et le grand surplomb. Le schéma de conception angulaire réapparaît dans le mur écran en polycarbonate de l'escalier et dans les poutres qui divisent les pièces. Le studio indépendant, enveloppé de bardeaux de cèdre de couleur sombre, flotte au-dessus des fondations, révélant le plan d'étage oblique.

Das Clogston Wohnhaus und das unabhängige Studio befinden sich im Herzen des Greenlake-Viertels von Seattle und wurden unter Berücksichtigung der örtlichen Gegebenheiten und des Programms entworfen. Die Reaktion auf den Standort beginnt mit der Neigung des Grundrisses, um den Blick auf die benachbarten Gebäude zu vermeiden, den Blick auf den Park zu maximieren und natürliches Licht zu erhalten. Der Raum zwischen dem Wohnhaus und dem Atelier bildet einen geschützten Innenhof, der für Aktivitäten im Freien geeignet ist. Der Hauptraum und der Eingang mit den schrägen, volumetrischen Dachebenen entsprechen dem schrägen Grundriss. Am Haupteingang wurden Zedernschindeln verwendet, um die doppelte Höhe des Gebäudes und den großen Überhang zu betonen. Das schräge Gestaltungsschema findet sich in der Polycarbonatwand des Treppenhauses und in den raumteilenden Balken wieder. Das freistehende Atelier, das mit dunkel gebeizten Zedernschindeln verkleidet ist, schwebt über den Fundamenten und offenbart den schrägen Grundriss.

Situada en el corazón del barrio Greenlake de Seattle, la residencia Clogston y el estudio independiente se diseñaron en respuesta a las condiciones del lugar y al programa. La respuesta al lugar comienza con la inclinación de la planta para omitir las vistas de las estructuras vecinas, maximizar las vistas del parque y proporcionar luz natural. El espacio entre la residencia y el estudio crea un patio protegido y acondicionado para actividades al aire libre. El espacio principal y la entrada, con planos de techo volumétricos en ángulo, se corresponden con la planta sesgada. Las tejas de cedro se utilizan en la entrada principal para resaltar el volumen de doble altura y el gran voladizo. El esquema de diseño anguloso reaparece en el muro pantalla de policarbonato de la escalera y en las vigas que dividen las habitaciones. El estudio independiente, envuelto en tejas de cedro teñidas de oscuro, flota sobre los cimientos, revelando la planta sesgada.

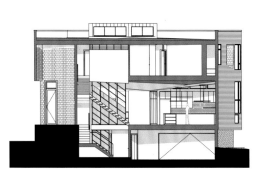

Section A

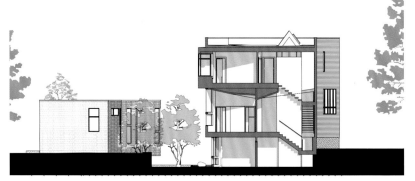

Section B

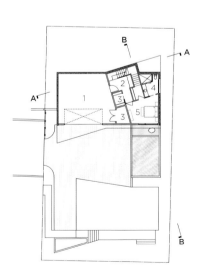

Ground floor plan

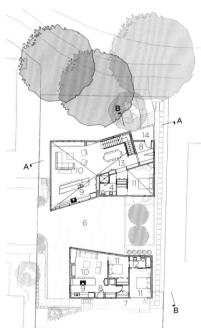

Second floor plan

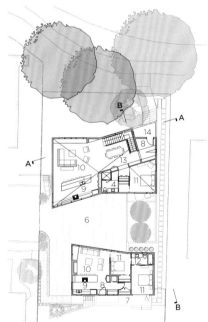

Third floor plan

1. Garage
2. Mudroom
3. Closet
4. Bathroom
5. Guest suite
6. Courtyard
7. Terrace
8. Entry
9. Kitchen
10. Living area
11. Bedroom
12. Bathroom
13. Dining area
14. Entry porch
15. Primary suite
16. Nursery
17. Laundry room
18. Bedroom suite

MAPLE LEAF RESIDENCE

Seattle, Washington, United States // Lot area: 7,006 sq ft; building area: 3,722 sq ft

The Maple Leaf Residence, located on a bustling Seattle street, was designed to acknowledge the mixed-use neighborhood, filtering street noise and maximizing visual privacy by utilizing thick walls, unique massing, and rigid exterior materials. The street-facing facade acts as a filter between public and private. The filter concept is used throughout the home. The entry path is recessed between steel plates, slopes to the door, and angled to preserve a large evergreen tree. The entry is compressed to help dramatize the volumetric living room space located on the second level. Perforated steel screens line the staircase, screening the living room from the kitchen while creating a sculptural piece within the space. Perforated exterior siding filters natural light from street-facing glazing. Interior spaces were designed to take in the views of the distant Olympic Mountain range and beautiful sunsets.

La résidence Maple Leaf, située dans une rue animée de Seattle, a été conçue pour reconnaître le quartier à usage mixte en filtrant le bruit de la rue et en maximisant l'intimité visuelle grâce à des murs épais, une masse unique et des matériaux extérieurs rigides. La façade donnant sur la rue agit comme un filtre entre le public et le privé. Le concept de filtre est utilisé dans toute la maison. L'allée est placée entre des plaques d'acier, elle est en pente vers la porte et est inclinée pour préserver un grand arbre à feuilles persistantes. L'entrée est comprimée pour aider à dramatiser l'espace volumétrique du salon situé au deuxième niveau. Des écrans en acier perforé bordent l'escalier, séparant le salon de la cuisine et créant une pièce sculpturale dans l'espace. Le revêtement extérieur perforé filtre la lumière naturelle des fenêtres donnant sur la rue. Les espaces intérieurs ont été conçus pour profiter des vues sur la chaîne de montagnes olympiques au loin et des magnifiques couchers de soleil.

Die Maple Leaf Residence an einer belebten Straße in Seattle wurde so entworfen, dass sie die gemischte Nachbarschaft berücksichtigt, indem sie den Straßenlärm filtert und die visuelle Privatsphäre durch die Verwendung dicker Wände, einer einzigen Masse und fester Außenmaterialien maximiert. Die der Straße zugewandte Fassade fungiert als Filter zwischen öffentlich und privat. Das Filterkonzept zieht sich durch das ganze Haus. Die Einfahrt ist zwischen Stahlplatten eingelassen, fällt zur Tür hin ab und ist geneigt, um einen großen immergrünen Baum zu erhalten. Der Eingang ist komprimiert, um den volumetrischen Raum des auf der zweiten Ebene gelegenen Wohnzimmers zu dramatisieren. Perforierte Stahlschirme begrenzen die Treppe, schirmen das Wohnzimmer von der Küche ab und schaffen ein skulpturales Element im Raum. Die perforierte Außenverkleidung filtert das natürliche Licht aus den zur Straße hin gelegenen Fenstern. Die Innenräume wurden so gestaltet, dass man die Aussicht auf die entfernten Olympic Mountains und die wunderschönen Sonnenuntergänge genießen kann.

La residencia Maple Leaf, situada en una bulliciosa calle de Seattle, fue diseñada para reconocer el barrio de uso mixto, filtrando el ruido de la calle y maximizando la privacidad visual mediante la utilización de muros gruesos, una masa única y materiales exteriores rígidos. La fachada que da a la calle actúa como filtro entre lo público y lo privado. El concepto de filtro se utiliza en toda la casa. El camino de entrada está situado entre placas de acero, se inclina hacia la puerta y se inclina para preservar un gran árbol de hoja perenne. La entrada se comprime para ayudar a dramatizar el espacio volumétrico del salón situado en el segundo nivel. Las pantallas de acero perforado bordean la escalera, protegiendo la sala de estar de la cocina y creando una pieza escultórica dentro del espacio. El revestimiento exterior perforado filtra la luz natural de los cristales que dan a la calle. Los espacios interiores se diseñaron para disfrutar de las vistas de la lejana cordillera olímpica y de las hermosas puestas de sol.

Section A

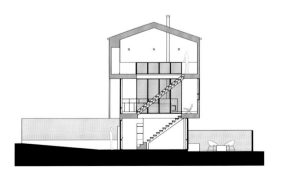

Section B

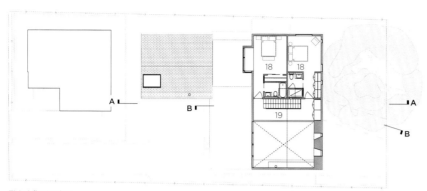

Third floor plan

Second floor plan

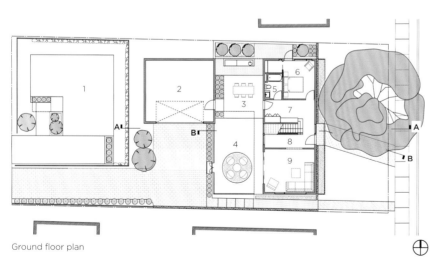

Ground floor plan

1. Guest house
2. Garage
3. Dining terrace
4. Courtyard
5. Bathroom
6. Bedroom
7. Mudoom
8. Entry
9. Den
10. Closet
11. Primary suite
12. Dining area
13. Laundry room
14. Powder room
15. Study
16. Kitchen
17. Living area
18. Kid's suite
19. Loft

COATES DESIGN
ARCHITECTURE + INTERIORS

TANNER OFFICE BUILDING

Architecture Design Team:
Coates Design Architecture + Interiors
Landscape Architect:
Outdoor Studio LA
Civil Engineer:
Team 4 Enginnering
Structural Engineer:
Quantum Consulting Enginers
Electrical and Mechanical Engineer:
WSP Flack + Kurtz
Photographer:
© David W Cohen, William Wright

SEAVIEW ESCAPE

Architecture Design Team:
Coates Design Architecture + Interiors
Civil Engineer:
Browne Wheeler Engineers, Inc
Structural Engineer:
Quantum Consulting Enginners
General Contractor:
Fairbank Construction
Photographer:
© Lara Swimmer

ISLAND RETREAT

Architecture Design Team:
Coates Design Architecture + Interiors
Civil Engineer:
Browne Wheeler Engineers, Inc
Geotechnical Engineer:
Earth Solutions NW, LLC
Environmental Engineer:
BGE Environmental, LLC
Landscape Enginner:
Brian Syndberg Landscaping, Inc
Structural and Mechanical Engineer:
Quantum Consulting Enginners
General Contractor:
Fairbank Construction
Photographer:
© Lara Swimmer

Coates Design Architects is an architectural firm located on Bainbridge Island near Seattle, Washington. The firm's managing partner, Matthew Coates, achieved international acclaim by winning the "Cradle to Cradle (C2C)" Home Design Competition in 2005. He captured the momentum from this accomplishment to create a firm dedicated to "Responsible Architecture." Coates Design Architects addresses the reality that people spend 80% of their lives indoors by contributing buildings and spaces that are provocative, healthful, and inspiring to our communities. Team members with backgrounds in design, construction, and the fine arts work together to transform complex design challenges into elegant solutions, revealing creative design strategies and technological innovation inspired by their clients, the site, and the ecological context. Coates Design Architects believes that better design leads to better living, which leads the team to create buildings that have a positive impact on the environment and the people who use them.

Coates Design Architects ist ein Architekturbüro mit Sitz auf Bainbridge Island in der Nähe von Seattle, Washington. Der geschäftsführende Gesellschafter der Firma, Matthew Coates, erlangte 2005 mit dem Gewinn des „Cradle to Cradle (C2C)"-Wohndesignwettbewerbs internationale Anerkennung. Coates Design Architects gehen auf die Tatsache ein, dass Menschen 80 % ihres Lebens in Innenräumen verbringen, indem sie provokative, gesunde und inspirierende Gebäude in unsere Gemeinschaften einbringen. Teammitglieder mit einem Hintergrund in Design, Konstruktion und bildender Kunst arbeiten zusammen, um komplexe Designherausforderungen in elegante Lösungen umzuwandeln und kreative Designstrategien und technologische Innovationen zu enthüllen, die von ihren Kunden, dem Standort und dem ökologischen Kontext inspiriert sind. Coates Design Architects glaubt, dass besseres Design zu einem besseren Leben führt, was das Team dazu veranlasst, Gebäude zu schaffen, die sich positiv auf die Umwelt und die Menschen auswirken, die sie nutzen.

Coates Design Architects est un cabinet d'architectes situé sur Bainbridge Island, près de Seattle, dans l'État de Washington. L'associé directeur de l'entreprise, Matthew Coates, a acquis une renommée internationale en remportant le concours de conception de logements « Cradle to Cradle (C2C) » en 2005. Il a utilisé l'élan de cette réalisation pour créer un cabinet dédié à l'« architecture responsable ». Coates Design Architects répond à la réalité selon laquelle les gens passent 80 % de leur vie à l'intérieur en fournissant des bâtiments et des espaces qui sont provocants, sains et inspirants pour nos communautés. Les membres de l'équipe, issus du monde du design, de la construction et des beaux-arts, travaillent ensemble pour transformer des défis de conception complexes en solutions élégantes, révélant des stratégies de conception créatives et une innovation technologique inspirées par leurs clients, le lieu et le contexte écologique. Coates Design Architects est convaincu qu'une meilleure conception permet de mieux vivre, ce qui conduit l'équipe à construire des bâtiments qui ont un impact positif sur l'environnement et les personnes qui les utilisent.

Coates Design Architects es un estudio de arquitectura situado en la isla de Bainbridge, cerca de Seattle, Washington. El socio director de la empresa, Matthew Coates, alcanzó la fama internacional al ganar el concurso de diseño de viviendas «Cradle to Cradle (C2C)» en 2005. Aprovechó el impulso de este logro para crear una empresa dedicada a la «Arquitectura Responsable». Coates Design Architects hace frente a la realidad de que las personas pasan el 80% de sus vidas en el interior, aportando edificios y espacios que sean provocativos, saludables e inspiradores para nuestras comunidades. Los miembros del equipo, con formación en diseño, construcción y bellas artes, trabajan juntos para transformar complejos retos de diseño en soluciones elegantes, revelando estrategias de diseño creativo e innovación tecnológica inspiradas en sus clientes, el lugar y el contexto ecológico. Coates Design Architects cree que un mejor diseño conduce a una mejor vida, lo que lleva al equipo a construir edificios que tienen un impacto positivo en el medio ambiente y en las personas que los utilizan.

TANNER OFFICE BUILDING

Kingston, Washington, United States // Lot area: 9,583 sq ft; building area: 6,000 sq ft

This highly visible landmark in the growing community of Kingston is situated on a prominent site that captures a beautiful view of Puget Sound. Large windows let in optimal natural sunlight, and a ventilation system brings in air to create a comfortable office space open to the surrounding environment. A rain garden retains water until it is absorbed into the soil, creating a lively planted area. Built to LEED Gold standards, this project provides its owners with an open, healthy, and well-lit work environment while at the same time reducing operating costs significantly with sustainable design solutions. As day turns into night, the mechanically-operated shading louvers open up, and lights are turned on to transform this glass tower into a glowing beacon of warm light.

Ce bâtiment très visible dans la communauté croissante de Kingston est situé sur un site proéminent qui offre une vue magnifique sur le Puget Sound. De grandes fenêtres laissent entrer une lumière naturelle optimale et un système de ventilation apporte de l'air pour créer un espace de bureau confortable et ouvert sur son environnement. Un jardin de pluie retient l'eau jusqu'à ce qu'elle soit absorbée par le sol, créant ainsi une zone de plantation vivante. Construit selon les normes LEED Gold, ce projet offre à ses propriétaires un environnement de travail ouvert, sain et bien éclairé, tout en réduisant considérablement les coûts d'exploitation grâce à des solutions de conception durable. Lorsque le jour se transforme en nuit, des volets d'ombrage à commande mécanique s'ouvrent et des lumières s'allument pour transformer cette tour de verre en un phare de lumière chaude.

Dieses unübersehbare Gebäude in der wachsenden Gemeinde Kingston befindet sich an einem prominenten Standort, von dem aus man einen schönen Blick auf den Puget Sound hat. Große Fenster sorgen für einen optimalen natürlichen Lichteinfall, und ein Belüftungssystem sorgt für die Luftzufuhr, so dass ein komfortabler, zur Umgebung hin offener Büroraum entsteht. Ein Regengarten hält das Wasser zurück, bis es im Boden versickert, und schafft so eine lebendige Pflanzfläche. Das nach LEED-Gold-Standards errichtete Projekt bietet seinen Eigentümern ein offenes, gesundes und gut beleuchtetes Arbeitsumfeld und senkt gleichzeitig die Betriebskosten durch nachhaltige Designlösungen erheblich. Wenn der Tag in die Nacht übergeht, öffnen sich die mechanisch betriebenen Beschattungslamellen und die Beleuchtung wird eingeschaltet, um den Glasturm in ein glühendes Leuchtfeuer zu verwandeln, das warmes Licht spendet.

Este edificio de gran visibilidad en la creciente comunidad de Kingston está situado en un lugar prominente que ofrece una hermosa vista de Puget Sound. Los grandes ventanales dejan entrar la luz natural de forma óptima, y un sistema de ventilación aporta aire para crear un espacio de oficinas confortable y abierto al entorno. Un jardín de lluvia retiene el agua hasta que es absorbida por el suelo, creando una animada zona de plantación. Construido según las normas LEED Gold, este proyecto proporciona a sus propietarios un entorno de trabajo abierto, saludable y bien iluminado, al tiempo que reduce considerablemente los costes de funcionamiento con soluciones de diseño sostenibles. Cuando el día se convierte en noche, las lamas de sombreado accionadas mecánicamente se abren y las luces se encienden para transformar esta torre de cristal en un faro resplandeciente de luz cálida.

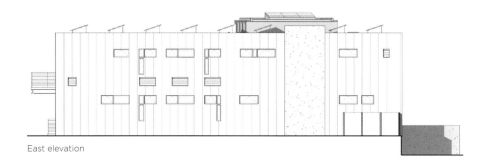

East elevation

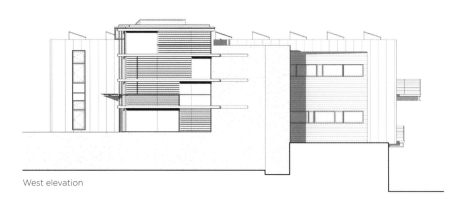

West elevation

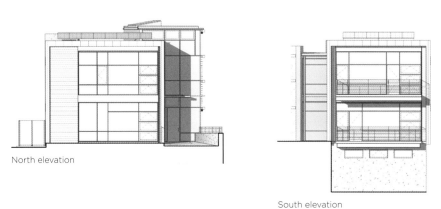

North elevation

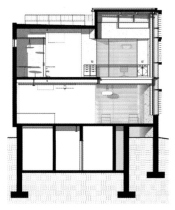

South elevation

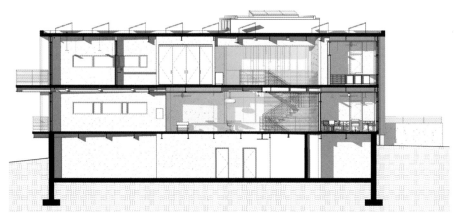

Longitudinal section

Cross section

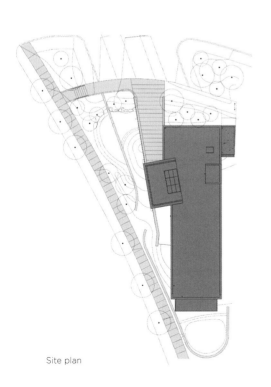

Site plan

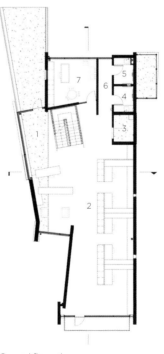

Ground floor plan

1. Reception
2. Open office
3. Elevator
4. Water closet
5. Corridor
6. Office
7. Accounting
8. Storage
9. Break room
10. Deck

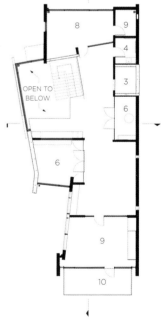

Second floor plan

SEAVIEW ESCAPE

Bainbridge Island, Washington, United States // Lot area: 10,890 sq ft; building area: 2,800 sq ft

This shoreline Pacific Northwest-style house is anchored into a steeply sloped site. There is an open-concept living, dining, and kitchen area that opens directly to the outdoors with a corner bi-fold door system. A stone mass wall divides the public and private spaces of the house while enclosing the stairs, support areas, and powder room. Two siblings wanted a pair of homes designed in conjunction with one another on the site, wishing to use the houses—just 50 feet apart—for big family gatherings. Each home includes a material palette of stone, concrete, wood, and metal, utilizes the existing topography, and complements one another while defining the subtle differences in the siblings' tastes. A communal drive leads to the two homes, providing a unique overlook of the ocean and green roof.

Cette maison de style Pacific Northwest est nichée sur un site en pente raide. Il y a un salon, une salle à manger et une cuisine à aire ouverte qui s'ouvrent directement sur l'extérieur avec un système de porte pliante en coin Un mur de pierre divise les espaces publics et privés de la maison tout en enfermant les escaliers, les zones de soutien et salle d'eau. Deux frères et sœurs voulaient une paire de maisons conçues conjointement sur le site, souhaitant utiliser les maisons - à seulement 15 metrès l'une de l'autre - pour de grandes réunions de famille. Chaque maison comprend une palette de matériaux de pierre, de béton, de bois et de métal, utilisant la topographie existante et se complétant tout en définissant les différences subtiles dans les goûts de la fratrie. Une allée commune mène aux deux maisons, offrant une vue unique sur l'océan et le toit vert.

Dieses Haus im typischen Stil des pazifischen Nordwestens liegt auf einem steil abfallenden Grundstück. Es gibt einen offenen Wohn-, Ess- und Küchenbereich, der sich mit einem Eck-Falttürsystem direkt ins Freie öffnet. Eine Steinmauer trennt die öffentlichen und privaten Bereiche des Hauses und umschließt die Treppe, die Stützbereiche und die Gästetoilette. Zwei Geschwister wollten ein Paar Häuser, die gemeinsam auf dem Gelände entworfen wurden, und wollten die Häuser – nur 50 Meter voneinander entfernt – für große Familienfeiern nutzen. Jedes Haus umfasst eine Materialpalette aus Stein, Beton, Holz und Metall, nutzt die vorhandene Topographie und ergänzt sich gegenseitig, während es die subtilen Unterschiede im Geschmack der Geschwister definiert. Eine gemeinsame Zufahrt führt zu den beiden Häusern und bietet einen einzigartigen Blick auf das Meer und das grüne Dach.

Esta casa de estilo típico del noroeste del Pacífico está anclada en un terreno con una pendiente pronunciada. Hay un área de sala, comedor y cocina de concepto abierto que se abre directamente al exterior con un sistema de puertas plegables en las esquinas Un muro de masa de piedra divide los espacios públicos y privados de la casa mientras encierra las escaleras, las áreas de apoyo y sala de polvo. Dos hermanos querían un par de casas diseñadas en conjunto en el sitio, con el deseo de usar las casas, a solo 15 metros de distancia, para grandes reuniones familiares. Cada hogar incluye una paleta de materiales de piedra, hormigón, madera y metal, que utilizan la topografía existente y se complementan entre sí al tiempo que definen las diferencias sutiles en los gustos de los hermanos. Un camino de acceso común conduce a las dos casas, proporcionando una vista única del océano y del techo verde.

Cross section

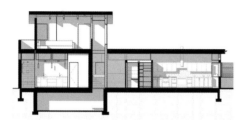

Longitudinal section

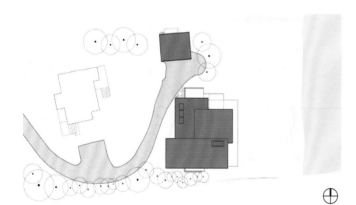

Site plan

Ground floor plan

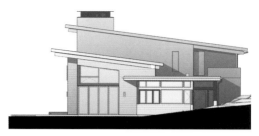

North elevation

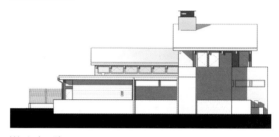

West elevation

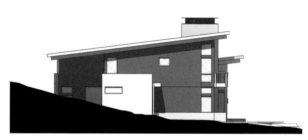

South elevation

East elevation

Second floor plan

1. Entry
2. Closet
3. Office
4. Family room
5. Dining area
6. Kitchen
7. Pantry
8. Powder room
9. Laundry room
10. Mechanical room
11. Master bathroom
12. Water closet
13. Master bedroom
14. Master closet
15. Staircase
16. Guest bedroom
17. Closet
18. Bathroom
19. Media room
20. Den

ISLAND RETREAT

Bainbridge Island, Washington // Lot area: 21,780 sq ft; building area: 2,600 sq ft

This two-bedroom hillside retreat allows the family to enjoy a regular island getaway. Wood floors and expansive two-story glazing bestow a view of the mountains from the upper balcony. Cantilevered wood "floating" stair treads lead to a library overlooking the double-height living and dining spaces below. Beach glass and nautical light fixtures, chosen for the bathrooms, bring a coastal feel indoors. A stone mass wall with Corten panels provides the focal point of the living space, housing a fireplace and media center while providing separation from the master suite. A wooded pathway connects the home to the beach, creating a natural transition from home to the outdoors. A communal drive, shared between the two siblings' retreat homes, provides a unique overlook of the cantilevered green roof.

Cette retraite de deux chambres à coucher à flanc de colline permet à la famille de profiter régulièrement d'une escapade sur l'île. Les sols en bois et les grandes baies vitrées des deux étages offrent une vue sur les montagnes depuis le balcon supérieur. Les marches de l'escalier en bois en porte-à-faux mènent à une bibliothèque qui surplombe le salon et à une salle à manger à double hauteur en contrebas. Des motifs de plage et des lampes nautiques, choisis pour les salles de bains, apportent une touche côtière à l'intérieur. Un mur de pierre avec des panneaux en acier Corten est le point central du salon, qui abrite une cheminée et un centre multimédia, tout en séparant la suite parentale. Un chemin bordé d'arbres relie la maison à la plage, créant une transition naturelle entre la maison et l'extérieur. Un chemin commun, partagé par les deux abris, offre une vue unique sur le toit vert en porte-à-faux.

Dieser Rückzugsort mit zwei Schlafzimmern am Hang ermöglicht es der Familie, regelmäßig einen Inselaufenthalt zu genießen. Holzböden und großzügige Verglasungen auf beiden Etagen bieten vom oberen Balkon aus einen Blick auf die Berge. Eine freitragende Holztreppe führt zu einer Bibliothek mit Blick auf das Wohnzimmer und ein darunter liegendes, doppelt so hohes Esszimmer. Strandmotive und nautische Lampen, die für die Bäder ausgewählt wurden, bringen ein Küstengefühl in die Einrichtung. Eine Steinwand mit Corten-Stahlpaneelen bildet den Mittelpunkt des Wohnzimmers, das einen Kamin und eine Mediathek beherbergt und gleichzeitig die Master-Suite abtrennt. Ein von Bäumen gesäumter Weg verbindet das Haus mit dem Strand und schafft einen natürlichen Übergang zwischen dem Haus und der freien Natur. Ein gemeinsamer Weg, der von den beiden Unterkünften genutzt wird, bietet einen einzigartigen Blick auf das auskragende Gründach.

Este refugio de dos dormitorios en la ladera de la colina permite a la familia disfrutar de una escapada a la isla de forma habitual. Los suelos de madera y el amplio acristalamiento de las dos plantas ofrecen una vista de las montañas desde el balcón superior. Los peldaños de la escalera de madera en voladizo conducen a una biblioteca con vistas al salón y a un comedor de doble altura en la parte inferior. Los motivos playeros y las lámparas náuticas, elegidas para los baños, aportan una sensación costera al interior. Un muro de piedra con paneles de acero Corten es el centro de atención del salón, que alberga una chimenea y un centro multimedia, a la vez que separa la suite principal. Un camino arbolado conecta la casa con la playa, creando una transición natural entre la vivienda y el exterior. Un camino común, compartido por los dos refugios, ofrece una vista única del tejado verde en voladizo.

South elevation

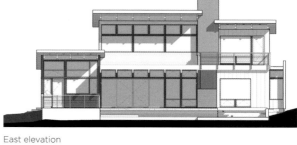

East elevation

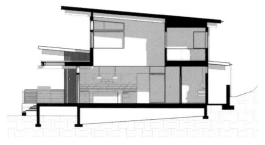

Section through dining area and guest bedroom

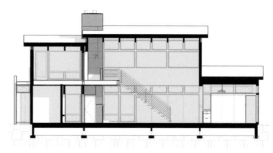

Section through staircase

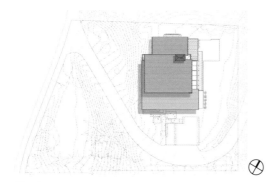

Site plan

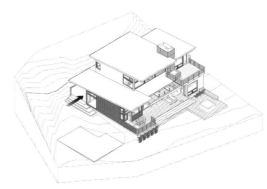

Axonometric view

Ground floor plan

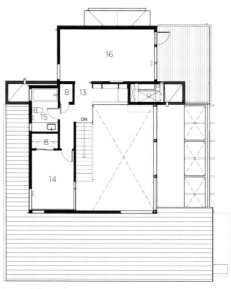

Second floor plan

1. Entry
2. Powder room
3. Mud/laundry room
4. Kitchen
5. Dining area
6. Living area
7. Office
8. Closet
9. Master bedroom
10. Master bathroom
11. Master closet
12. Mechanical room
13. Library
14. Bedroom
15. Bathroom
16. Media room

FINNE
ARCHITECTS

074
˅

078
˅

082
˅

DESCHUTES HOUSE

Architect and interior Designer:
Nils Finne, AIA, Design Principal;
Chris Hawley, Project Manager
Custom Steel Kitchen Light Bar:
Design by Nils Finne; fabrication by
Landbridge Lighting Llc
Custom Bathroom Accessories:
VRI Series of twisted steel bath accessories;
design by Nils Finne; fabrication by 5-STAR
Industries Llc
Custom Wood Ceiling Clouds:
Design by Nils Finne
VG Douglas Fir lift-Slide Doors:
Quantum Windows and Doors
General Contractor:
Duey Built Inc
Structural Engineer:
Swenson Say Fagét Structural Engineering
Photographer:
© Benjamin Benschneider

VENICE HOUSE

Architect and interior Designer:
Nils Finne, AIA, Design Principal;
Chris Hawley and Chris Graesser,
Project Managers
Custom Steel Kitchen Pendant Light Fixture:
Design by Nils Finne; fabrication by
Landbridge Lighting Llc
Custom Cast Glass Breakfast Counter:
Design by Nils Finne; Fabrication by
Glassworks Inc
Custom Bathroom Accessories:
VRI Series of twisted steel bath accessories;
design by Nils Finne; fabrication by 5-STAR
Industries Llc
General Contractor:
Bruder Construction
Structural Engineer:
Parker Resnick Structural Engineering
Photographer:
© Tom Bonner

MAZAMA HOUSE

Architect and interior Designer:
Nils Finne, AIA, Design Principal;
Chris Hawley, Project Architect/Manager;
Mary Rowe; Ross Determan, project Team
Custom Wood Cabinets:
Taylor Made Furniture
Custom Wood Furniture:
Seaboard Cabinets Co
General Contractor:
Steve Roeter, Principal; Randy Kolhase,
Project Superintendent/
Rimmer & Roeter Construction
Metal Fabrications and Custom Light
Fixtures:
5-STAR Industries Llc and
Landbridge Lighting Llc
Structural Engineer:
Monte Clark Engineering
Photographer:
© Benjamin Benschneider

Raised in the United States and Norway, Nils Finne established FINNE Architects in Seattle to bring a Scandinavian understanding of craft and landscape to the Pacific Northwest. The firm has practiced smart sustainable design for twenty-five years, designing new custom homes and renovation projects in Washington, Oregon, California, Michigan, Massachusetts, Virginia, Rhode Island, and Norway. FINNE is a member of the Green Building Council. Dedicated to the idea of Crafted Modernism, Nils Finne typically designs custom lighting, furniture, cabinets, and hardware for every project. FINNE has produced more than 80 custom fabrication pieces, which are available for purchase as stand-alone items.

Aufgewachsen in den Vereinigten Staaten und Norwegen, gründete Nils Finne FINNE Architects in Seattle, um das skandinavische Verständnis von Handwerk und Landschaft in den pazifischen Nordwesten zu bringen. Das Unternehmen praktiziert seit fünfundzwanzig Jahren intelligentes, nachhaltiges Design und entwirft neue Eigenheime und Renovierungsprojekte in Washington, Oregon, Kalifornien, Michigan, Massachusetts, Virginia, Rhode Island und Norwegen. FINNE ist Mitglied des Green Building Council. Nils Finne, der sich der Idee des handwerklichen Modernismus verschrieben hat, entwirft für jedes Projekt maßgeschneiderte Leuchten, Möbel, Schränke und Beschläge. FINNE hat mehr als 80 Sonderanfertigungen hergestellt, die auch als Einzelstücke erworben werden können.

Élevé aux États-Unis et en Norvège, Nils Finne a fondé FINNE Architects à Seattle pour apporter la compréhension scandinave de l'artisanat et du paysage au nord-ouest du Pacifique. L'entreprise pratique la conception durable intelligente depuis vingt-cinq ans, concevant de nouvelles maisons personnalisées et des projets de rénovation dans les États de Washington, de l'Oregon, de Californie, du Michigan, du Massachusetts, de Virginie, de Rhode Island et de Norvège. FINNE est membre du Green Building Council. Dédié à l'idée du modernisme artisanal, Nils Finne conçoit souvent des éclairages, des meubles, des armoires et des ferrures sur mesure pour chaque projet. FINNE a produit plus de 80 pièces sur mesure, qui peuvent être achetées en tant qu'articles autonomes.

Criado en Estados Unidos y Noruega, Nils Finne fundó FINNE Architects en Seattle para llevar al noroeste del Pacífico la comprensión escandinava de la artesanía y el paisaje. La empresa lleva veinticinco años practicando el diseño sostenible inteligente, diseñando nuevas casas a medida y proyectos de renovación en Washington, Oregón, California, Michigan, Massachusetts, Virginia, Rhode Island y Noruega. FINNE es miembro del Green Building Council. Dedicado a la idea del modernismo artesanal, Nils Finne suele diseñar iluminación, muebles, armarios y herrajes a medida para cada proyecto. FINNE ha producido más de 80 piezas de fabricación a medida, que se pueden adquirir como artículos independientes.

DESCHUTES HOUSE

Bend, Oregon, United States // Lot area: 7,122 sq ft; building area: 2,950 sq ft

The Deschutes House wraps around a south-facing, grassy court-yard, with dramatic second-story spaces cantilevered toward the river. The living ceiling plane has CNC-milled wood ceiling panels inspired by the landscape morphology. The house is clad with two contrasting siding materials: tightly spaced red cedar and corrugated metal. The fireplace chimney is clad in Montana ledge stone. The house has many sustainable building features: 2 x 8 construction—40% greater insulation value—, large glass areas to provide natural lighting and ventilation, roof overhangs for sun and snow protection, metal siding for durability, and radiant floor heating. The house also has solar hot water panels.

La Deschutes House s'étend autour d'une cour herbeuse orientée au sud, avec des espaces spectaculaires au deuxième étage, en porte-à-faux vers la rivière. Le plan de la toiture de la maison est constitué de panneaux de bois fraisé CNC inspirés par la morphologie du paysage. La maison est revêtue de deux matériaux de revêtement contrastés : du cèdre rouge largement espacé et de la tôle ondulée. La cheminée est habillée de pierre du Montana. La maison présente de nombreuses caractéristiques de construction durable : construction en 2 x 8 (valeur d'isolation supérieure de 40 %), grandes surfaces vitrées pour assurer un éclairage et une ventilation naturels, débords de toit pour protéger du soleil et de la neige, bardage métallique pour la durabilité et chauffage par le sol. La maison est également équipée de panneaux solaires pour l'eau chaude.

Das Deschutes House erstreckt sich um einen grasbewachsenen, nach Süden ausgerichteten Innenhof und bietet im zweiten Stock spektakuläre Räume, die zum Fluss hin auskragen. Die Dachebene des Hauses besteht aus CNC-gefrästen Holzplatten, die von der Morphologie der Landschaft inspiriert sind. Das Haus ist mit zwei kontrastierenden Verkleidungsmaterialien verkleidet: rote Zeder in großen Abständen und Wellblech. Der Kamin ist mit Montana-Stein verkleidet. Das Haus verfügt über viele nachhaltige Konstruktionsmerkmale: 2 x 8-Konstruktion (40 % mehr Dämmwert), große Glasflächen für natürliche Beleuchtung und Belüftung, Dachüberstände zum Schutz vor Sonne und Schnee, Metallverkleidung für Langlebigkeit und Fußbodenheizung. Das Haus verfügt außerdem über eine Solaranlage zur Warmwasserbereitung.

La Deschutes House se extiende alrededor de un patio herboso orientado al sur, con espectaculares espacios en el segundo piso en voladizo hacia el río. El plano del techo de la vivienda tiene paneles de madera fresados con CNC inspirados en la morfología del paisaje. La casa está revestida con dos materiales de revestimiento que contrastan: cedro rojo muy espaciado y metal ondulado. La chimenea está revestida de piedra de Montana. La casa tiene muchas características de construcción sostenible: construcción en 2 x 8 (un 40 % más de valor de aislamiento), grandes zonas acristaladas para proporcionar iluminación y ventilación naturales, voladizos en el tejado para proteger del sol y la nieve, revestimiento metálico para mayor durabilidad y calefacción por suelo radiante. La casa también cuenta con paneles solares de agua caliente.

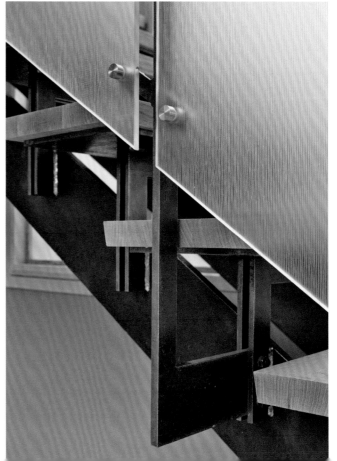

VENICE HOUSE

Los Angeles, California, United States // Lot area: 10,895 sq ft; building area: 4,900 sq ft

The Venice House is a garden sanctuary on a narrow lot. It consists of a series of folded roof planes and a collage of textured metal and wood exterior surfaces. The wood living pavilion projects into the garden along the wester edge of the site, with a soaring hyperbolic paraboloid roof formed by exposed Douglas fir beams. Oversized 8 feet by 10 feet sliding glass doors open the dining area to the pool. Interior finishes are simple, with rift-sawn white oak cabinets and floors combined with white plaster walls. A custom steel light fixture hangs over the quartz kitchen island and cast-glass breakfast counter. The house is highly energy-efficient, with deep roof overhangs, natural lighting and ventilation, LED lighting, and drought-tolerant landscaping.

La Venice House est un sanctuaire paysager situé sur un terrain étroit. Il se compose d'une série de plans de toit pliés et d'un collage de surfaces extérieures texturées en métal et en bois. Le pavillon en bois s'avance dans le jardin le long du bord ouest du site, avec un toit hyperbolique surélevé formé par des poutres apparentes en sapin de Douglas. Des portes en verre coulissantes de 2,5 x 3 mètres s'ouvrent de la salle à manger à la piscine. Les finitions intérieures sont simples, avec des armoires et des sols en chêne scié blanc combinés à des murs en plâtre blanc. Un lustre en acier personnalisé est suspendu au-dessus de l'îlot de cuisine en quartz et du bar du petit-déjeuner en verre moulé. La maison est très économe en énergie, avec de profonds débords de toit, un éclairage et une ventilation naturels, un éclairage LED et un aménagement paysager tolérant à la sécheresse.

Das Venice House ist ein landschaftlich gestaltetes Heiligtum auf einem schmalen Grundstück. Es besteht aus einer Reihe von gefalteten Dachebenen und einer Collage aus strukturierten Metall- und Holzaußenflächen. Der Holzpavillon ragt am westlichen Rand des Grundstücks in den Garten hinein und hat ein erhöhtes, hyperbolisches Parabeldach aus freiliegenden Douglasienbalken. Glasschiebetüren von 2,5 x 3 Meter öffnen sich vom Essbereich zum Pool. Die Innenausstattung ist schlicht, mit weiß gesägten Eichenschränken und -böden in Kombination mit weißen Gipswänden. Über der Kücheninsel aus Quarz und der Frühstücksbar aus Gussglas hängt ein maßgeschneiderter Stahlkronleuchter. Das Haus ist äußerst energieeffizient, mit tiefen Dachüberständen, natürlicher Beleuchtung und Belüftung, LED-Beleuchtung und trockenheitstoleranter Bepflanzung.

La Venice House es un santuario ajardinado en un terreno estrecho. Está formada por una serie de planos de tejado plegados y un collage de superficies exteriores de metal y madera con textura. El pabellón de madera se proyecta en el jardín a lo largo del borde occidental del terreno, con un elevado techo parabólico hiperbólico formado por vigas de abeto Douglas expuestas. Unas puertas correderas de cristal de 2,5 x 3 metros abren el comedor a la piscina. Los acabados interiores son sencillos, con armarios y suelos de roble blanco aserrado combinados con paredes de yeso blanco. Una lámpara de acero personalizada cuelga sobre la isla de cocina de cuarzo y la barra de desayuno de vidrio fundido. La casa es muy efciente desde el punto de vista energético, con profundos voladizos en el tejado, iluminación y ventilación naturales, iluminación LED y un paisaje tolerante a la sequía.

MAZAMA HOUSE

Winthrop, Washington, United States // Lot area: 4 acres; building area: 4,300 sq ft

The house is located in a copse of trees at the easterly end of a large meadow on the North Cascades' eastern edge. Two building volumes indicate the house organization. A grounded two-story bedroom wing anchors a raised living pavilion, lifted off the ground by a series of exposed steel columns. The raised floor level provides enhanced views and keeps the main living level well above the winter snow accumulation. The house reflects the continuing FINNE investigation into the idea of crafted modernism, with cast bronze inserts at the front door, variegated laser-cut steel railing panels, a curvilinear cast-glass kitchen counter, waterjet-cut aluminum light fixtures, and custom furniture pieces.

La maison est située dans un bosquet d'arbres à l'extrémité orientale d'une grande prairie, à l'est des Cascades du Nord. Deux volumes de construction indiquent l'organisation de la maison. Une aile de chambre à coucher de deux étages sert d'ancrage à un pavillon d'habitation surélevé, surélevé du sol par une série de colonnes d'acier apparentes. Le niveau surélevé du sol offre de meilleures vues et maintient le niveau de vie principal bien au-dessus de l'accumulation de neige en hiver. La maison reflète la recherche permanente de FINNE sur l'idée de modernisme artisanal, avec des inserts en bronze coulé dans la porte d'entrée, des panneaux de balustrade en acier découpé au laser, un comptoir de cuisine en verre coulé curviligne, des luminaires en aluminium découpé au jet d'eau et des meubles personnalisés.

Das Haus liegt in einer Baumgruppe am östlichen Ende einer großen Wiese am östlichen Rand der North Cascades. Zwei Baukörper weisen auf die Organisation des Hauses hin. Ein zweigeschossiger Schlaftrakt verankert einen erhöhten Wohnpavillon, der durch eine Reihe von freiliegenden Stahlstützen vom Boden abgehoben ist. Das erhöhte Erdgeschoss bietet eine bessere Aussicht und hält die Hauptwohnebene im Winter weit über der Schneelast. Das Haus spiegelt FINNEs fortwährende Erforschung der Idee des handwerklichen Modernismus wider, mit Bronzegusseinsätzen in der Eingangstür, bunten lasergeschnittenen Stahlgeländerpaneelen, einer geschwungenen Küchenarbeitsplatte aus Gussglas, wasserstrahlgeschnittenen Aluminiumleuchten und maßgefertigten Möbelstücken.

La casa está situada en un bosquecillo de árboles en el extremo oriental de una gran pradera en el borde oriental de las Cascadas del Norte. Dos volúmenes de construcción indican la organización de la casa. Un ala de dormitorios de dos pisos ancla un pabellón de estar elevado, levantado del suelo por una serie de columnas de acero expuestas. El nivel de suelo elevado ofrece mejores vistas y mantiene el nivel principal de la vivienda muy por encima de la acumulación de nieve en invierno. La casa refleja la continua investigación de FINNE sobre la idea del modernismo artesanal, con inserciones de bronce fundido en la puerta principal, paneles de barandilla de acero cortados con láser abigarrado, una encimera de cocina curvilínea de vidrio fundido, lámparas de aluminio cortadas con chorro de agua y piezas de mobiliario personalizadas.

ROBERT HUTCHISON
ARCHITECTURE

COURTYARD HOUSE ON A RIVER

Architecture Design Team:
Robert Hutchison, Scott Claassen,
Wenjing Zhang
Structural Engineer:
Swenson Say Faget
General Contractor:
Owner
Steel fireplace fabrication:
Dovetail General Contractors
Photographer:
© Mark Woods Photography

Awards:
2017 Canadian Wood Council Award

CANTILEVER HOUSE

Architecture Design Team:
Robert Hutchison, Scott Claassen
Interior Designer:
Carla Allbee
Landscape Architect:
The Berger Partnership
Structural Engineer:
Perbix Bykonen
General Contractor:
Dolan Built LLC
Photographer:
© Mark Woods Photography

COURTYARD DADU

Architecture Design Team:
Robert Hutchison, Sean Morgan
Structural Engineer:
Bykonen Carter Quinn Structural Engineers
General Contractor:
IHS Contractors
Photographer:
© Eirik Johnson

Awards:
2021 AIA Seattle Home of Distinction

Robert Hutchison Architecture (RHA) is an architecture and design studio based in Seattle, Washington, specializing in projects that explore the relationship between elegance and economy. For RHA, buildings are approached less as objects and more as interludes in space and time, enhancing the connection to the natural environment and between people. RHA explores the boundaries of architecture, balancing the permanent with the ephemeral to create works evoking a strong sense of place. The firm's projects range from custom residences, cabins, art studios, and commercial interiors to temporary installations, speculative projects, and community-based research projects. The firm's growing collection of DADUs (Detached Accessory Dwelling Units) manifest RHA's concern with finding economical ways to live and work more efficiently in compact footprints, contributing to discussions around increasing urban density in sustainable, human-centered ways.

Robert Hutchison Architecture (RHA) ist ein Architektur- und Designbüro mit Sitz in Seattle, Washington, das sich auf Projekte spezialisiert hat, die das Verhältnis zwischen Eleganz und Wirtschaftlichkeit untersuchen. Für RHA werden Gebäude weniger als Objekte betrachtet, sondern eher als Zwischenspiele in Raum und Zeit, wodurch die Verbindung zur natürlichen Umgebung und zwischen Menschen verstärkt wird. RHA untersucht die Grenzen der Architektur und balanciert das Beständige mit dem Vergänglichen aus, um Werke zu schaffen, die ein starkes Ortsgefühl hervorrufen. Die Projekte des Unternehmens reichen von individuellen Wohnhäusern, Landhäusern, Kunstateliers und kommerziellen Innenräumen bis hin zu temporären Installationen, spekulativen Projekten und gemeinschaftsbasierten Forschungsprojekten. Die wachsende Sammlung von Nebenwohneinheiten unterstreicht das Anliegen von RHA, wirtschaftliche Wege zu finden, um auf kompaktem Raum effizienter zu leben und zu arbeiten, und damit einen Beitrag zu den Diskussionen über die Erhöhung der städtischen Dichte auf nachhaltige und menschenzentrierte Weise zu leisten.

Robert Hutchison Architecture (RHA) est un cabinet d'architecture et de design basé à Seattle, Washington, spécialisé dans les projets qui explorent la relation entre élégance et économie. Pour la RHA, les bâtiments sont abordés moins comme des objets que comme des interludes dans l'espace et le temps, renforçant le lien avec l'environnement naturel et entre les personnes. RHA explore les frontières de l'architecture, équilibrant le permanent et l'éphémère pour créer des œuvres qui évoquent un fort sentiment de lieu. Les projets de l'entreprise vont des résidences personnalisées, des cottages, des studios d'art et des intérieurs commerciaux aux installations temporaires, projets spéculatifs et projets de recherche communautaires. La collection croissante d'unités d'habitations accessoires de l'entreprise souligne le souci de la RHA de trouver des moyens économiques de vivre et de travailler plus efficacement dans des espaces compacts, contribuant ainsi aux discussions sur l'augmentation de la densité urbaine d'une manière durable et centrée sur l'homme.

Robert Hutchison Architecture (RHA) es un estudio de arquitectura y diseño con sede en Seattle, Washington, especializado en proyectos que exploran la relación entre elegancia y economía. Para RHA, los edificios se enfocan más como interludios en el espacio y el tiempo que como objetos, mejorando la conexión con el entorno natural y entre las personas. RHA explora los límites de la arquitectura, equilibrando lo permanente con lo efímero para crear obras que evocan un fuerte sentido del lugar. Los proyectos de la empresa abarcan desde residencias personalizadas, cabañas, estudios de arte e interiores comerciales hasta instalaciones temporales, proyectos especulativos y proyectos de investigación basados en la comunidad. La creciente colección de unidades de vivineda accesorias de la empresa pone de manifiesto la preocupación de RHA por encontrar formas económicas de vivir y trabajar de forma más eficiente en espacios compactos, contribuyendo a los debates sobre el aumento de la densidad urbana de forma sostenible y centrada en el ser humano.

COURTYARD HOUSE ON A RIVER

Greenwater, Washington, United States // Lot area: 1 acre; building area: 2,000 sq ft

The home was designed for a couple who relocated to this rural location where they could enjoy skiing and mountain biking year-round. It is clad in a custom-run Western red cedar rainscreen blending into the surrounding forest along the banks of the glacier-fed White River in the shadow of Mount Rainier. The owners served as general contractors and self-performed much of the work to maintain a tight construction budget. With the architect and homeowners/contractors working together diligently throughout the design and construction process, the building was kept as compact as possible, minimizing site disturbance. Through thoughtfully planned spaces and views, carefully considered natural lighting, and a warm material palette, the residence emphasizes design over size.

Cette maison a été conçue pour un couple qui s'est installé dans cet endroit rural pour profiter du ski et du VTT toute l'année. Il est revêtu d'un écran pare-pluie en cèdre rouge de l'Ouest fabriqué sur mesure qui se fond dans la forêt environnante, le long des rives de la rivière White alimentée par des glaciers, à l'ombre du mont Rainier. Les propriétaires ont fait office d'entrepreneurs et ont réalisé eux-mêmes une grande partie des travaux afin de respecter un budget de construction serré. L'architecte et les propriétaires/entrepreneurs ont travaillé ensemble avec diligence pendant le processus de conception et de construction, et le bâtiment a été maintenu aussi compact que possible, minimisant ainsi la perturbation du terrain. Grâce à la planification des espaces et des vues, à un éclairage naturel soigneusement étudié et à une palette de matériaux chaleureux, la résidence met l'accent sur le design.

Dieses Haus wurde für ein Paar entworfen, das in diese ländliche Gegend gezogen ist, um das ganze Jahr über Skifahren und Mountainbiken zu können. Es ist mit einer speziell angefertigten Regenwand aus westlicher Rotzeder verkleidet, die sich in den umliegenden Wald am Ufer des gletschergespeisten White River im Schatten des Mount Rainier einfügt. Die Eigentümer traten als Bauunternehmer auf und führten einen Großteil der Arbeiten selbst aus, um ein knappes Baubudget einzuhalten. Der Architekt und die Eigentümer/Auftragnehmer arbeiteten während des Planungs- und Bauprozesses sorgfältig zusammen, und das Gebäude wurde so kompakt wie möglich gehalten, um den Eingriff in den Boden zu minimieren. Durch die Planung von Räumen und Ausblicken, eine sorgfältig durchdachte natürliche Beleuchtung und eine Palette von warmen Materialien unterstreicht das Haus das Design.

Esta casa se diseñó para una pareja que se trasladó a este lugar rural para disfrutar del esquí y el ciclismo de montaña durante todo el año. Está revestida con una pantalla de lluvia de cedro rojo occidental hecha a medida que se integra en el bosque circundante a lo largo de las orillas del río White, alimentado por glaciares, a la sombra del monte Rainier. Los propietarios actuaron como contratistas y realizaron ellos mismos gran parte del trabajo para mantener un presupuesto de construcción ajustado. El arquitecto y los propietarios/contratistas trabajaron juntos con diligencia durante el proceso de diseño y construcción, y el edificio se mantuvo lo más compacto posible, reduciendo al mínimo la alteración del terreno. Gracias a la planificación de los espacios y las vistas, la iluminación natural cuidadosamente considerada y una paleta de materiales cálidos, la residencia hace hincapié en el diseño.

East elevation

West elevation

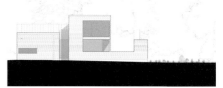

South elevation

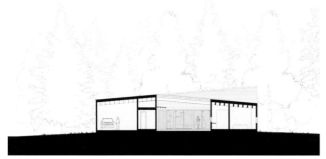

Section A

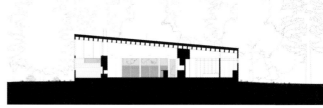

Section B

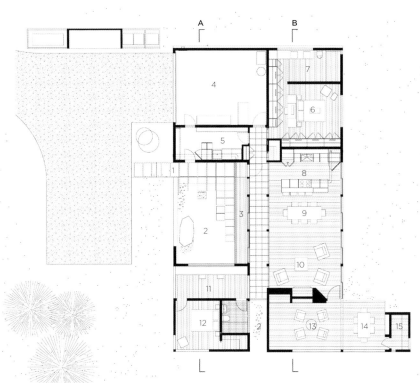

Floor plan

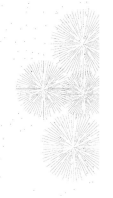

1. Entry
2. Courtyard
3. Deck
4. Ski and mountain bike workshop
5. Mud room
6. Master bedroom
7. Master bathroom
8. Kitchen
9. Dining
10. Living area
11. Study
12. Guest bedroom
13. Covered patio
14. Patio
15. Sauna

CANTILEVER HOUSE

Seattle, Washington, United States // Buiding area: 2,100 sq ft (residence), 800 sq ft (ADU)

The clients had lived in a compact Seattle bungalow for fifteen years on a small site overlooking Portage Bay. They loved the convenient location close to downtown Seattle and the water views, but the bungalow was difficult to heat and cool, had poor natural light, and suffered from water intrusion problems. They decided to construct a new house on the same property that distilled their urban lifestyle into an equally small footprint, a light-filled, and private home, yet transparent and oriented toward the water and city views. The primary architectural strategy connects the exterior entry, primary interior living areas, and exterior patio as a continuous spatial experience. To generate additional income, they devoted a third of the available living area to a rentable mother-in-law unit.

Les clients vivaient depuis quinze ans dans un bungalow à Seattle, sur un petit terrain donnant sur baie de Portage. Ils aimaient le bon emplacement, proche du centre-ville, et la vue sur l'eau, mais le bungalow était difficile à chauffer et à refroidir, avait peu de lumière naturelle et souffrait de problèmes d'intrusion d'eau. Ils ont décidé de construire une nouvelle maison sur la même propriété qui distillerait leur style de vie urbain dans un espace tout aussi petit, une maison lumineuse et privée, mais transparente et orientée vers la vue sur l'eau et la ville. La stratégie architecturale principale relie l'entrée extérieure, les principaux espaces de vie intérieurs et la cour extérieure en une seule expérience spatiale continue. Pour générer des revenus supplémentaires, ils ont consacré un tiers de l'espace habitable disponible à une unité louable.

Die Bauherren lebten seit fünfzehn Jahren in einem Bungalow in Seattle, der auf einem kleinen Grundstück mit Blick auf die Portage Bay stand. Sie schätzten die gute Lage in der Nähe des Stadtzentrums und den Blick aufs Wasser, aber der Bungalow war schwer zu heizen und zu kühlen, hatte wenig natürliches Licht und litt unter Wassereinbrüchen. Sie beschlossen, auf demselben Grundstück ein neues Haus zu bauen, das ihren urbanen Lebensstil auf ebenso kleinem Raum unterbringen sollte, ein Haus, das hell und privat, aber dennoch transparent und auf das Wasser und den Blick auf die Stadt ausgerichtet sein sollte. Die architektonische Hauptstrategie verbindet den Außeneingang, die Hauptwohnbereiche im Inneren und den Außenhof zu einem durchgehenden Raumerlebnis. Um zusätzliche Einnahmen zu erzielen, wurde ein Drittel der verfügbaren Wohnfläche als vermietbare Einheit genutzt.

Los clientes llevaban quince años viviendo en un bungaló en Seattle, en un pequeño terreno con vistas a la bahía de Portage. Les encantaba la buena ubicación, cerca del centro, y las vistas al agua, pero el bungaló era difícil de calentar y refrescar, tenía poca luz natural y sufría problemas de intrusión de agua. Decidieron construir una nueva casa en la misma propiedad que destilara su estilo de vida urbano en un espacio igualmente pequeño, una casa luminosa y privada, pero transparente y orientada hacia el agua y las vistas de la ciudad. La estrategia arquitectónica principal conecta la entrada exterior, las principales zonas de estar interiores y el patio exterior como una experiencia espacial continua. Para generar ingresos adicionales, dedicaron un tercio de la superficie habitable disponible a una unidad alquilable.

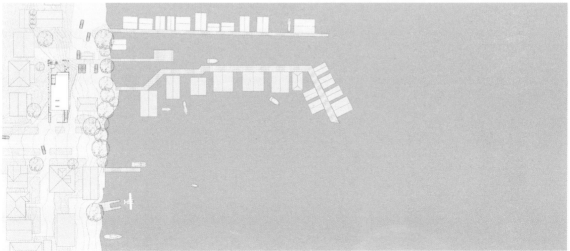

Site plan

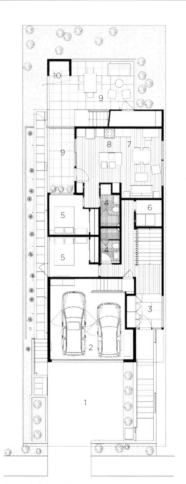

Ground floor plan

Second floor plan

1. Driveway
2. Garage
3. Entry foyer
4. Bathroom
5. Bedroom
6. Laundry room
7. Living/dining area
8. Kitchen
9. Patio
10. BBQ
11. Driveway below
12. Exterior stair below
13. Master bedroom
14. Master bathroom
15. Office
16. Powder room
17. Dining area
18. Kitchen
19. Living area
20. Patio below
21. BBQ below

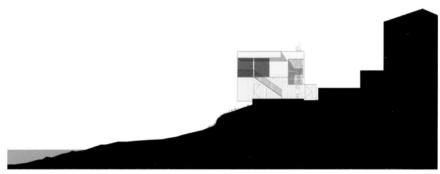

North elevation

South elevation

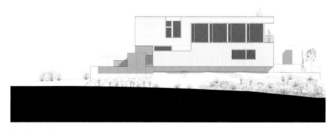

East elevation

Cross section

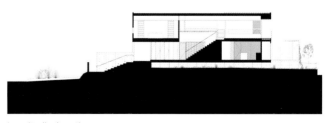

Longitudinal section

COURTYARD DADU

Seattle, Washington, United States // Lot area: 5,000 sq ft; building area: 760 sq ft

Courtyard DADU sits in the backyard of an early 1900s farmhouse in an urban Seattle neighborhood. It was designed as a living space for the property owner who planned to rent out the main house. Oriented around a north-facing courtyard, the DADU's U-shaped layout establishes a quiet outdoor space, creating protection and a sound barrier from the nearby freeway. The design steps down the site to create a diverse collection of interior spaces, moving from the bedroom and bathroom on the west side, stepping down to the kitchen and entry in the middle, and terminating in the more expansive living and dining area at the lowest portion of the site. The sleeping loft above the living and dining area and the custom stair add value while maintaining economy.

La Courtyard DADU est située dans l'arrière-cour d'une ferme du début des années 1900, dans un quartier urbain de Seattle. Il a été conçu comme une maison pour le propriétaire, qui prévoyait de louer la maison principale. Disposé autour d'une cour orientée au nord, le plan en U crée un espace extérieur calme, qui fait office de tampon et d'écran acoustique par rapport à l'autoroute voisine. La conception descend le long du site pour créer un ensemble diversifié d'espaces intérieurs, allant de la chambre et de la salle de bain sur le côté ouest, à la cuisine et à l'entrée au centre, pour se terminer par le grand salon et la salle à manger dans la partie la plus basse du site. Le loft au-dessus du salon et de la salle à manger et l'escalier personnalisé ajoutent de la valeur tout en restant économiques.

Courtyard DADU befindet sich im Hinterhof eines Bauernhauses aus der Zeit um 1900 in einem städtischen Viertel von Seattle. Es war als Wohnhaus für den Eigentümer gedacht, der das Haupthaus vermieten wollte. Der U-förmige Grundriss um einen nach Norden ausgerichteten Innenhof schafft einen ruhigen Außenbereich, der einen Puffer und eine Schallschutzwand zur nahe gelegenen Autobahn bildet. Der Entwurf ist absteigend angelegt, um verschiedene Innenräume zu schaffen, die vom Schlafzimmer und dem Bad auf der Westseite über die Küche und den Eingang in der Mitte bis hin zum großen Wohn- und Esszimmer im untersten Teil des Grundstücks reichen. Das Loft über dem Wohn- und Esszimmer und die maßgefertigte Treppe erhöhen den Wert des Hauses bei gleichzeitiger Wirtschaftlichkeit.

Courtyard DADU se encuentra en el patio trasero de una casa de campo de principios de 1900 en un barrio urbano de Seattle. Se diseñó como vivienda para el propietario, que tenía previsto alquilar la casa principal. Colocada en torno a un patio orientado al norte, la disposición en forma de U establece un espacio exterior tranquilo, creando una protección y una barrera acústica frente a la cercana autopista. El diseño desciende por el solar para crear un conjunto diverso de espacios interiores, que van desde el dormitorio y el cuarto de baño en el lado oeste, descienden hasta la cocina y la entrada en el centro, y terminan en el salón y el comedor más amplios en la parte más baja del solar. El altillo sobre el salón y el comedor y la escalera personalizada añaden valor al tiempo que mantienen la economía.

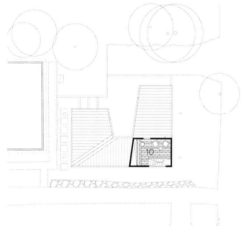

Upper floor plan

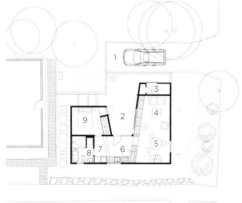

Lower floor plan

1. Driveway
2. Courtyard
3. Storage/utilities
4. Living area
5. Dining area
6. Kitchen
7. Laundry room
8. Bathroom
9. Bedroom
10. Office

South elevation

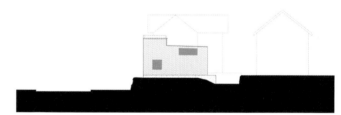

East elevation

Section East-West through kitchen

Section East-West through courtyard

CAST
ARCHITECTURE

102
v

106
v

110
v

BEAR CREEK BASECAMP

Architecture Design Team: CAST architecture/ Tim Hammer, Principal
Contractor: Phil Dietz/Lost River Construction
Landscape Designer: Cathy Habermehl/ Windy Valley Landscaping
Cabinetry and Casework: Phil Woraz/ Woraz Woodworking
Photographer:
© CAST architecture

CEDAR COTTAGE

Architecture Design Team:
CAST architecture/ Stefan Hampden, Principal; Matt Hutchins, AIA, CPHD, Principal; Adam Clements, Project Architect
Photographer:
© Cindy Apple Photography

RAINIER BEACH URBAN FARM AND WETLANDS

Architecture Design Team: CAST architecture/ Matt Hutchins, AIA CPHD and Forrest Murphy, LEED AP BD+C
Owner: City of Seattle Parks and Recreation, Seattle Tilth
Landscape Architect: Berger Partnership
Kitchen Designer: Bundy and Associates
Civil Engineer: Anchor QEA
Structural Engineer: Smith Lubke Engineering
Electrical Engineer: Sparling
Mechanical Engineer: The Greenbusch Group
Photographers:
© Built Work Photography, CAST architecture

Awards:
2020 AIA Washington Council Civic Design Merit Award
2020 AIA Seattle Honor Awards, Honorable Mention
2021 Washington ASLA, Award of Merit

🌐 www.castarchitecture.com ◎ cast.arch

Forrest Murphy | Matt Hutchins | Stefan Hampden | Tim Hammer

CAST architecture is a Seattle-based firm with extensive experience designing contemporary spaces throughout the Northwest. Specializing in modern and sustainable projects, the firm is committed to improving the lives of individuals, families, and communities through thoughtful and vibrant design. Founded in 1999, CAST has created inspired places—within the residential, commercial, and public sectors—that embody the Northwest region's unique vitality, intelligence, and lifestyle. CAST is an active part of this community and strives to make it a better place with every project, whether it is a serene house or a bustling public space. Their work is sensitive to site and climate and responds with thoughtful, intuitive solutions that make the most of its environment.

CAST Architecture ist ein in Seattle ansässiges Studio mit umfassender Erfahrung in der Gestaltung zeitgenössischer Räume im gesamten Nordwesten. Das Unternehmen hat sich auf moderne, nachhaltige Projekte spezialisiert und setzt sich dafür ein, das Leben von Einzelpersonen, Familien und Gemeinden durch durchdachtes und lebendiges Design zu verbessern. Das 1999 gegründete Unternehmen CAST hat Räume im Wohn-, Geschäfts- und öffentlichen Sektor geschaffen, die die einzigartige Vitalität, Intelligenz und den Lebensstil der Region Nordwest verkörpern. CAST ist ein aktiver Teil dieser Gemeinschaft und ist bestrebt, sie mit jedem Projekt zu einem besseren Ort zu machen, ob es sich nun um ein ruhiges Haus oder einen belebten öffentlichen Raum handelt. Ihre Arbeit ist sensibel für Ort und Klima und reagiert mit durchdachten und intuitiven Lösungen, die das Beste aus ihrer Umgebung machen.

CAST Architecture est un studio basé à Seattle qui possède une grande expérience dans la conception d'espaces contemporains dans tout le Nord-Ouest. Spécialisée dans les projets modernes et durables, l'entreprise s'engage à améliorer la vie des individus, des familles et des communautés grâce à une conception réfléchie et dynamique. Fondée en 1999, CAST a créé des espaces dans les secteurs résidentiel, commercial et public qui incarnent la vitalité, l'intelligence et le style de vie uniques de la région du Nord-Ouest. CAST est une partie active de cette communauté et s'efforce d'en faire un endroit meilleur avec chaque projet, qu'il s'agisse d'une maison tranquille ou d'un espace public animé. Leur travail est sensible au lieu et au climat et répond par des solutions réfléchies et intuitives qui tirent le meilleur parti de leur environnement.

CAST Achitecture es un estudio con sede en Seattle que cuenta con una amplia experiencia en el diseño de espacios contemporáneos en todo el noroeste. Especializada en proyectos modernos y sostenibles, la empresa se compromete a mejorar la vida de las personas, las familias y las comunidades a través de un diseño reflexivo y vibrante. Fundada en 1999, CAST ha creado espacios en los sectores residencial, comercial y público que encarnan la vitalidad, la inteligencia y el estilo de vida únicos de la región del Noroeste. CAST es una parte activa de esta comunidad y se esfuerza por hacerla un lugar mejor con cada proyecto, ya sea una casa tranquila o un espacio público bullicioso. Su trabajo es sensible al lugar y al clima y responde con soluciones reflexivas e intuitivas que aprovechan al máximo su entorno.

BEAR CREEK BASECAMP

Winthrop, Washington, United States // Lot area: 20 acres; building area: 2,800 sq ft

When a young family of five decided to build a second home in Washington's Methow Valley, they envisioned a house that would provide an intimate connection with the landscape while allowing them to accommodate friends and family for extended stays. The home needed to be comfortable, low-maintenance, and endure in a climate that ranges from winter snowpacks and freezing temperatures to sun-baked summers. The home seeks a minimally intrusive presence in the sparsely populated landscape through open-air verandas and glazed corridors join the home's three living vessels and connect occupants to the adjacent landscapes, lake below, and distant North Cascades peaks. The balance of durable materials, an experiential plan, and a modest scale help focus this mountain retreat on the place, people, and adventures.

Lorsqu'une jeune famille de cinq personnes a décidé de construire une résidence secondaire dans la vallée de Methow, dans l'État de Washington, elle a imaginé une maison qui lui permettrait d'avoir un lien intime avec le paysage tout en pouvant accueillir des amis et de la famille pour des séjours prolongés. La maison devait être confortable, nécessiter peu d'entretien et résister à un climat qui oscille entre les neiges hivernales et des températures glaciales et des étés ensoleillés. La maison cherche à s'immiscer le moins possible dans le paysage peu peuplé a travers des terrasses en plein air et des passerelles vitrées relient les trois baies habitables de la maison et connectent les occupants aux paysages adjacents, au lac et aux sommets lointains des Cascades du Nord. Un équilibre entre des matériaux durables, un plan expérimental et une échelle modeste permet de concentrer cette retraite en montagne sur le lieu, les personnes et l'aventure.

Als eine junge fünfköpfige Familie beschloss, im Methow Valley in Washington ein zweites Haus zu bauen, schwebte ihnen ein Haus vor, das eine enge Verbindung zur Landschaft herstellt und gleichzeitig die Möglichkeit bietet, Freunde und Familie für längere Zeit zu beherbergen. Das Haus sollte komfortabel und wartungsarm sein und einem Klima standhalten, das zwischen Schnee im Winter und eisigen Temperaturen und sonnigen Sommern schwankt. Das Haus sucht eine minimal aufdringliche Präsenz in der dünn besiedelten Landschaft durch Open-Air-Veranden und verglaste Korridore, die die drei Wohnschiffe des Hauses verbinden und die Bewohner mit den angrenzenden Landschaften, dem darunter liegenden See und den fernen Gipfeln der North Cascades verbinden. Ein ausgewogenes Verhältnis von langlebigen Materialien, ein experimenteller Plan und ein bescheidener Maßstab tragen dazu bei, dass sich dieser Rückzugsort in den Bergen auf Ort, Menschen und Abenteuer konzentriert.

Cuando una joven familia de cinco miembros decidió construir una segunda vivienda en el valle de Methow, en Washington, imaginó una casa que proporcionara una conexión íntima con el paisaje y que, al mismo tiempo, les permitiera alojar a amigos y familiares en estancias prolongadas. La casa tenía que ser cómoda, de bajo mantenimiento, y resistir a un clima que oscila entre las nevadas invernales y las temperaturas gélidas y los veranos soleados. La casa busca una presencia mínimamente intrusiva en el paisaje escasamente poblado a traves de terrazas al aire libre y los pasillos acristalados unen las tres naves habitables de la casa y conectan a los ocupantes con los paisajes adyacentes, el lago y los lejanos picos de las Cascadas del Norte. El equilibrio de materiales duraderos, un plan experimental y una escala modesta ayudan a centrar este refugio de montaña en el lugar, las personas y las aventuras.

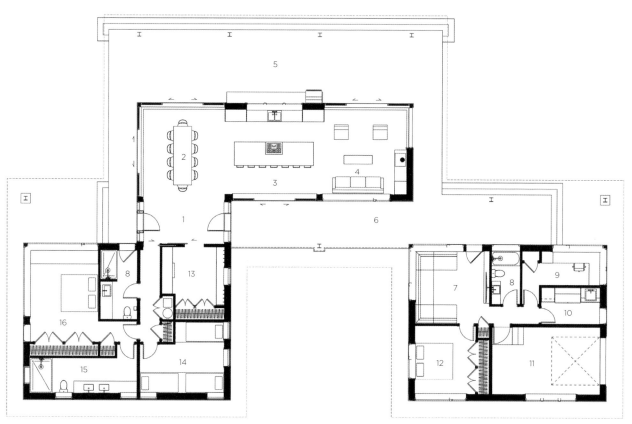

Floor plan

1. Entry
2. Dining area
3. Kitchen
4. Living area
5. Patio
6. Entry veranda
7. Family room
8. Bathroom
9. Office
10. Laundry room
11. Garage/utilities
12. Guest bedroom
13. Pantry/mud room
14. Bunkroom
15. Master bathroom
16. Master bedroom

CEDAR COTTAGE

Seattle, Washington, United States // Building area: 467 sq ft (One-bedroom option)/631 sq ft (two-bedroom option)

The Cedar Cottage is a super-efficient, bright, modern backyard cottage design that can be configured as a one or two-bedroom, oriented for privacy, daylight, or solar access. It is designed with practical, conventional construction in mind. All on one level, it is ideal for seniors looking to downsize but not compromise on the quality of life. At only 467 square feet of interior floor area, the Cedar Cottage has an extremely efficient footprint, providing well-daylit space for living, necessary storage, flexibility in many sites—including sloped ones—covered outdoor porch space, plus easy expandability for families or roommates with a two-bedroom model. The Cedar Cottage has a compact form, a solar-ready sloped roof, and a slab-on-grade foundation.

Le Cedar Cottage est une conception d'arrière-cour super efficace, lumineuse et moderne qui peut être configurée comme une ou deux chambres à coucher, orientée pour l'intimité, la lumière du jour ou l'accès solaire. Il est conçu dans une optique de construction pratique et conventionnelle. Tout sur un seul étage, il est idéal pour les personnes âgées qui cherchent à réduire leur taille sans compromettre leur qualité de vie. Avec seulement 44 m² de surface intérieure, la cabine présente une empreinte extrêmement efficace, offrant un espace de vie bien éclairé, les rangements nécessaires, une flexibilité en de nombreux points, y compris les pentes, un espace de porche extérieur couvert, ainsi que la facilité d'extension pour les familles ou les colocataires avec un modèle à deux chambres. Le Cedar Cottage a une forme compacte, un toit en pente prêt pour l'énergie solaire et une fondation en dalle sur sol.

Das Cedar Cottage ist ein super-effizientes, helles und modernes Hinterhof-Design, das als Ein- oder Zweizimmerhaus konfiguriert werden kann und auf Privatsphäre, Tageslicht oder Sonneneinstrahlung ausgerichtet ist. Es wurde mit Blick auf eine praktische und konventionelle Konstruktion entworfen. Die Wohnung befindet sich auf einer Etage und ist ideal für Senioren, die sich verkleinern möchten, ohne dabei auf Lebensqualität verzichten zu müssen. Mit einer Innenfläche von nur 44 m² ist die Hütte äußerst effizient und bietet einen gut beleuchteten Wohnraum, den notwendigen Stauraum, Flexibilität an vielen Stellen, einschließlich Schrägen, eine überdachte Veranda im Freien sowie die Möglichkeit der Erweiterung für Familien oder Mitbewohner mit einem Modell mit zwei Schlafzimmern. Das Cedar Cottage hat eine kompakte Form, ein solartaugliches Schrägdach und ein ebenerdiges Fundament.

La Cedar Cottage es un diseño situado en un patio trasero súper eficiente, luminoso y moderno, que puede configurarse como de uno o dos dormitorios, orientado a la privacidad, la luz del día o el acceso solar. Está diseñada pensando en una construcción práctica y convencional. Todo en una sola planta, es ideal para las personas mayores que buscan reducir el tamaño pero sin comprometer la calidad de vida. Con solo 44 m² de superficie interior, la cabaña tiene una huella extremadamente eficiente, proporcionando un espacio bien iluminado para la vida, el almacenamiento necesario, la flexibilidad en muchos puntos, incluyendo los inclinados, un espacio de porche cubierto al aire libre, además de la facilidad de expansión para las familias o compañeros de cuarto con un modelo de dos dormitorios. El Cedar Cottage tiene una forma compacta, un tejado inclinado preparado para la energía solar y unos cimientos de losa sobre suelo.

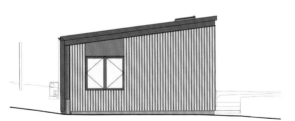

North elevation

West elevation

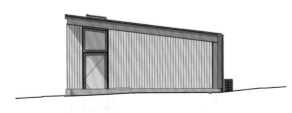

South elevation

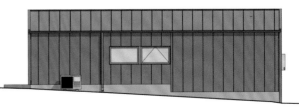

East elevation

Perspective section

One-bedroom floor plan

Two-bedroom floor plan

RAINIER BEACH URBAN FARM AND WETLANDS (RBUFW)

Seattle, Washington, United States // Lot area: 7 acres; building area: 1,800 sq ft

RBUFW is a partnership between Seattle Tilth Alliance and the City of Seattle Parks and Recreation to transform a lakefront parcel into a regional center for the promotion of urban agriculture and local food production. At the heart of the farm is the new Classroom Building. Simple and durable, it combines a community gathering area, a large demonstration kitchen, and space for processing produce harvested on-site. The farm inspires and educates people to safeguard our natural resources while building an equitable and sustainable local food system. It also hosts fresh food-related programs for community-supported agriculture, gardening, beekeeping, and food production. The Classroom Building's canopy is wrapped in translucent polycarbonate, linking this building to its agricultural heritage among the greenhouses.

Le RBUFW est un partenariat entre la Seattle Tilth Alliance et la ville de Seattle Parks and Recreation pour la transformation d'une parcelle en bord de lac en un centre régional de promotion de l'agriculture urbaine et de la production alimentaire locale. Au cœur de la ferme se trouve le nouveau bâtiment de classe. Le bâtiment simple et durable combine une zone de réunion communautaire, une grande cuisine de démonstration et un espace pour la transformation des produits récoltés sur place. La ferme inspire et éduque les gens à sauvegarder nos ressources naturelles tout en construisant un système alimentaire local équitable et durable. La ferme accueille des programmes liés aux aliments frais pour l'agriculture soutenue par la communauté, le jardinage, l'apiculture et la production alimentaire. L'auvent du bâtiment des classes est enveloppé de polycarbonate translucide, reliant ce bâtiment à son héritage agricole parmi les serres.

Das RBUFW ist eine Partnerschaft zwischen der Seattle Tilth Alliance und den City of Seattle Parks and Recreation, um eine Parzelle am Seeufer in ein regionales Zentrum zu verwandeln, das die städtische Landwirtschaft und die lokale Lebensmittelproduktion fördert. Herzstück des Hofes ist das neue Schulgebäude. Das einfache und langlebige Gebäude kombiniert einen Besprechungsbereich, eine große Demonstrationsküche und einen Raum zur Verarbeitung von vor Ort geernteten Produkten. Die Farm inspiriert und erzieht Menschen dazu, natürliche Ressourcen zu schützen und gleichzeitig ein gerechtes und nachhaltiges lokales Ernährungssystem aufzubauen. Es beherbergt auch Programme im Zusammenhang mit frischen Lebensmitteln für die von der Gemeinschaft unterstützte Landwirtschaft, Gartenarbeit, Bienenzucht und Lebensmittelproduktion. Das Vordach des Klassenzimmergebäudes ist mit durchscheinendem Polycarbonat bedeckt und verbindet dieses Gebäude mit seinem landwirtschaftlichen Erbe inmitten der Gewächshäuser.

La RBUFW es una asociación entre la Seattle Tilth Alliance y el Ayuntamiento de Seattle Parks and Recreation para transformar una parcela frente al lago en un centro regional que promueve la agricultura urbana y la producción local de alimentos. En el corazón de la granja se encuentra el nuevo edificio de aulas. El edificio, sencillo y duradero, combina una zona de reunión, una gran cocina de demostraciónes y un espacio para procesar los productos cosechados in situ. La granja inspira y educa a la gente para salvaguardar los recursos naturales al tiempo que construye un sistema alimentario local equitativo y sostenible. También alberga programas relacionados con los alimentos frescos para la agricultura respaldada por la comunidad, la jardinería, la apicultura y la producción de alimentos. La marquesina del edificio de aulas está recubierta de policarbonato translúcido, lo que vincula este edificio con su patrimonio agrícola entre los invernaderos.

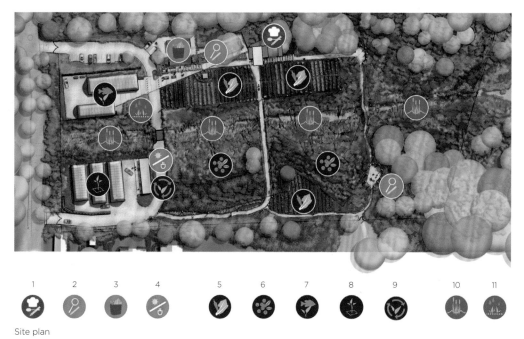

Site plan

1. Classroom/
   Community kitchen
2. Outdoor class
3. Market stand
4. PV roof
5. In-ground farming:
   Vegetables
6. Wetland buffer:
   Blueberry farming
7. Greenhouse: Aquaponics
8. Greenhouse: Starts
9. Site compost
10. Wetlands
11. Rain garden

North-south section

1. Community kitchen
2. Multi-purpose classroom
3. Classroom storage
4. Produce wash and pack

East-west section

1. Multi-purpose classroom
2. Covered terrace

SIGNAL
Architecture + Research

COTTONWOOD CANYON EXPERIENCE CENTER

Owner: Oregon State Parks
Fundraising and Partnerships: Oregon Parks Forever
Master Plan and Landscape Architecture: Walker Macy
Structural Engineer: Lund Opsahl
General Contractor: Tapani Underground
Solar Consulting and Installation: Sunbridge Solar
Photographer: © Gabe Border

🌐 signalarch.com ◎ signal_arch

Seattle-based studio Signal Architecture + Research strives to bring meaning to built environments. Founded in 2014 by architect Mark Johnson, Signal's award-winning structures amplify the stories of people and place through an artful blend of inquiry and architecture. From cultural landmarks to educational spaces, the firm is energized by discovery, communication, and collaboration to increase public access to design excellence. Focusing on projects that provide a common good and emphasize the power of location, history, and narrative, Signal creates thoroughly researched, thoughtful spaces that directly respond to their communities and surroundings. In an industry defined by aesthetics, Signal is guided by research, community engagement, and environmental consciousness to create an architecture of clarity and longevity.

Das in Seattle ansässige Büro Signal Architecture + Research bemüht sich, der gebauten Umwelt einen Sinn zu geben. Die preisgekrönten Strukturen von Signal, das 2014 von dem Architekten Mark Johnson gegründet wurde, erzählen die Geschichten von Menschen und Orten durch eine raffinierte Mischung aus Forschung und Architektur. Von kulturellen Wahrzeichen bis hin zu Bildungseinrichtungen setzt das Unternehmen auf Entdeckung, Kommunikation und Zusammenarbeit, um der Öffentlichkeit den Zugang zu exzellentem Design zu erleichtern. Signal konzentriert sich auf Projekte, die dem Gemeinwohl dienen und die Kraft des Ortes, der Geschichte und der Erzählung betonen, und schafft sorgfältig recherchierte und durchdachte Räume, die direkt auf ihre Gemeinden und Umgebungen reagieren. In einer Branche, die sich durch Ästhetik definiert, lässt sich Signal von Forschung, gesellschaftlichem Engagement und Umweltbewusstsein leiten, um eine klare und langlebige Architektur zu schaffen.

Signal Architecture + Research, studio basé à Seattle, s'efforce de donner un sens à l'environnement bâti. Fondée en 2014 par l'architecte Mark Johnson, les structures primées de Signal amplifient les histoires des gens et des lieux grâce à un mélange ingénieux de recherche et d'architecture. Qu'il s'agisse de points de repère culturels ou d'espaces éducatifs, l'entreprise mise sur la découverte, la communication et la collaboration pour permettre au public d'accéder à l'excellence en matière de conception. En se concentrant sur des projets qui fournissent un bien commun et soulignent le pouvoir de l'emplacement, de l'histoire et de la narration, Signal crée des espaces soigneusement étudiés et réfléchis qui répondent directement à leurs communautés et environnements. Dans un secteur défini par l'esthétique, Signal est guidé par la recherche, l'engagement communautaire et la conscience environnementale pour créer une architecture claire et durable.

El estudio Signal Architecture + Research, con sede en Seattle, se esfuerza por dar sentido a los entornos construidos. Fundado en 2014 por el arquitecto Mark Johnson, las premiadas estructuras de Signal amplifican las historias de las personas y los lugares a través de una ingeniosa mezcla de investigación y arquitectura. Desde los hitos culturales hasta los espacios educativos, la empresa se nutre del descubrimiento, la comunicación y la colaboración para aumentar el acceso del público a la excelencia del diseño. Centrándose en proyectos que proporcionan un bien común y enfatizan el poder de la ubicación, la historia y la narrativa, Signal crea espacios cuidadosamente investigados y pensados que responden directamente a sus comunidades y entornos. En una industria definida por la estética, Signal se guía por la investigación, el compromiso con la comunidad y la conciencia medioambiental para crear una arquitectura de claridad y longevidad.

COTTONWOOD CANYON EXPERIENCE CENTER

Wasco, Oregon, United States // Lot area: 8,000 acres; building area: 1,500 sq ft

Cottonwood Canyon Experience Center is a multiuse facility in Cottonwood Canyon State Park, the second largest state park in Oregon. In 2016, Oregon State Parks brought on Portland-based Walker Macy to develop a master plan—including six cabins, a shower/bath facility, and the Cottonwood Canyon Experience Center—for a unique recreation experience. Signal Architecture + Research was selected to design the center, prioritizing the story of the place and the language of the landscape. The building references the ranch vernacular of the region with shaded outdoor space, windbreaks, wood stove hearth, and walkways. Interior spaces allow for maximum adaptability. Honest materials, durability, and weather protection informed the placement of the building to create a multipurpose facility that frames the past and the future in a timeless venue.

Le centre est une installation polyvalente située au Cottonwood Canyon State Park, le deuxième plus grand parc d'État de l'Oregon. En 2016, les parcs de l'État de l'Oregon ont engagé la société Walker Macy, basée à Portland, pour élaborer un plan directeur comprenant six cabanes, une installation de douches et de toilettes et le centre de loisirs pour une expérience unique. Signal Architecture + Research a été choisi pour concevoir le centre, en donnant la priorité à l'histoire du site et au langage du paysage. Le bâtiment fait référence aux ranchs de la région, avec des espaces extérieurs ombragés, des brise-vent, des cuisinières à bois et des allées. Les espaces intérieurs permettent une adaptabilité maximale. L'emplacement du bâtiment a été choisi en fonction de l'honnêteté des matériaux, de la durabilité et de la protection contre les intempéries afin de créer une installation polyvalente qui encadre le passé et l'avenir dans un lieu intemporel.

Das Zentrum ist eine Mehrzweckanlage im Cottonwood Canyon State Park, Oregons zweitgrößtem Staatspark. Im Jahr 2016 beauftragte Oregon State Parks den in Portland ansässigen Walker Macy mit der Entwicklung eines Masterplans, der sechs Kabinen, eine Dusch- und Toiletteneinrichtung sowie das Erholungszentrum für ein einzigartiges Erlebnis umfasste. Signal Architecture + Research wurde mit der Gestaltung des Zentrums beauftragt, wobei die Geschichte des Ortes und die Sprache der Landschaft im Vordergrund standen. Das Gebäude nimmt Bezug auf die Sprache der Ranches in der Region, mit schattigen Außenbereichen, Windschutz, Holzkochern und Wegen. Die Innenräume ermöglichen maximale Anpassungsfähigkeit. Ehrliche Materialien, Langlebigkeit und Wetterschutz bestimmten die Platzierung des Gebäudes, um eine Mehrzweckanlage zu schaffen, die Vergangenheit und Zukunft an einem zeitlosen Ort einrahmt.

El Centro es una instalación multiuso en el Parque Estatal del Cañón Cottonwood, el segundo parque estatal más grande de Oregón. En 2016, los Parques Estatales de Oregón contrataron a Walker Macy, con sede en Portland, para desarrollar un plan maestro que incluye seis cabañas, una instalación de duchas/baños y el Centro de Recreo, para una experiencia única. Signal Architecture + Research fue seleccionada para diseñar el centro, dando prioridad a la historia del lugar y al lenguaje del paisaje. El edificio hace referencia a los ranchos de la región, con espacios exteriores sombreados, cortavientos, estufas de leña y caminos. Los espacios interiores permiten la máxima adaptabilidad. La colocación del edificio se basó en la honestidad de los materiales, la durabilidad y la protección contra la intemperie para crear una instalación polivalente que enmarca el pasado y el futuro en un lugar intemporal.

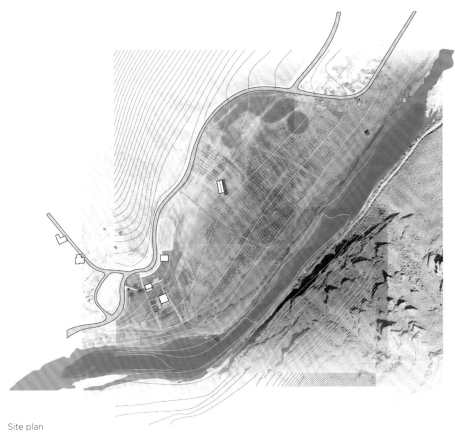

Site plan

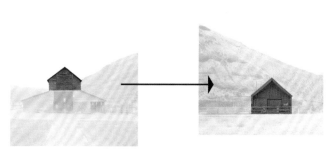

Structure shape inspiration diagram

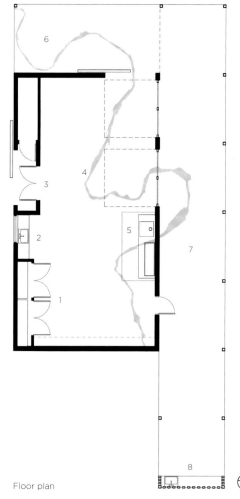

Floor plan

1. Storage
2. Indoor kitchen/sink
3. Entry/storage
4. John Day River etched in concrete floor
5. Wood-burning stove
6. Covered patio
7. Shaded patio
8. Outdoor kitchen/sink

CHADBOURNE + DOSS
ARCHITECTS

CYCLE HOUSE

Architecture Design Team:
Lisa Chadbourne and Daren Doss
General Contractor:
Fackler Construction
Photographer:
© Benjamin Benschneider

THE PERCH

Architecture Design Team:
Lisa Chadbourne and Daren Doss
Landscape Architect:
Land Morphology
General Contractor, concrete, metalwork,
and costum casework fabrication:
Dovetail
Photographer:
© Kevin Scott

WOOD BLOCK RESIDENCE

Architecture and Interior Design Team:
Lisa Chadbourne and Daren Doss
Landscape Architect:
Alchemie
General Contractor:
Constantly Building
Photographer:
© Ben Benschneider

Lisa Chadbourne and Daren Doss met in their first-year studio studying for Master of Architecture degrees at the University of Washington. Their collaboration in life and work quickly began. They established chadbourne + doss architects in Seattle, Washington in 2001, and Astoria, Oregon, in 2002. With different backgrounds, experiences, and design perspectives, they work together in a genuine collaboration that is investigative, thoughtful, and critical. They take a holistic approach to creating unique environments that are relevant to their place and deeply responsive to a client's needs and desires. Their work embodies a fascination with the contrasting relationships of everyday life – inside/outside, public/private, technology/nature – through the innovative use of form, materials, and light. Taking on creative projects at all scales, they have a particular interest in work that engages the environment, craft, and community.

Lisa Chadbourne und Daren Doss lernten sich im ersten Jahr ihres Masterstudiums der Architektur an der University of Washington kennen. Ihre Zusammenarbeit in Leben und Arbeit begann schnell. Sie gründeten 2001 Chadbourne + Doss Architects in Seattle, Washington, und 2002 in Astoria, Oregon. Mit ihren unterschiedlichen Hintergründen, Erfahrungen und Designperspektiven arbeiten sie in einer echten Zusammenarbeit zusammen, die investigativ, reflektierend und kritisch ist. Sie verfolgen einen ganzheitlichen Ansatz, um einzigartige Umgebungen zu schaffen, die für den jeweiligen Ort relevant sind und auf die Bedürfnisse und Wünsche der Kunden eingehen. Ihre Arbeiten verkörpern eine Faszination für die Kontraste des Alltags, innen/außen, öffentlich/privat, Technik/Natur, durch den innovativen Einsatz von Form, Material und Licht. Sie sind an kreativen Projekten aller Größenordnungen beteiligt und haben ein besonderes Interesse an Arbeiten, die sich mit der Umwelt, dem Handwerk und der Gemeinschaft befassen.

Lisa Chadbourne et Daren Doss se sont rencontrés lors de leur première année d'études pour l'obtention d'un master en architecture à l'université de Washington. Leur collaboration dans la vie et le travail a rapidement commencé. Ils ont fondé Chadbourne + Doss Architects à Seattle, Washington, en 2001, et à Astoria, Oregon, en 2002. Avec des formations, des expériences et des perspectives de conception différentes, ils travaillent ensemble dans une véritable collaboration qui est investigatrice, réfléchie et critique. Ils adoptent une approche holistique pour créer des environnements uniques, adaptés au lieu où ils se trouvent et profondément sensibles aux besoins et aux désirs des clients. Leur travail incarne une fascination pour les contrastes de la vie quotidienne, intérieur/extérieur, public/privé, technologie/nature, à travers l'utilisation innovante de la forme, des matériaux et de la lumière. Ils s'intéressent aux projets créatifs à toutes les échelles et plus particulièrement à ceux qui concernent l'environnement, l'artisanat et la communauté.

Lisa Chadbourne y Daren Doss se conocieron en su primer año de estudio para obtener un máster de arquitectura en la Universidad de Washington. Rápidamente comenzó su colaboración en la vida y en el trabajo. Fundaron Chadbourne + Doss Architects en Seattle, Washington, en 2001, y en Astoria, Oregón, en 2002. Con diferentes formaciones, experiencias y perspectivas de diseño, trabajan juntos en una auténtica colaboración que es investigadora, reflexiva y crítica. Adoptan un enfoque holístico para crear entornos únicos que sean relevantes para su lugar y respondan profundamente a las necesidades y deseos de los clientes. Su trabajo encarna la fascinación por los contrastes de la vida cotidiana, dentro/fuera, público/privado, tecnología/naturaleza, mediante el uso innovador de la forma, los materiales y la luz. Aceptando proyectos creativos a todas las escalas, tienen un interés particular en el trabajo que involucra al medio ambiente, la artesanía y la comunidad.

CYCLE HOUSE

Seattle, Washington, United States // Lot area: 5,563 sq ft; building area: 2,400 sq ft residence + 540 sq ft studio

This urban infill residence is located at the intersection of two major bike routes in the Mount Baker neighborhood of Seattle. The lot is narrow and has panoramic views of Lake Washington and the Cascade Mountain Range, including Mount Rainier. The owners, an active couple, wanted their house to have storage and maintenance space for their eighteen bicycles, a strong connection to the exterior, a good flow for entertaining, and cozy spaces for reading and relaxation. Their engagement during the design process provided the architects with scent vials to evoke sensibilities they wished to experience in their home—cool ocean, woody comfort, industrial, and quiet. Iceland was the inspiring metaphor that guided the design for a refined, natural, and stark palette of materials.

Cette résidence urbaine est située à l'intersection de deux grandes pistes cyclables dans le quartier de Mount Baker à Seattle. Le terrain est étroit et offre des vues panoramiques sur le lac Washington et la chaîne de montagnes des Cascades, notamment le mont Rainier. Les propriétaires, un couple actif, souhaitaient que leur maison dispose d'un espace pour ranger et entretenir leurs dix-huit bicyclettes, d'un lien fort avec l'extérieur, d'une bonne circulation pour recevoir et d'espaces accueillants pour la lecture et la relaxation. Leur engagement au cours du processus de conception a permis aux architectes de disposer de flacons parfumés évoquant les sensibilités qu'ils souhaitaient retrouver dans leur maison : fraîcheur de l'océan, confort boisé et tranquillité. L'Islande a été la métaphore inspirante qui a guidé la conception d'une palette de matériaux raffinés, naturels et austères.

Dieses städtische Wohnhaus liegt an der Kreuzung zweier wichtiger Fahrradrouten in Seattles Mount Baker-Viertel. Das Grundstück ist schmal und bietet einen Panoramablick auf den Lake Washington und das Kaskadengebirge, einschließlich des Mount Rainier. Die Bauherren, ein aktives Paar, wünschten sich ein Haus, das Platz für die Unterbringung und Wartung ihrer achtzehn Fahrräder bietet, eine starke Verbindung zur Natur, einen guten Fluss für die Unterhaltung und einladende Räume zum Lesen und Entspannen. Ihr Engagement während des Entwurfsprozesses lieferte den Architekten Duftflakons, die die Empfindungen hervorrufen sollten, die sie in ihrem Haus erleben wollten: frisches Meer, holzige Behaglichkeit und Ruhe. Island war die inspirierende Metapher, die das Design einer raffinierten, natürlichen und strengen Materialpalette leitete.

Esta residencia urbana está situada en la intersección de dos importantes rutas para bicicletas en el barrio de Mount Baker de Seattle. El terreno es estrecho y tiene vistas panorámicas del lago Washington y la cordillera de las Cascadas, incluido el monte Rainier. Los propietarios, una pareja activa, querían que su casa tuviera espacio para guardar y mantener sus dieciocho bicicletas, una fuerte conexión con el exterior, un buen flujo para el entretenimiento y espacios acogedores para la lectura y la relajación. Su compromiso durante el proceso de diseño proporcionó a los arquitectos frascos de aromas para evocar las sensibilidades que deseaban experimentar en su casa: océano fresco, confort amaderado y tranquilidad. Islandia fue la metáfora inspiradora que guió el diseño de una paleta de materiales refinada, natural y austera.

Section

Third floor plan

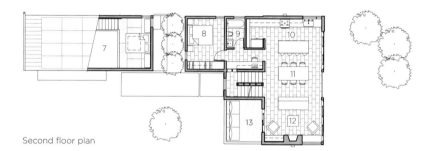

Second floor plan

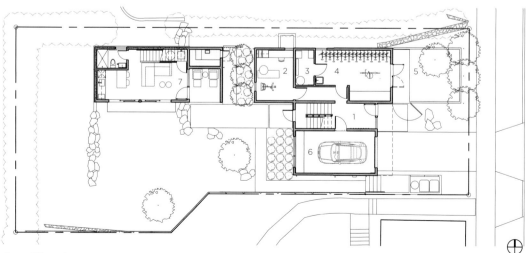

Ground floor plan

1. Entry
2. Office/exercise room
3. Mechanical room
4. Bike shop and storage
5. Work yard
6. Garage
7. Backyard studio
8. Bedroom
9. Bathroom
10. Kitchen
11. Dining area
12. Living area
13. Roof deck
14. Laundry room
15. Walk-in closet

THE PERCH

Seattle, Washington, United States // Lot area: 7,253 sq f t; building area: 5,500 sq ft

The owners' design brief asked for an adventurous sanctuary inspired by the forest, sea, and skies of the Salish Sea. They also wanted a house that would age well, support their active lifestyle, and adapt as they age. Occupying a corner lot in Seattle's Queen Anne hill, the house opens to expansive west views of the sea and the Olympic Mountains while encircling a courtyard that encapsulates an idealized atmosphere of the Pacific Northwest. The rigorous architecture modulates the experience of the natural and urban world beyond and the occupants' desire for privacy or exposure. Exterior materials—concrete, zinc siding, painted aluminum panel, and western red cedar—were selected for a timeless character and durability over time. Interior materials reference the Puget Sound forests with walnut floors and cedar ceilings.

Les propriétaires souhaitaient un sanctuaire aventureux inspiré par la forêt, la mer et le ciel de la mer de Salish. Ils voulaient également une maison qui vieillisse bien, qui soutienne leur style de vie actif et qui soit adaptée à leur âge. La maison, qui se trouve à l'angle de la colline Queen Anne de Seattle, s'ouvre sur des vues imprenables sur la mer et les Olympic Mountains à l'ouest, tout en entourant une cour qui renferme une atmosphère idéalisée du nord-ouest du Pacifique. L'architecture rigoureuse module l'expérience du monde naturel et urbain environnant et le désir d'intimité ou d'exposition des occupants. Les matériaux extérieurs, tels que le béton, le bardage en zinc, les panneaux en aluminium peint et le cèdre rouge de l'Ouest, ont été choisis pour leur caractère intemporel et leur durabilité. Les matériaux intérieurs font référence aux forêts de Puget Sound avec des sols en noyer et des plafonds en cèdre.

Die Bauherren wünschten sich einen abenteuerlichen Zufluchtsort, der von den Wäldern, dem Meer und dem Himmel der Salish Sea inspiriert ist. Außerdem wollten sie ein Haus, das gut altert, ihren aktiven Lebensstil unterstützt und ihrem Alter entspricht. Das Haus, das an der Ecke von Seattles Queen Anne Hill liegt, bietet einen weiten Blick auf das Meer und die Olympic Mountains im Westen und umgibt einen Innenhof, der eine idealisierte Atmosphäre des pazifischen Nordwestens vermittelt. Die rigorose Architektur moduliert die Erfahrung der natürlichen und urbanen Welt und den Wunsch der Bewohner nach Privatsphäre oder Offenheit. Außenmaterialien wie Beton, Zinkverkleidungen, lackierte Aluminiumpaneele und Western Red Cedar wurden aufgrund ihres zeitlosen Charakters und ihrer Haltbarkeit ausgewählt. Die Materialien für die Innenausstattung mit Walnussholzböden und Zedernholzdecken nehmen Bezug auf die Wälder des Puget Sound.

Las instrucciones de diseño de los propietarios pedían un santuario aventurero inspirado en el bosque, el mar y los cielos del mar de Salish. También querían una casa que envejeciera bien, que apoyara su estilo de vida activo y que se adaptara a su edad. La casa, que hace esquina en la colina Queen Anne de Seattle, se abre a unas amplias vistas del mar y las montañas olímpicas hacia el oeste, mientras rodea un patio que encierra una atmósfera idealizada del noroeste del Pacífico. La rigurosa arquitectura modula la experiencia del mundo natural y urbano más allá y el deseo de privacidad o exposición de los ocupantes. Los materiales exteriores, como el hormigón, el revestimiento de zinc, el panel de aluminio pintado y el cedro rojo occidental, se seleccionaron por su carácter intemporal y su durabilidad. Los materiales interiores hacen referencia a los bosques de Puget Sound con suelos de nogal y techos de cedro.

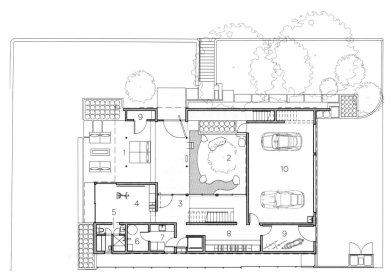

Ground floor plan

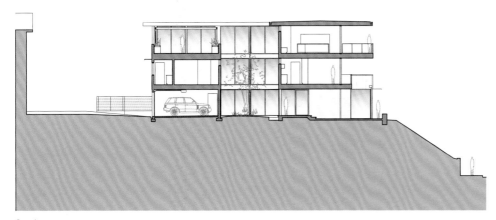

Section

1. Patio
2. Courtyard
3. Entry
4. Gym
5. Spa bathroom
6. Mechanical room
7. Laundry room
8. Mudroom
9. Storage
10. Garage
11. Bedroom
12. dressing room
13. Bathroom
14. Sleeping porch
15. Office
16. Storage
17. Kitchen
18. Living area
19. Deck
20. Dining area
21. Scullery
22. Media room

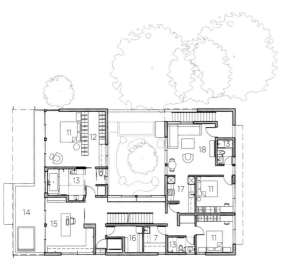

Second floor plan

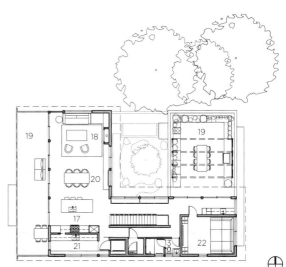

Third floor plan

WOOD BLOCK RESIDENCE

Winthrop, Washington, United States // Lot area: 9,636 sq ft; building area: 3,000 sq ft

The Wood Block Residence is a domestic transformation that mixes existing mid-century modern bones with new materials, new program interventions, and precise craftsmanship to create something entirely new. With respect for the original architecture by iconic Seattle architect Fred Bassetti, the structure was reimagined to reflect its owners, respond to its time and place, and provide a protected sanctuary for family life. Years of renovations were peeled back to the studs, revealing the modernist post-and-beam structure in the interior where new program elements inspired by a metaphor of wood toy blocks were inserted. New block form interventions contain, articulate, and separate programmatic functions. The materiality, the combination of old and new, and the setting create a warm and atmospheric refuge for modern living.

La maison est une transformation domestique qui mélange la fondation moderne existante du milieu du siècle avec de nouveaux matériaux, de nouvelles interventions de programme et un savoir-faire précis pour créer quelque chose d'entièrement nouveau. Tout en respectant l'architecture originale de Fred Bassetti, architecte emblématique de Seattle, la structure a été repensée pour refléter les propriétaires, répondre à l'époque et au lieu, et offrir un sanctuaire pour la vie de famille. Des années de rénovations ont été épluchées jusqu'aux poteaux, révélant la structure moderniste à poteaux et poutres à l'intérieur où de nouveaux éléments de programme inspirés par une métaphore de blocs de jouets en bois ont été insérés. Les nouvelles interventions en forme de blocs contiennent, articulent et séparent les fonctions programmatiques. La matérialité, la combinaison de l'ancien et du nouveau et l'environnement créent un havre atmosphérique chaleureux pour une vie moderne.

Die Wood Block Residence ist eine häusliche Transformation, die bestehende moderne Knochen aus der Mitte des Jahrhunderts mit neuen Materialien, neuen Programminterventionen und präziser Handwerkskunst mischt, um etwas Neues zu schaffen. Mit Respekt vor der ursprünglichen Architektur des berühmten Seattle-Architekten Fred Bassetti wurde die Struktur neu gestaltet, um ihre Besitzer widerzuspiegeln und auf ihre Zeit und ihren Ort zu reagieren. Jahrelange Renovierungsarbeiten wurden bis auf die Stollen zurückgeführt und enthüllten die modernistische Pfosten-und-Balken-Struktur im Inneren, wo neue Programmelemente eingefügt wurden, die von einer Metapher aus Holzspielzeugblöcken inspiriert waren. Die neuen blockartigen Interventionen enthalten, gliedern und trennen die programmatischen Funktionen. Die Materialität, die Kombination von Alt und Neu und die Umgebung schaffen einen warmen, atmosphärischen Hafen für modernes Wohnen.

La vivienda es una transformación doméstica que mezcla la base existente de mediados de siglo con nuevos materiales, nuevas intervenciones en el programa y una artesanía precisa para crear algo totalmente nuevo. Respetando la arquitectura original del emblemático arquitecto de Seattle Fred Bassetti, la estructura fue reimaginada para reflejar a sus propietarios, responder a su tiempo y lugar, y proporcionar un santuario para la vida familiar. Se despojó la estructura de renovaciones acumuladas, revelando un esqueleto de postes y vigas en el interior, donde se insertaron nuevos elementos del programa inspirados en una metáfora de bloques de juguete de madera. Las nuevas intervenciones en forma de bloque contienen, articulan y separan las funciones programáticas. La materialidad, la combinación de lo antiguo y lo nuevo y el entorno crean un refugio de atmósfera cálida para la vida moderna.

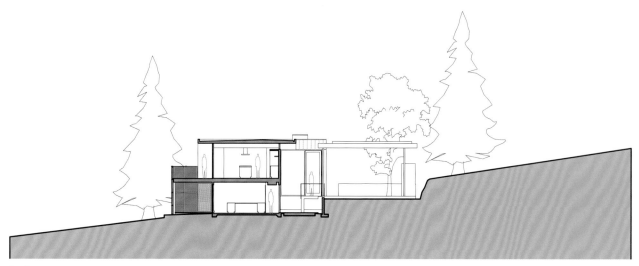

Section

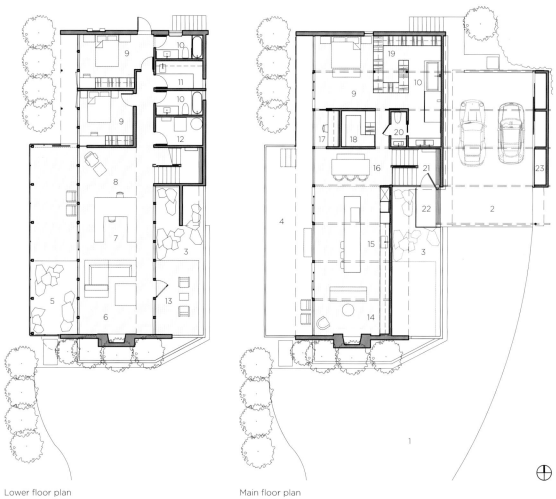

Lower floor plan   Main floor plan

1. Driveway   7. Hobby desck   13. Courtyard deck   19. Dressing room
2. Carport   8. Library   14. Living area   20. Powder room
3. Courtyard   9. Bedroom   15. Kitchen   21. Entry
4. Deck   10. Bathroom   16. Dining area   22. Entry patio
5. Screened porch   11. Laundry room   17. Office   23. Storage
6. Media room   12. Mechanical room   18. Pantry

134

NATHAN GOOD
ARCHITECTS

CANNON BEACH RESIDENCE

Architecture Design team:
Nathan Good, FAIA/Nathan Good Architects
Interior Designer:
Georgia Erdenberger IIDA/
Czopek & Erdenberger
Landscape Architect:
George Erdenberger ASLA
General Contractor:
Rich Elstrom Construction
Energy and Commissioning Consultant:
Charlie Stephens/Oregon Department
of Energy
Structural Engineer:
Andy Stricker/Stricker Engineering
Green Home Certification:
Randy Hansell/Earth Advantage
Energy Monitoring:
Bob Rogers/Oregon Institute of Technology
Solar Consultant:
Doug Boleyn/Cascade Solar Consulting
Mechanical Engineer:
Gene Johnson/Solar AE
Photographer:
© Nathan Good, Dan Morrison,
and Daniel Root

LIVE EDGE RESIDENCE

Architecture Design team:
Nathan Good Architects
Interior Designer:
Nathan Good Architects
Landscape Designer:
Heart Springs Landscape Design
General Contractor:
Leader Builders
Energy and Mechanical Consultant:
Charlie Stephens
Structural Engineer:
Walker Engineering
Green Home Certification:
Matt Douglas/Earth Advantage
Energy Modeling:
Earth Advantage
Photographer:
© Nathan Good and Rick Keating

PORTLAND SKYLINE RESIDENCE

Architecture Design team:
Nathan Good Architects
Interior Designer:
Nathan Good Architects
Landscape Designer:
Cynthia Woodyard
General Contractor:
Don Young & Associates
Energy Consultant:
Charlie Stephens
Structural Engineer:
Nordling Engineering
Green Home Certification:
Randy Hansell/Earth Advantage
Energy Modeling:
Earth Advantage
Photographer:
© Nathan Good and Jeremy Bittermann

🌐 www.nathangoodarchitects.com ⦿ nathan.good.architects

Nathan Good Architects is an architecture and interior design firm located in Salem, Oregon, with projects throughout the Pacific Northwest. The firm was founded by Nathan Good in 2005 to provide clients with thoughtful design solutions that enhance the lives of those who experience their spaces. Their architecture reflects the unique needs and aspirations of their clients, the climate, and the land. Leadership in environmentally responsible design is woven into all their work. Craftsmanship, durability, and pragmatic solutions are characteristic of Nathan Good Architects' designs. The firm values environmental stewardship, creative problem solving, and that which is visually delightful. Their projects have received regional, national, and international design awards and have been published in several books, periodicals, and online news sources. Nathan Good Architects continues to evolve as leaders in sustainable and resilient design.

Nathan Good Architects ist ein Architektur- und Innenarchitekturbüro mit Sitz in Salem, Oregon, das Projekte im gesamten pazifischen Nordwesten betreut. Das Unternehmen wurde 2005 von Nathan Good gegründet, um seinen Kunden durchdachte Designlösungen zu bieten, die das Leben der Menschen verbessern, die ihre Räume erleben. Ihre Architektur spiegelt die einzigartigen Bedürfnisse und Wünsche ihrer Kunden, das Klima und das Gelände wider. Die Vorreiterrolle im Bereich des umweltfreundlichen Designs zieht sich wie ein roter Faden durch ihre Arbeit. Handwerkliches Können, Langlebigkeit und pragmatische Lösungen sind die Markenzeichen der Entwürfe von Nathan Good Architects. Das Unternehmen legt Wert auf Umweltschutz, kreative Problemlösungen und visuell ansprechende Lösungen. Ihre Projekte wurden mit regionalen, nationalen und internationalen Designpreisen ausgezeichnet und sind in verschiedenen Büchern, Zeitschriften und Online-Artikeln veröffentlicht worden. Nathan Good Architects entwickelt sich weiter zu einem führenden Unternehmen für nachhaltiges und dauerhaftes Design.

Nathan Good Architects est un cabinet d'architecture et de décoration intérieure situé à Salem, dans l'Oregon, qui réalise des projets dans tout le nord-ouest du Pacifique. Le cabinet a été fondé par Nathan Good en 2005 pour offrir à ses clients des solutions de conception réfléchies qui améliorent la vie de ceux qui vivent dans leurs espaces. Son architecture reflète les besoins et les aspirations uniques de ses clients, le climat et le terrain. Le leadership en matière de conception respectueuse de l'environnement se retrouve dans tout leur travail. L'artisanat, la durabilité et les solutions pragmatiques sont les marques de fabrique des conceptions de Nathan Good Architects. L'entreprise accorde de l'importance au respect de l'environnement, à la résolution créative des problèmes et à ce qui est visuellement agréable. Leurs projets ont reçu des prix de design régionaux, nationaux et internationaux et ont été publiés dans divers livres, périodiques et articles en ligne. Nathan Good Architects continue d'évoluer en tant que leader en matière de conception durable et pérenne.

Nathan Good Architects es un estudio de arquitectura y diseño de interiores situado en Salem, Oregón, con proyectos en todo el noroeste del Pacífico. La empresa fue fundada por Nathan Good en 2005 para ofrecer a los clientes soluciones de diseño bien pensadas que mejoren la vida de quienes experimentan sus espacios. Su arquitectura refleja las necesidades y aspiraciones únicas de sus clientes, el clima y el terreno. El liderazgo en el diseño responsable con el medio ambiente está entretejido en todo su trabajo. La artesanía, la durabilidad y las soluciones pragmáticas son características de los diseños de Nathan Good Architects. La empresa valora el cuidado del medio ambiente, la resolución creativa de problemas y lo que es visualmente encantador. Sus proyectos han recibido premios de diseño regionales, nacionales e internacionales y han sido publicados en varios libros, publicaciones periódicas y artículos en internet. Nathan Good Architects sigue evolucionando como líderes en diseño sostenible y perdurable.

CANNON BEACH RESIDENCE

Cannon Beach, Oregon, United States // Lot area: .23 acres; building area: 2,268 sq ft

The Cannon Beach Residence has served as a refuge for the owners, their family, and friends. Tucked into a wooded hillside overlooking the Pacific Ocean and the village of Cannon Beach, the curvilinear wood-clad house focuses on the views to the surrounding landscape and captures its owners' love of natural materials and forms. The environmentally responsive design promotes a healthy indoor environment, has an energy-efficient envelope, and utilizes recycled and salvaged materials to create a longlasting home. The Cannon Beach Residence is the recipient of many awards, including the "Custom Green of the Year" by the National Association of Home Builders and an "Honor Design Award" and "People's Choice Award" by the Oregon chapters of the American Institute of Architects. In 2019, it received a Stephen Kellert Biophilic Design Award by the International Living Futures Institute.

La Cannon Beach Residence a servi de refuge pour les propriétaires, leur famille et leurs amis. La maison curviligne, revêtue de bois, située sur une colline boisée surplombant l'océan Pacifique et le village de Cannon Beach, met l'accent sur les vues du paysage environnant et traduit l'amour des propriétaires pour les matériaux et les formes de la nature. La conception écologique favorise un environnement intérieur sain, possède une enveloppe économe en énergie et utilise des matériaux recyclés et récupérés pour créer une maison durable. La résidence Cannon Beach a reçu de nombreux prix, notamment le prix « Custom Green of the Year » décerné par la National Association of Home Builders, ainsi que les prix « Honor Design Award » et « People's Choice Award » décernés par les sections de l'Oregon de l'American Institute of Architects. En 2019, il a reçu le prix Stephen Kellert Biophilic Design Award de l'Institut international Living Futures.

Die Cannon Beach Residence diente den Besitzern, ihrer Familie und Freunden als Zufluchtsort. Das geschwungene, mit Holz verkleidete Haus liegt an einem bewaldeten Hang mit Blick auf den Pazifik und das Dorf Cannon Beach. Es konzentriert sich auf die Aussicht auf die umliegende Landschaft und spiegelt die Liebe der Eigentümer zu den Materialien und Formen der Natur wider. Das umweltfreundliche Design fördert ein gesundes Raumklima, hat eine energieeffiziente Hülle und verwendet recycelte und geborgene Materialien, um ein langlebiges Zuhause zu schaffen. Die Cannon Beach Residence wurde mit zahlreichen Preisen ausgezeichnet, darunter „Custom Green of the Year" von der National Association of Home Builders und ein „Honor Design Award" und „People's Choice Award" von den Oregon Chapters des American Institute of Architects. Im Jahr 2019 erhielt er den Stephen Kellert Biophilic Design Award des International Living Futures Institute.

La Cannon Beach Residence ha servido como refugio para los propietarios, su familia y sus amigos. La casa curvilínea de madera, situada en una ladera boscosa con vistas al Pacífico y al pueblo de Cannon Beach, se centra en las vistas del paisaje circundante y capta el amor de sus propietarios por los materiales y las formas naturales. El diseño, respetuoso con el medio ambiente, fomenta un entorno interior saludable, ofrece una envoltura eficiente y utiliza materiales reciclados para crear un hogar duradero. La Cannon Beach Residence ha recibido numerosos premios, entre ellos el «Custom Green of the Year» de la Asociación Nacional de Constructores de Viviendas, un «Honor Design Award» y un «People's Choice Award» de las secciones de Oregón del Instituto Americano de Arquitectos. En 2019, recibió el premio Stephen Kellert Biophilic Design Award del International Living Futures Institute.

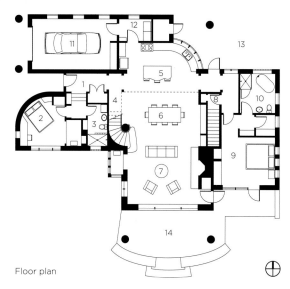

Floor plan

1. Entry
2. Guest bedroom
3. Guest bathroom
4. Stairs to loft
5. Kitchen
6. Dining area
7. Living area
8. Stairs to basement
9. Primary bedroom
10. Primary bathroom
11. Garage
12. Utility room
13. Northeast covered porch
14. South covered porch

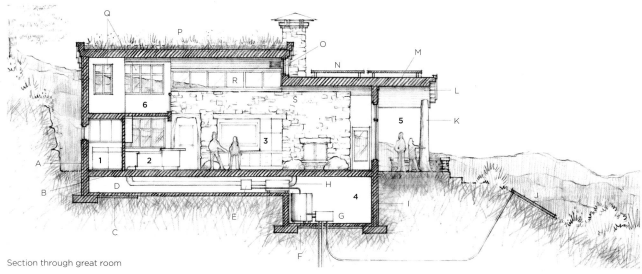

Section through great room

1. Clean room
2. Kitchen
3. Great room
4. Mechanical room
5. South porch
6. Loft

A. R-30 Durisol Exterior wall-forming system
B. FSC interior framing floors, walls, roof, cabinetry, and formwork
C. Sub-slab rigid insulation
D. Unconditioned "shortened" basement

E. In-line fan coil
F. Hot water storage tanks
G. Heat pump
H. Energy recovery ventilator
I. R-24 Durisol retaining walls
J. Solar-thermal panels
K. Salvaged "windfallen" Incense cedar columns

L. FSC cedar fascia soffits and shakes
M. R-50 insulated roofs
N. Solar-electric panels
O. South-facing clerestory windows
P. Vegetative roof

Q. U= .32 high-performance glazing with cedar frames
R. Clerestory windows
S. Internal thermal-mass stone wall
T. Modified Rumford masonry fireplace

© Craig Holmes

LIVE EDGE RESIDENCE

Bend, Oregon, United States // Lot area: 1.65 acres; building area: 4,150 sq ft

Nestled into a bluff above the scenic Deschutes River sits the LEED for Homes, Platinum-Certified, Live Edge Residence. The house—complete with an attached greenhouse—combines a modern design aesthetic with an intricate molding to the terrain, weaving around rock outcroppings and ragged juniper trees in the arid open-range environment. Extensive exterior terraces merge indoor and outdoor spaces while encouraging outdoor living. Live Edge was designed with resilience in mind, enabling the residents to prepare for the unexpected. The 15 kW Tesla "Power Wall" battery back-up system, wood-burning fireplace, 1,800-gallon potable water cistern, and attached greenhouse provide an array of self-sustaining resources for the occupants.

Perchée sur une falaise au-dessus de la pittoresque rivière Deschutes se trouve la Live Edge Residence, certifiée LEED for Homes Platinum. La maison, avec un jardin d'hiver attenant, allie un design moderne à une adaptation complexe au terrain, s'insérant dans des affleurements rocheux et des genévriers déchirés dans un environnement aride. De vastes terrasses extérieures fusionnent les espaces intérieurs et extérieurs et encouragent la vie en plein air. La Live Edge Residence a été conçu dans un souci de résilience, permettant aux résidents de se préparer à l'inattendu. Le système de batterie Tesla « Power Wall » de 15 kW, le foyer à bois, la citerne d'eau potable de 1 800 litres et la serre offrent une série de ressources autosuffisantes aux occupants.

Auf einer Klippe oberhalb des malerischen Deschutes River liegt die LEED for Homes Platinum-zertifizierte Live Edge Residence. Das Haus mit angebautem Wintergarten verbindet eine moderne Designästhetik mit einer komplizierten Anpassung an das Terrain, indem es sich um Felsen und Wacholderbäume herumschlängelt, die in eine karge Umgebung gerissen wurden. Ausgedehnte Außenterrassen verschmelzen Innen- und Außenräume und laden zum Leben im Freien ein. Live Edge wurde unter dem Aspekt der Widerstandsfähigkeit entwickelt, damit die Bewohner auf das Unerwartete vorbereitet sind. Das 15-kW-Tesla-Batteriesystem „Power Wall", ein holzbefeuerter Kamin, eine 1.800-Liter-Trinkwasserzisterne und ein Gewächshaus bieten den Bewohnern eine Reihe von Selbstversorgungsmöglichkeiten.

Enclavada en un acantilado sobre el pintoresco río Deschutes se encuentra la Live Edge Residencia, con certificación «LEED for Homes Platinum». La casa, con un invernadero anexo, combina una estética de diseño moderno con un intrincado amoldamiento al terreno, tejiendo alrededor de afloramientos rocosos y enebros desgarrados en un árido entorno. Las amplias terrazas exteriores fusionan los espacios interiores con los exteriores y fomentan la vida al aire libre. La Live Edge Residence se diseñó teniendo en cuenta la capacidad de recuperación, lo que permite a los residentes prepararse para lo inesperado. El sistema de baterías Tesla «Power Wall» de 15 kW, la chimenea de leña, la cisterna de agua potable de 1800 litros de agua potable y un invernadero proporcionan una serie de recursos autosuficientes para los ocupantes.

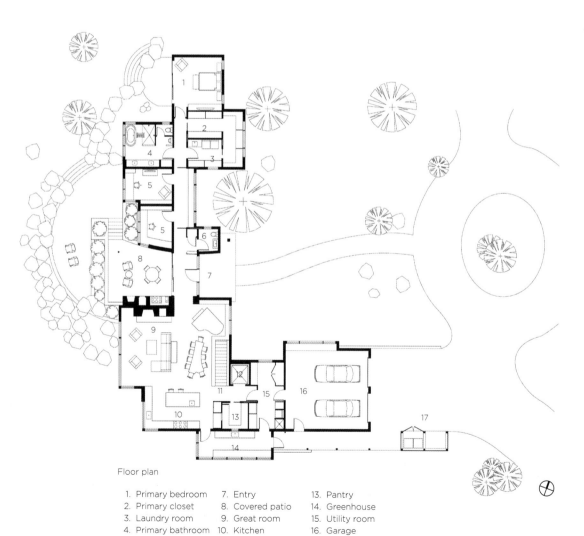

Floor plan

1. Primary bedroom
2. Primary closet
3. Laundry room
4. Primary bathroom
5. Office
6. Guest bathroom

7. Entry
8. Covered patio
9. Great room
10. Kitchen
11. Staircase
12. Elevator

13. Pantry
14. Greenhouse
15. Utility room
16. Garage
17. Firewood

PORTLAND SKYLINE RESIDENCE

Portland, Oregon, United States // Lot area: 1.7 acres; building area: 4,800 sq ft

The site for the Portland Skyline Residence was purchased by the owners for its sun exposure and proximity to downtown Portland. The home's elongated layout in the east-west direction maximizes solar exposure. This also optimized visual connection to the land on the home's south side and reduced the sound pollution from the access road. The residence is stacked into three levels to minimize the building footprint on the site. The Portland Skyline Residence, which was designed and built to generate as much energy as it consumes annually, also includes other sustainable practices such as enhanced insulation levels, ultra-efficient HVAC systems, and exemplary utilization of natural light. The Portland Skyline Residence has achieved a LEED for Homes Platinum Certification.

Le site de la résidence Portland Skyline a été choisi par les propriétaires pour son exposition au soleil et sa proximité avec le centre-ville de Portland. La disposition allongée est-ouest de la maison maximise l'exposition solaire. Cela a également permis d'optimiser la connexion visuelle avec le terrain situé au sud de la maison et de réduire les nuisances sonores de la route d'accès. La résidence est superposée sur trois niveaux afin de minimiser l'empreinte du bâtiment sur le site. La résidence, qui a été conçue et construite pour générer autant d'énergie qu'elle en consomme annuellement, comprend également d'autres pratiques durables telles que des niveaux d'isolation améliorés, des systèmes CVC ultra-efficaces et une utilisation exemplaire de la lumière naturelle. La résidence Skyline à Portland a obtenu la certification LEED for Homes Platinum.

Der Standort der Portland Skyline Residence wurde von den Eigentümern wegen der Sonneneinstrahlung und der Nähe zum Stadtzentrum von Portland gewählt. Der langgestreckte Ost-West-Grundriss des Hauses maximiert die Sonneneinstrahlung. Dadurch wurde auch die Sichtverbindung zum Grundstück auf der Südseite des Hauses optimiert und die Lärmbelästigung durch die Zufahrtsstraße reduziert. Das Wohnhaus ist auf drei Ebenen gestapelt, um die Grundfläche des Gebäudes auf dem Grundstück zu minimieren. Das Wohnhaus, das so konzipiert und gebaut wurde, dass es so viel Energie erzeugt, wie es jährlich verbraucht, umfasst auch andere nachhaltige Praktiken wie eine verbesserte Isolierung, hocheffiziente HLK-Systeme und eine vorbildliche Nutzung des natürlichen Lichts. Die Skyline Residence in Portland hat das LEED for Homes Platin-Zertifikat erhalten.

El emplazamiento de la residencia Portland Skyline fue adquirido por los propietarios por su exposición al sol y su proximidad al centro de Portland. La disposición alargada de la casa en dirección este-oeste maximiza la exposición solar. Esto también optimizó la conexión visual con el terreno del lado sur de la casa y redujo la contaminación acústica de la carretera de acceso. La residencia está apilada en tres niveles para minimizar la huella del edificio en el terreno. La residencia, que se diseñó y construyó para generar tanta energía como la que consume anualmente, también incluye otras prácticas sostenibles, como niveles de aislamiento mejorados, sistemas de calefacción, ventilación y aire acondicionado ultraeficientes y una utilización ejemplar de la luz natural. La residencia Skyline de Portland ha obtenido la certificación LEED for Homes Platinum.

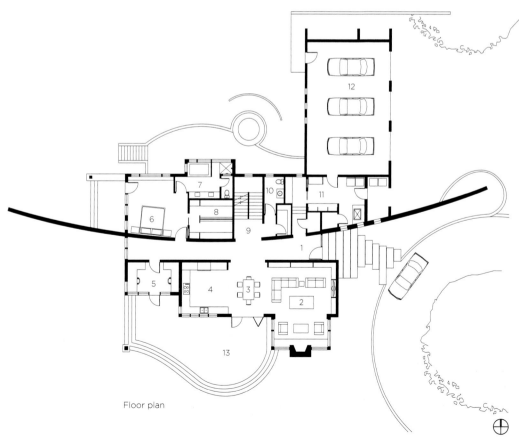

Floor plan

1. Entry
2. Living area
3. Dining area
4. Kitchen
5. Office
6. Primary bedroom
7. Primary bathroom
8. Primary closet
9. Staircase
10. Guest bathroom
11. Utility room
12. Garage
13. South patio

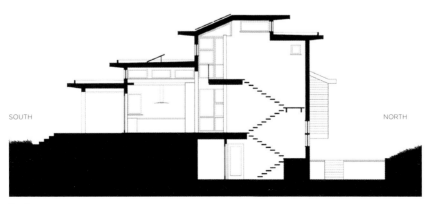

SOUTH

NORTH

Section

ATELIERJONES

CLTHOUSE

Architecture Design Team:
Susan Jones, FAIA; Brian Gerich; Joe Swain;
Maria Ibarlucia; Mesa Sherriff;
Marisol Foreman; Megumi Migita
Structural Engineer:
Harriott Valentine Engineers
Geotechnical Engineer:
Pan Geo
Surveyor:
Jouni Paavola
Built Green Certifier:
Evergreen Certified
Passive House Consultant:
Brett Holverstott
CLT Consultants:
WoodWorks, ARUP
CLT Fabrication/CNC:
Structurlam
General Contractor:
Cascade Built Llc
Photographer:
© Lara Swimmer Photography

Constitution SHED

Architecture and Interior Design Team:
Susan Jones, FAIA; Lenore Wan
Owner:
Susan Jones and Marco Zangari
General Contractor:
Happy Acres Construction
Photographer:
© Lara Swimmer Photography

R & D MODULAR

Architecture and Interior Design Team:
Susan Jones, FAIA; Olga Amigud;
Ian Maples; Lenore Wan; Meghan Doring;
Chester Weir; Alex Zink
Owner:
Susan Jones and Marco Zangari
Visualizations:
© atelierjones

Susan Jones is a Seattle architect and founder of atelierjones. Her solely woman-owned architectural firm designs mass timber prefabricated single-family houses and urban infill residential homes. atelierjones also designs large, mass timber middle-income residential buildings, which specifically advance new building codes allowing lower carbon construction, which Susan helped craft and guide through the ICC Tall Wood Building Code regulatory processes. Her prolific work over the last nine years to advance and restructure the carbon-intensive construction industry towards lower carbon materials exemplifies the role that architects can play to innovate at all scales and urgently lower carbon footprint. She regularly partakes in cross-disciplinary dialogues—locally and internationally—to help understand and better promote sustainable forest practices while managing her family-owned 140-acre forest in the San Juan Islands.

Susan Jones ist eine in Seattle ansässige Architektin und Gründerin von atelierjones. Ihr Architekturbüro, das sich in weiblichem Besitz befindet, entwirft vorgefertigte Einfamilienhäuser aus Massivholz und städtische Wohnhäuser. atelierjones entwirft auch große Wohngebäude aus Holz, die neue Bauvorschriften fördern, die eine kohlenstoffärmere Bauweise ermöglichen, und die Susan mitgestaltet und durch das Regulierungsverfahren des ICC für große Holzgebäude geleitet hat. Ihre erfolgreiche Arbeit der letzten neun Jahre zur Förderung und Umstrukturierung der kohlenstoffintensiven Bauindustrie hin zu kohlenstoffärmeren Materialien ist ein Beispiel für die Rolle, die Architekten bei der Innovation auf allen Ebenen und der dringenden Reduzierung des ökologischen Fußabdrucks spielen können. Er nimmt regelmäßig an interdisziplinären Dialogen auf lokaler und internationaler Ebene teil, um das Verständnis und die Förderung nachhaltiger Forstwirtschaftspraktiken zu verbessern, während er den 56 ha großen Wald seiner Familie auf den San Juan Islands bewirtschaftet.

Susan Jones est une architecte basée à Seattle et fondatrice d'atelierjones. Son cabinet d'architecture, qui appartient à elle-même, conçoit des maisons préfabriquées en bois massif et des logements urbains intercalaires. atelierjones conçoit également de grands bâtiments résidentiels en bois, qui favorisent les nouveaux codes de construction permettant une construction à faible émission de carbone, et que Susan a contribué à élaborer et à guider à travers les processus réglementaires du code de construction en bois de grande hauteur de l'ICC. Le travail prolifique qu'elle a accompli au cours des neuf dernières années pour faire progresser et restructurer l'industrie de la construction à forte intensité de carbone en faveur de matériaux à faible teneur en carbone illustre le rôle que les architectes peuvent jouer pour innover à toutes les échelles et réduire de toute urgence l'empreinte écologique. Elle participe régulièrement à des dialogues interdisciplinaires, tant au niveau local qu'international, pour aider à mieux comprendre et à promouvoir les pratiques forestières durables, tout en gérant la forêt de 56 ha de sa famille dans les îles San Juan.

Susan Jones es una arquitecta de Seattle y fundadora de atelierjones. Su estudio de arquitectura, propiedad exclusivamente de una mujer, diseña casas unifamiliares prefabricadas de madera en masa y viviendas residenciales de relleno urbano. atelierjones también diseña grandes edificios residenciales de madera, que promueven específicamente los nuevos códigos de construcción que permiten una construcción con menos emisiones de carbono, y que Susan ayudó a elaborar y guiar a través de los procesos normativos del Código de Construcción de Madera Alta del ICC. Su prolífico trabajo durante los últimos nueve años para hacer avanzar y reestructurar la industria de la construcción, intensiva en carbono, hacia materiales más bajos en este elemento, ejemplifica el papel que pueden desempeñar los arquitectos para innovar a todas las escalas y reducir urgentemente la huella. Participa con regularidad en diálogos interdisciplinares, tanto a nivel local como internacional, para ayudar a entender y promover mejor las prácticas forestales sostenibles mientras gestiona el bosque de 56 ha que posee su familia en las Islas San Juan.

CLTHOUSE

Seattle, Washington, United States // Lot area: 2,560 sq ft; building area: 1,500 sq ft

The design for the CLTHouse was driven by the different parameters of a small, triangular lot, the need for a light-filled, urban cabin, and the desire for heritage Pacific Northwest materials. Cross-laminated timber (CLT) was a natural choice to fulfill these requirements. Triangular, facing an industrial alley and parking lot, the site was once submerged under an urban lake, and then crafted into development conditions as a result of twentieth-century marine infrastructure work. Experienced as a new Northwest beach cabin, the house has dark exterior wood skin and light wood interior walls, opened and revealing an orthogonal court. Interior spatial sequences recall complexities of Josef Frank's beach houses, where dynamic views are screened, then revealed upwards and outwards around the core to a roof deck overlooking the lake.

La conception de la CLTHouse s'est appuyée sur les différents paramètres d'une petite parcelle triangulaire, sur le besoin d'une cabine urbaine lumineuse et sur le désir d'utiliser des matériaux du nord-ouest du Pacifique. Le bois lamellé-croisé (CLT) était un choix naturel pour répondre à ces exigences. Triangulaire, donnant sur une allée industrielle et un parking, le site était autrefois immergé sous un lac urbain, transformé ensuite en un espace issu des travaux d'infrastructure maritime du XXe siècle. Vécue comme une nouvelle cabane de plage du nord-ouest, la maison présente une peau en bois sombre à l'extérieur et des murs intérieurs en bois clair, qui s'ouvrent pour révéler une cour orthogonale. Les séquences spatiales intérieures rappellent les complexités des maisons de plage de Josef Frank, dans lesquelles les vues dynamiques sont tamisées pour se révéler vers le haut et vers l'extérieur autour du noyau jusqu'à une terrasse surplombant le lac.

Der Entwurf des CLTHouse basierte auf den verschiedenen Parametern eines kleinen, dreieckigen Grundstücks, dem Bedürfnis nach einem lichtdurchfluteten Stadthaus und dem Wunsch, Materialien aus dem pazifischen Nordwesten zu verwenden. Brettsperrholz (CLT) war die natürliche Wahl, um diese Anforderungen zu erfüllen. Das dreieckige Gelände, das eine Industrieallee und einen Parkplatz überragt, war einst unter einem städtischen See versunken und wurde später in einen Raum umgewandelt, der aus den maritimen Infrastrukturarbeiten des 20. Das als neue nordwestliche Strandhütte empfundene Haus hat außen eine dunkle Holzhaut und innen helle Holzwände, die sich zu einem orthogonalen Innenhof hin öffnen. Die räumlichen Abläufe im Inneren erinnern an die Komplexität der Strandhäuser von Josef Frank, in denen sich dynamische Ausblicke nach oben und nach außen um den Kern herum zu einem Deck mit Blick auf den See auffächern.

El diseño de la CLTHouse se basó en los diferentes parámetros de una parcela pequeña y triangular, la necesidad de una cabaña urbana llena de luz y el deseo de utilizar materiales del noroeste del Pacífico. La madera laminada cruzada (CLT) fue una elección natural para cumplir estos requisitos. Triangular, con vistas a un callejón industrial y a un aparcamiento, el solar estuvo en su día sumergido bajo un lago urbano, para transformarse más adelante en un espacio resultado de las obras de infraestructura marítima del siglo XX. Experimentada como una nueva cabaña de playa del noroeste, la casa tiene una piel de madera oscura en el exterior y paredes interiores de madera clara, que se abren y revelan un patio ortogonal. Las secuencias espaciales interiores recuerdan las complejidades de las casas de playa de Josef Frank, en las que las vistas dinámicas se tamizan para revelarse posteriormente hacia arriba y hacia el exterior alrededor del núcleo hasta una cubierta con vistas al lago.

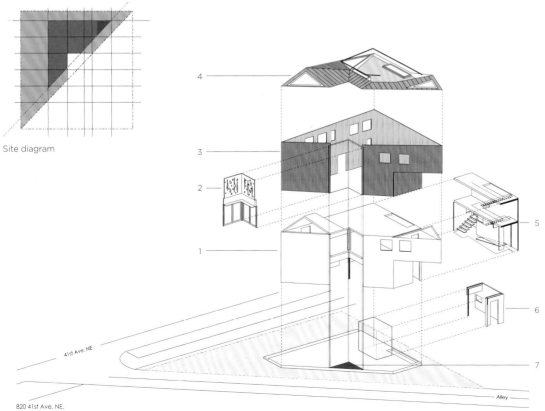

Site diagram

Building diagram

820 41st Ave. NE.

41st Ave. NE

Alley

4

3

2

1

5

6

7

1. White CLT interior
2. CNC routed pine wood screens
3. Dark shou sugi ban pine cladding
4. Standing seam metal roofing
5. Building circulation
6. Double-height kitchen area surrounded by circulation core
7. Courtyard

North elevation

Section A

East elevation

Section B

South elevation

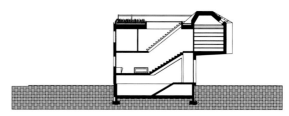

Section 1.1

West elevation

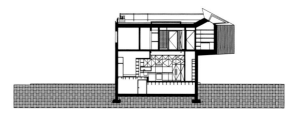

Section 1.2

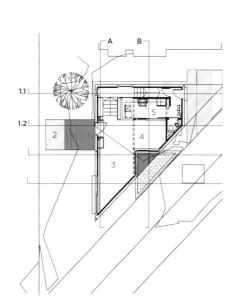

Basement floor plan

Ground floor plan

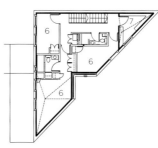

Second floor plan

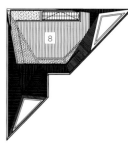

Roof plan

1. Basement
2. Entry
3. Living room
4. Dining area
5. Kitchen
6. Bedroom
7. Library
8. Roof deck

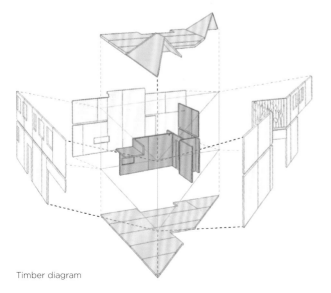

Timber diagram

3-ply   7,028 sq ft = 22 panels
             = 27,411 board feet

5-ply   4,091 sq ft = 13 panels
             = 20,385 board feet

Total   4,091 sq ft = 35 panels
             = 47,796 board feet

Constitution SHED

Orcas Island, Washington, United States // Lot area: 144 acres; building area: 72 sq ft

Constitution SHED layers built reflections of site, ecologies, memory, and legacy. Located high on a remote mountaintop, the simple SHED had lost its functional purpose as a support structure for a large water tank. The grandfather of the owner/architect had built the SHED as a protection against fires. Decades later, the owner/architect had the SHED relocated to a local workshop, where its stalwart proportions and 80-year-old Douglas fir boards, once milled on-site, could be restored and find new life as a writer's retreat. The new boards were cut from windfall trees found on-site to reflect the exact dimensions of the existing wood. Off-grid and well-wrapped with insulation, Constitution SHED stands up well in harsh winters while being wired for solar and carrying its water source on its roof.

Le cabane est construit en plusieurs couches en relation avec les réflexions sur le lieu, les écologies, la mémoire et l'héritage. Situé au sommet d'une montagne isolée, ce simple hangar avait perdu sa fonction de structure de support pour un grand réservoir d'eau. Le grand-père du propriétaire/architecte l'avait construit comme protection contre les incendies. Des dizaines d'années plus tard, il l'a fait déménager dans un atelier local, où ses proportions robustes et ses planches de sapin Douglas de 80 ans, autrefois travaillées sur place, ont pu être restaurées et trouver une nouvelle vie en tant que refuge pour écrivains. Les nouvelles planches ont été coupées à partir d'arbres trouvés sur le site afin de refléter les dimensions exactes du bois existant. Hors réseau et bien isolée, la cabane, reliée à l'énergie solaire et dotée d'un système de recyclage de l'eau sur le toit, résiste bien aux hivers rigoureux de la région.

Ein schichtweise aufgebauter Schuppen, der sich auf Überlegungen zu Ort, Ökologie, Erinnerung und Erbe bezieht. Der einfache Schuppen, der auf einem abgelegenen Berggipfel steht, hatte seine Funktion als Stützkonstruktion für einen großen Wassertank verloren. Der Großvater des Eigentümers/Architekten hatte es zum Schutz vor Feuer gebaut. Jahrzehnte später ließ er es in eine örtliche Werkstatt bringen, wo seine robusten Proportionen und die 80 Jahre alten Douglasienbretter, die einst an Ort und Stelle gefräst wurden, restauriert werden konnten und ein neues Leben als Schriftstellerunterkunft fanden. Die neuen Bretter wurden aus vor Ort gefundenen Bäumen geschnitten, um die exakten Abmessungen des vorhandenen Holzes zu erhalten. Die netzunabhängige und gut isolierte Hütte, die an die Solarenergie angeschlossen ist und über ein Wasserrecycling-System auf dem Dach verfügt, hält den harten Wintern der Region gut stand.

Cobertizo construido en capas en relación a las reflexiones del lugar, las ecologías, la memoria y el legado. Situado en la cima de una montaña remota, el sencillo cobertizo había perdido su propósito funcional como estructura de soporte para un gran tanque de agua. El abuelo del propietario/arquitecto lo había construido como protección contra los incendios. Décadas más tarde, hizo que se trasladara a un taller local, donde sus robustas proporciones y sus tablas de abeto Douglas de 80 años, que en su día se fresaron in situ, pudieran restaurarse y encontrar una nueva vida como refugio para escritores. Los nuevos tablones se cortaron de árboles encontrados en el lugar para reflejar las dimensiones exactas de la madera existente. Sin conexión a la red eléctrica y con un buen aislamiento, la caseta, conectada a la energía solar y con un sistema de reciclaje de aguas en el tejado, resiste bien los duros inviernos de la zona.

Orcas Island site map

View looking north

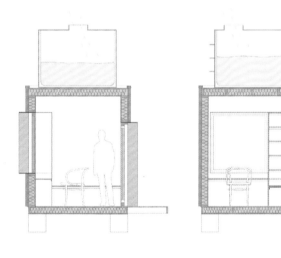

Floor plan and sections

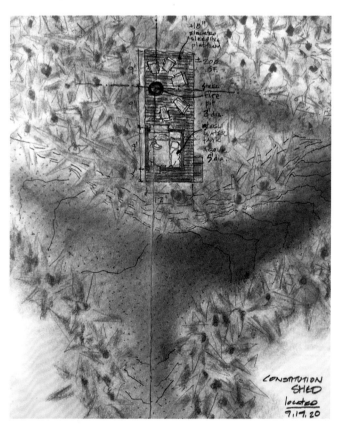

Site plan

R&D MODULAR

Seattle, Washington, United States // Lot area: 3,300 sq ft; building area: 4,110 sq ft

Cities are seeking a greater range of delivery methods for multi-family housing. R&D Modular is a case study on the execution of a self-developed, five-unit, lower-carbon, workforce mass timber modular housing project. With the prefabricated capacity of mass timber, whose material origin can be found in local communities near Pacific Northwest cities, there is a real opportunity to marry urban needs with regional, bio-genic resources. As designed, the project provides four modular mass timber loft units on top of an at-grade family-sized unit, using multiple prefabricated elements, from mass timber, to bathroom/kitchen units, to wood arcade shading and privacy elements.

Les villes recherchent une plus grande variété de méthodes de livraison pour les logements multi familiaux. R&D Modular est une étude sur la mise en œuvre d'un projet de cinq unités de logement modulaire en bois de masse avec des émissions de carbone et une main-d'œuvre réduites. Avec la capacité de préfabrication du bois de masse, dont les origines matérielles peuvent être trouvées dans les communautés locales près des villes du PNW, il existe une réelle opportunité de marier les besoins urbains avec les ressources régionales et biogéniques. Tel que conçu, le projet propose quatre lofts modulaires en bois massif au-dessus d'une unité familiale au niveau du sol, utilisant plusieurs éléments préfabriqués, du bois massif aux unités de salle de bain/cuisine, en passant par l'ombrage des arcades en bois et les éléments d'intimité.

Die Städte sind auf der Suche nach einer breiteren Palette von Bereitstellungsmethoden für Mehrfamilienhäuser. R&D Modular ist eine Studie über die Umsetzung eines modularen Wohnbauprojekts mit fünf Wohneinheiten aus Massivholz, das weniger Kohlenstoffemissionen und weniger Arbeit verursacht. Mit der Vorfertigungskapazität von Massivholz, dessen Material in den Gemeinden in der Nähe der PNW-Städte zu finden ist, besteht eine echte Chance, städtische Bedürfnisse mit regionalen und biogenen Ressourcen zu verb inden. Wie geplant, bietet das Projekt vier modulare Dachgeschosseinheiten aus Massivholz auf einer familiengroßen Einheit in der gleichen Klasse, wobei mehrere vorgefertigte Elemente verwendet werden, von Massivholz über Badezimmer-/Kücheneinheiten bis hin zu hölzernen Arkadenbeschattungen und Sichtschutzelementen.

Las ciudades buscan una mayor variedad de métodos de entrega de viviendas multi familiares. R&D Modular es un estudio sobre la ejecución de un proyecto de viviendas modulares de madera en masa, de cinco unidades, con menos emisiones de carbono y mano de obra. Con la capacidad de prefabricación de la madera en masa, cuyo origen material puede encontrarse en las comunidades locales cercanas a las ciudades del PNW, existe una oportunidad real de conjugar las necesidades urbanas con los recursos regionales y bio génicos. Tal como se diseñó, el proyecto proporciona cuatro unidades de loft modulares de madera en masa sobre una unidad de tamaño familiar a nivel, utilizando múltiples elementos prefabricados, desde madera en masa hasta unidades de baño/cocina, sombreado de arcada de madera y elementos de privacidad.

South elevation

West elevation

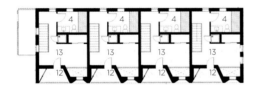

Third floor plan

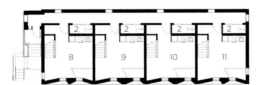

Second floor plan

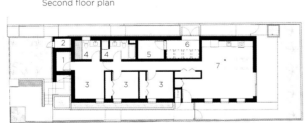

Ground floor plan

1. Closet
2. Storage
3. Bedroom
4. Bathroom
5. Mechanical room
6. Trash
7. Living/dining
8. Unit 1
9. Unit 2
10. Unit 3
11. Unit 4
12. Balcony
13. Loft

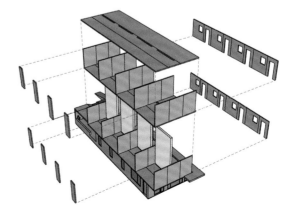

Prefabricated elements diagram

Cross-laminated timber diagram

PAUL MICHAEL DAVIS
ARCHITECTS

164

168

172

THE EULBERG RESIDENCE

Architecture Design Team:
Paul Michael Davis, Terence Wong, Tiffany
Chow, Mariana Gutheim, Graham Day,
John Passmore
General Contractor:
Jason Reid and Andy Watts/Boom Builders
Landscape Architect:
Dan Dizazzo
Art consultant:
Lele Barnett
Landscape Contractor:
Casey McCormick/Cyan Landscapes
Structural and Civil Engineer:
Mark Leingang, P.E. S.E./TransOlympic
Engineering, Inc
Cabinet builder:
Justin Souers/Hyland Cabinetworks, Inc
HVAC Consultant:
Northwest Mechanical
Photographer:
© Mark Woods Photography

THE WYSS FAMILY CONTAINER HOUSE

Architecture Design Team:
Paul Michael Davis, Tiffany Chow
General Contractor:
Dick McDonald, Roger Reynolds/
Karlstrom Associates
Landscape Architect:
Scott Hallquist/Performance
Landscape Company
Structural and Civil Engineer:
Mark Leingang, P.E. S.E./TransOlympic
Engineering, Inc
Shipping Containers:
ITS ConGlobal
Photographer:
© Mark Woods Photography

**WHOLE EARTH MONTESSORI
SCHOOL BUILDING**

Architecture Design Team:
Paul Michael Davis, Sharon Khosla, John
Passmore, Graham Day, Tiffany Chow
General Contractor:
Denis Holzknecht/Inglewood Construction Inc
Structural Engineer:
John Smith, P.E./Smith Company
Structural Engineers
Electrical Engineer:
Kevin Wartelle/Travis Fitzmaurice & Associates
HVAC Engineer:
Alex Abossein/ Abossein Engineering LLC
Photographer:
© Dale Lang, PhD

🌐 www.paulmichaeldavis.com   ⊙ paulmikedavis

Based in Seattle's Capitol Hill neighborhood, architect Paul Michael Davis and his team provide design services with a focus on innovative practicality. Founded in 2010, Paul Michael Davis Architects (PMDA) is staking out a middle ground between northwest regionalism and global formalism. Ranging in project types from homes to schools, the work is rooted in the practicalities of building in relation to location. The design team loves to think of these realities as opportunities to be innovative. The firm's award-winning projects have been featured in publications such as Dwell, Dezeen, Archinect, and The Seattle Times. Says Davis, "We are great at listening—nearly every client tells us this. We are great at taking a client's needs and hopes and translating them into something that they never would have imagined. We want to push design forward."

Der in Seattles Stadtteil Capitol Hill ansässige Architekt Paul Michael Davis und sein Team bieten Designdienstleistungen mit Schwerpunkt auf innovativer Zweckmäßigkeit. Das 2010 gegründete Architekturbüro Paul Michael Davis Architects (PMDA) bewegt sich irgendwo zwischen Nordwest-Regionalismus und globalem Formalismus. Ihre Arbeit, die vom Wohnungsbau bis hin zu Schulen reicht, basiert auf den praktischen Aspekten des Bauens in Verbindung mit dem Standort. Das Designteam betrachtet diese Gegebenheiten gerne als Chance, innovativ zu sein. Die preisgekrönten Projekte des Büros wurden in Publikationen wie Dwell, Dezeen, Archinect und The Seattle Times vorgestellt. „Wir können sehr gut zuhören", so Davis, „das sagt uns fast jeder Kunde. Wir sind sehr gut darin, die Bedürfnisse und Hoffnungen unserer Kunden in etwas zu verwandeln, das sie sich nie hätten vorstellen können. Wir wollen das Design voranbringen".

Installés dans le quartier Capitol Hill de Seattle, l'architecte Paul Michael Davis et son équipe proposent des services de conception axés sur l'aspect pratique et innovant. Fondé en 2010, Paul Michael Davis Architects (PMDA) se situe quelque part entre le régionalisme du Nord-Ouest et le formalisme mondial. Leur travail, qui va du logement aux écoles, est fondé sur les aspects pratiques de la construction en fonction du lieu. L'équipe de conception aime à considérer ces réalités comme des occasions d'être innovant. Les projets primés du cabinet ont été présentés dans des publications telles que Dwell, Dezeen, Archinect et le Seattle Times. Selon M. Davis, « nous sommes très bons dans l'écoute ; presque tous les clients nous le disent. Nous sommes très forts pour prendre les besoins et les espoirs d'un client et les traduire en quelque chose qu'il n'aurait jamais imaginé. Nous voulons faire avancer le design ».

Con sede en el barrio de Capitol Hill de Seattle, el arquitecto Paul Michael Davis y su equipo ofrecen servicios de diseño centrados en la practicidad innovadora. Fundado en 2010, Paul Michael Davis Architects (PMDA) se sitúa en un punto intermedio entre el regionalismo del noroeste y el formalismo global. Su trabajo, que abarca desde viviendas hasta escuelas, se basa en los aspectos prácticos de la construcción en relación con la ubicación. Al equipo de diseño le encanta pensar en estas realidades como oportunidades para ser innovadores. Los proyectos premiados de la empresa han aparecido en publicaciones como Dwell, Dezeen, Archinect y The Seattle Times. Según Davis, «somos muy buenos escuchando; casi todos los clientes nos lo dicen. Se nos da muy bien tomar las necesidades y esperanzas de un cliente y traducirlas en algo que nunca hubiera imaginado. Queremos impulsar el diseño».

THE EULBERG RESIDENCE

Clyde Hill, Washington, United States // Lot area: .44 acres; project area: 4,078 sq ft

The house sits on a gently sloping suburban lot bordered on three sides by streets and a driveway. The clients asked us to create a natural light-filled home that at the same time provides privacy within this otherwise exposed site. The house is sunken down on the exposed street sides, creating a private, green, southwest-facing courtyard. The design ensures that the indoors blend seamlessly with the outdoors. A forty-foot-long set of multi-slide doors opens up the great room to the private rear courtyard. Inside, an uncluttered modern design blends soft, warm materials—cedar, vertical grain fir, and wool—with modern industrial surfaces—gray brick, ground face concrete, and laminated white cabinetry—creating a comfortable and inviting atmosphere, addressing the cold Pacific Northwest climate.

La maison se trouve sur un terrain de banlieue en pente douce, bordé sur trois côtés par des rues et une allée. Les clients nous ont demandé de créer une maison pleine de lumière naturelle tout en assurant l'intimité sur ce terrain autrement exposé. La maison est en retrait sur les côtés faisant face à la rue, créant ainsi une cour privée, verte et orientée vers le sud-ouest. La conception garantit que l'intérieur s'harmonise parfaitement avec l'extérieur. Un ensemble de portes coulissantes de 12 mètres de long ouvre le grand salon sur la cour arrière privée. À l'intérieur, un design moderne et épuré associe des matériaux doux et chauds - cèdre, sapin à grain vertical et laine - à des surfaces industrielles modernes, brique grise, béton poli et armoires en stratifié blanc, créant ainsi un environnement confortable et accueillant qui résiste au climat froid du nord-ouest du Pacifique.

Das Haus steht auf einem leicht abfallenden Vorstadtgrundstück, das an drei Seiten von Straßen und einer Auffahrt begrenzt wird. Die Bauherren baten uns, ein Haus mit viel natürlichem Licht zu schaffen, das gleichzeitig Privatsphäre auf diesem ansonsten exponierten Grundstück bietet. Das Haus ist an den der Straße zugewandten Seiten versenkt, so dass ein privater, grüner, nach Südwesten ausgerichteter Innenhof entsteht. Das Design sorgt dafür, dass sich der Innenraum nahtlos in das Äußere einfügt. Ein Satz 12 Meter langer Schiebetüren öffnet das große Wohnzimmer zum privaten Hinterhof. Im Inneren kombiniert ein klares, modernes Design weiche, warme Materialien - Zeder, Tanne mit vertikaler Maserung und Wolle - mit modernen Industrieoberflächen, grauem Backstein, poliertem Beton und weißen Laminatschränken, wodurch eine komfortable und einladende Umgebung geschaffen wird, die dem kalten Klima des pazifischen Nordwestens standhält.

La casa se asienta en un terreno suburbano de suave pendiente, bordeado en tres de sus lados por calles y un camino de entrada. Los clientes nos pidieron que creáramos una casa llena de luz natural que, al mismo tiempo, proporcionara privacidad en este terreno que, de otro modo, estaría expuesto. La casa está hundida en los lados que dan a la calle, creando un patio privado, verde y orientado al suroeste. El diseño garantiza que el interior se integre a la perfección con el exterior. Un conjunto de puertas correderas de 12 metros. de largo abre el gran salón al patio trasero privado. En el interior, un diseño moderno y despejado combina materiales suaves y cálidos, cedro, abeto de vetas verticales y lana, con superficies industriales modernas, ladrillo gris, hormigón pulido y armarios blancos laminados, creando un ambiente cómodo y acogedor, que hace frente al frío clima del noroeste del Pacífico.

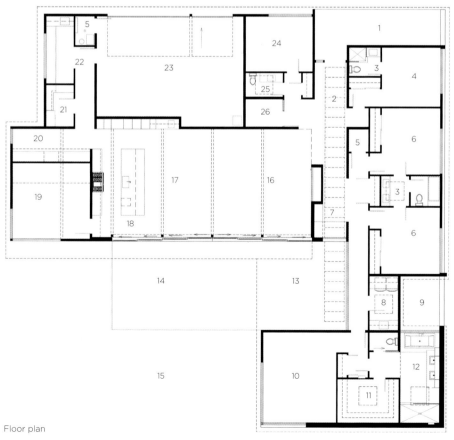

Floor plan

1. Front porch	14. Patio
2. Entry	15. Lawn
3. Bathroom	16. Living area
4. Guest bedroom	17. Dining area
5. Mechanical room	18. Kitchen
6. Bedroom	19. Playroom
7. Reading nook	20. Workstations
8. Laundry room	21. Pantry
9. Courtyard	22. Mud room
10. Master bedroom	23. Garage
11. Master closet	24. Study
12. Master bathroom	25. Powder room
13. Covered patio	26. Wine storage

THE WYSS FAMILY CONTAINER HOUSE

Mercer Island, Washington, United States // Lot area: 11,751 sq ft; building area: 3,238 sq ft

The clients wanted a bold, unusual, and adventurous addition to their existing 1950s split level where they could raise their three active boys. They loved the idea of repurposing shipping containers but, at the same time, they wanted the remodel to fit into the style of the existing traditional neighborhood while reflecting the unique history and development of the Seattle area and Pacific Northwest. The design focuses on the living room and kitchen as gathering centers connecting various parts of the house in a simple flow. It also provides quiet areas for contemplation and reflection. Because most of the existing house was to remain in place, and the neighborhood had a clear vernacular language, placing a big stack of shipping containers next to it seemed inadequate. Instead, the design sets out the containers like found objects.

Les clients voulaient un ajout audacieux, inhabituel et aventureux à leur maison à deux étages des années 1950, où ils pourraient élever leurs trois enfants. Ils ont adoré l'idée de réutiliser des conteneurs d'expédition, mais ils voulaient aussi que la rénovation s'intègre au style du quartier traditionnel existant tout en reflétant l'histoire et le développement uniques de la région de Seattle et du nord-ouest du Pacifique. Le design met l'accent sur le salon et la cuisine en tant que centres de rassemblement qui relient les différentes parties de la maison. Il offre également des zones de calme pour la contemplation et la réflexion. Étant donné que la majeure partie de la maison existante devait rester en place, et que le quartier avait un vernaculaire clair, placer une grande pile de conteneurs d'expédition à côté semblait inapproprié. Au lieu de cela, le design dispose les conteneurs comme s'il s'agissait d'objets trouvés.

Die Bauherren wünschten sich einen kühnen, ungewöhnlichen und abenteuerlichen Anbau an ihr zweistöckiges Haus aus den 1950er Jahren, in dem sie ihre drei Kinder großziehen konnten. Sie liebten die Idee, Schiffscontainer wiederzuverwenden, wollten aber auch, dass sich die Renovierung in den Stil der bestehenden traditionellen Nachbarschaft einfügt und gleichzeitig die einzigartige Geschichte und Entwicklung von Seattle und dem Nordwesten des Pazifiks widerspiegelt.Das Design betont das Wohnzimmer und die Küche als Treffpunkte, die verschiedene Teile des Hauses verbinden. Sie bietet auch ruhige Bereiche für Kontemplation und Reflexion. Angesichts der Tatsache, dass der größte Teil des bestehenden Hauses erhalten bleiben sollte und die Nachbarschaft eine eindeutige Sprache hatte, erschien es unangemessen, einen großen Stapel von Schiffscontainern daneben zu stellen. Stattdessen ordnet der Entwurf die Behälter wie Fundstücke an.

Los clientes querían un anexo atrevido, inusual y aventurero a su casa de dos plantas de los años 50, donde pudieran criar a sus tres hijos. Les encantaba la idea de reutilizar los contenedores de envío, pero también querían que la renovación encajara con el estilo del vecindario tradicional existente y al mismo tiempo reflejara la historia y el desarrollo únicos del área de Seattle y el noroeste del Pacífico. El diseño se centra en el salón y la cocina como centros de reunión que conectan varias partes de la casa. También ofrece zonas tranquilas para la contemplación y la reflexión. Dado que la mayor parte de la casa existente debía permanecer en su sitio, y que el barrio tenía un lenguaje vernáculo claro, colocar una gran pila de contenedores de transporte junto a ella parecía inadecuado. En lugar de ello, el diseño dispone los contenedores como si fueran objetos encontrados.

Second floor plan

EXISTING ROOF
BELOW

Ground floor plan

1. Garage
2. Mud room
3. Family room
4. Kitchen
5. Dining area
6. Outdoor deck
7. Living area
8. Entry
9. Bedroom
10. Laundry room
11. Rec room
12. Terrace
13. Shed (built with
    shipping containers)
14. Garage below
15. Family room below
16. Closet
17. Shipping container
    below

WHOLE EARTH MONTESSORI SCHOOL BUILDING

Bothell, Washington, United States // Lot area: 5-acre school campus; building area: 3,597 sq ft

Inspired by the trinomial cube, a primary teaching tool in Montessori education, Paul Michael Davis Architects designed an addition to a rural campus, merging the school's pedagogy with the surrounding natural environment. The Whole Earth Montessori envisioned a modern building that speaks not only to Montessori's history but also provides students with a stimulating environment to nurture their creativity and individuality. The site is classified as a critical habitat where no new development is allowed, but a 1980s concrete foundation offered an opportunity to build a simple cubic volume onto which a layer of complexity in the window design could be added. In addition to being energy efficient, the building's large windows, generous overhangs, and exterior staircases keep the students engaged with nature.

S'inspirant du cube trinomial, un outil pédagogique essentiel de l'éducation Montessori, Paul Michael Davis Architects a conçu une annexe à un campus rural, fusionnant la pédagogie de l'école avec l'environnement naturel. Whole Earth Montessori envisageait un bâtiment moderne qui non seulement reflète l'histoire de Montessori, mais offre également aux élèves un environnement stimulant pour nourrir leur créativité et leur individualité. Le site est classé comme habitat critique où aucun nouveau développement n'est autorisé, mais une fondation en béton des années 1980 offrait la possibilité de construire un volume cubique simple sur lequel une couche de complexité pouvait être ajoutée dans la conception des fenêtres. En plus de leur efficacité énergétique, les grandes fenêtres, les surplombs généreux et les escaliers extérieurs du bâtiment permettent aux étudiants de rester en contact avec la nature.

Inspiriert vom Trinomwürfel, einem wesentlichen Lehrmittel in der Montessori-Pädagogik, entwarfen Paul Michael Davis Architects einen Anbau an einen ländlichen Campus, der Schulpädagogik mit der natürlichen Umgebung verschmilzt. Whole Earth Montessori stellte sich ein modernes Gebäude vor, das nicht nur die Geschichte von Montessori widerspiegelt, sondern den Schülern auch eine fördernde Umgebung bietet, um ihre Kreativität und Individualität zu fördern. Das Gelände ist als kritischer Lebensraum eingestuft, wo keine Neuentwicklung erlaubt ist, aber ein Betonfundament aus den 1980er Jahren bot die Möglichkeit, ein einfaches kubisches Volumen zu bauen, auf dem eine Ebene der Komplexität in der Fenstergestaltung hinzugefügt werden konnte. Neben der Energieeffizienz ermöglichen die großen Fenster, großzügigen Überhänge und Außentreppen des Gebäudes den Kontakt zur Natur.

Inspirándose en el cubo trinomial, una herramienta de enseñanza primordial en la educación Montessori, Paul Michael Davis Architects diseñó la ampliación de un campus rural, fusionando la pedagogía de la escuela con el entorno natural. El Whole Earth Montessori imaginó un edificio moderno que hablara no solo de la historia de Montessori, sino que también proporcionara a los estudiantes un entorno estimulante para alimentar su creatividad e individualidad. El emplazamiento está clasificado como hábitat crítico donde no se permite ningún nuevo desarrollo, pero unos cimientos de hormigón de la década de 1980 ofrecían la oportunidad de construir un volumen cúbico sencillo sobre el que se podía añadir una capa de complejidad en el diseño de las ventanas. Además de ser eficiente desde el punto de vista energético, los grandes ventanales del edificio, los generosos voladizos y las escaleras exteriores mantienen a los estudiantes en contacto con la naturaleza.

1. Apply the trinomial cube, a staple montessori teaching tool, used as window module

2. Explode to the corners to dematerialize and open classrooms to the landscape

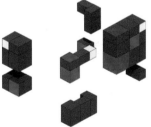

3. Move to the programmatic locations

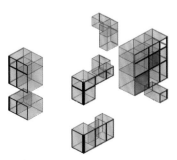

4. Translate blocks into real window details

5. Place in phase 1 structure

6. Repeat process in phase 2

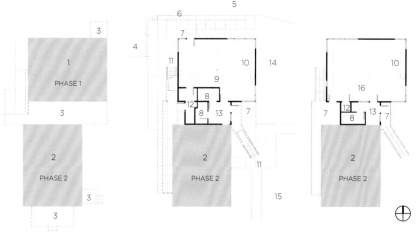

1. Phase 1: Repalce 1970s house previously converted to classroom and office
2. Phase 2: Replace 1970s garage previously converted to classroom and office
3. Decks, porches, and ramps to be removed
4. Drop-off parking area
5. Driveway
6. Bench
7. Entry
8. Restroom
9. Classroom
10. Kitchen and storage
11. Stairs to upper level
12. Mechanical room
13. Lobby
14. Lawn
15. Play yard
16. Office/flexible space

Existing ground floor plan   New ground floor plan   New second floor plan

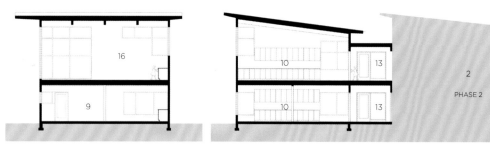

East-west section   North-south section

VictorEric
Design + Build

VENTURI RESIDENCE

Design/buildTeam:
VictorEric
Photographer:
© Barrie Underhill/Upper Left Photography

WILTSHIRE RESIDENCE

Design/buildTeam:
VictorEric
Photographer:
© Barrie Underhill/Upper Left Photography

TRIUMPH RESIDENCE

Design/buildTeam:
VictorEric
Photographer:
© Barrie Underhill/Upper Left Photography

🌐 www.victoreric.com ◎ victorericgroup

VictorEric Design + Build is a multiple-award-winning firm recognized for its high caliber design in architecture, interior design, and landscape design. At VictorEric, home building and design are approached from a human perspective to achieve the ultimate expression of each client's unique lifestyle. VictorEric's team is well-versed in the technical details that come with high-end design and has allowed the firm to deliver projects effectively from design to construction. With the team, process, and vision in place, VictorEric runs like a well-oiled machine, enabling Eric's role to evolve into Chief Visionary Officer. This role allows him to focus on exclusive projects that require the highest level of involvement and attention. These projects become VictorEric's E-Signature Series. This speaks to the dedication that ensures each series is a reflection of the client's vision and the team's relentless pursuit of excellence in design, craftsmanship, and service.

VictorEric Design + Build ist ein mehrfach preisgekröntes Unternehmen für hochkarätiges Design in den Bereichen Architektur, Innenarchitektur und Landschaftsarchitektur. Bei VictorEric werden Hausbau und Design aus einer menschlichen Perspektive betrachtet, um den einzigartigen Lebensstil eines jeden Kunden optimal zum Ausdruck zu bringen. Das Team von VictorEric ist mit den technischen Details des High-End-Designs bestens vertraut und hat das Unternehmen in die Lage versetzt, Projekte vom Entwurf bis zum Bau effizient umzusetzen. Mit dem Team, den Prozessen und der Vision vor Ort läuft VictorEric wie eine gut geölte Maschine, so dass sich Erics Rolle zum 'Visionary Director' entwickelt hat. Diese Rolle ermöglicht es ihm, sich auf einzigartige Projekte zu konzentrieren, die ein Höchstmaß an Engagement und Aufmerksamkeit erfordern. Diese Projekte werden zur E-Signatur-Serie von VictorEric. Dies spricht für die Hingabe, mit der jede Serie die Vision des Kunden widerspiegelt, und für das unermüdliche Streben des Teams nach Spitzenleistungen in Design, Handwerk und Service.

VictorEric Design + Build est une entreprise primée à plusieurs reprises pour son design de haut niveau en matière d'architecture, de décoration intérieure et d'architecture paysagère. Chez VictorEric, la construction et la conception de maisons sont abordées d'un point de vue humain afin d'obtenir l'expression maximale du style de vie unique de chaque client. L'équipe de VictorEric connaît bien les détails techniques liés à la conception haut de gamme et a permis à l'entreprise de réaliser efficacement des projets, de la conception à la construction. Avec l'équipe, le processus et la vision en place, VictorEric fonctionne comme une machine bien huilée, ce qui a permis à Eric de voir son rôle évoluer vers celui de « directeur visionnaire ». Ce rôle lui permet de se concentrer sur des projets uniques qui exigent le plus haut niveau d'implication et d'attention. Ces projets deviennent la série E-Signature de VictorEric. Cela témoigne du dévouement qui fait que chaque série est le reflet de la vision du client et de la recherche incessante de l'équipe de l'excellence en matière de conception, d'artisanat et de service.

VictorEric Design + Build es una empresa ganadora de múltiples premios por su diseño de alto calibre en arquitectura, diseño de interiores y paisajismo. En VictorEric, la construcción y el diseño de viviendas se abordan desde una perspectiva humana para lograr la máxima expresión del estilo de vida único de cada cliente. El equipo de VictorEric está bien versado en los detalles técnicos que vienen con el diseño de gama alta y ha permitido a la empresa conseguir entregar los proyectos con eficacia desde el diseño hasta la construcción. Con el equipo, el proceso y la visión establecidos, VictorEric funciona como una máquina bien engrasada, lo que ha permitido que el papel de Eric evolucione hasta convertirse en «Director Visionario». Este papel le permite centrarse en proyectos exclusivos que requieren el máximo nivel de implicación y atención. Estos proyectos se convierten en la serie E-Signature de VictorEric. Esto habla de la dedicación que asegura que cada serie es un reflejo de la visión del cliente y la búsqueda incesante del equipo de la excelencia en el diseño, la artesanía y el servicio.

VENTURI RESIDENCE

Vancouver, British Columbia, Canada // Lot area: 31,744 sq ft; building area: 13,272 sq ft

The Venturi Residence is a prime example of VictorEric's exclusive E-signature series, which takes VictorEric's award-winning design to the highest level of craftsmanship, design quality, and attention to detail. Venturi Residence satisfies the clients' need for high-level automation, security, and above all, creative expression. The clients wanted to steer clear of the boxed design prevalent in most modern architecture and wanted a design that incorporated flowing lines. This flowing design expression transitions seamlessly to the landscape and interiors. It is complemented with advanced technological features and luxurious finishes such as board-formed-concrete walls, thermo-formed countertops, and exquisite marble surfaces. A stunning double-height entry foyer with wavy forms and a sculptural staircase are created for high visual impact and a rich spatial experience.

La résidence Venturi est un exemple parfait de la série exclusive E-signature de VictorEric, qui porte le design primé de VictorEric au plus haut niveau d'artisanat, de qualité de conception et d'attention aux détails. La résidence Venturi répond au besoin des clients d'un haut niveau d'automatisation, de sécurité et, surtout, d'expression créative. Les clients souhaitaient s'éloigner de la conception carrée qui domine la plupart des architectures modernes et voulaient un design aux lignes fluides. Cette expression fluide du design se traduit de manière transparente dans le paysage et les intérieurs. Il est complété par des caractéristiques technologiques avancées et des finitions de luxe telles que des murs en béton formé, des plans de travail thermoformés et des surfaces en marbre exquis. Un impressionnant hall d'entrée à double hauteur aux formes ondulantes et un escalier sculptural ont été créés pour un fort impact visuel et une expérience spatiale riche.

Die Venturi Residence ist ein Paradebeispiel für die exklusive E-Signatur-Serie von VictorEric, die das preisgekrönte Design von VictorEric auf ein Höchstmaß an Handwerkskunst, Designqualität und Liebe zum Detail bringt. Die Venturi Residence entspricht dem Bedürfnis der Kunden nach einem hohen Maß an Automatisierung, Sicherheit und vor allem kreativem Ausdruck. Die Bauherren wollten weg von dem kastenförmigen Design, das in der modernen Architektur meist vorherrscht, und wünschten sich ein Design mit fließenden Linien. Dieser fließende Designausdruck überträgt sich nahtlos auf die Landschaft und die Innenräume. Hinzu kommen fortschrittliche technische Merkmale und luxuriöse Oberflächen wie geformte Betonwände, thermogeformte Arbeitsplatten und exquisite Marmoroberflächen. Eine beeindruckende, doppelhohe Eingangshalle mit wellenförmigen Formen und einer skulpturalen Treppe sorgt für eine hohe visuelle Wirkung und ein reichhaltiges Raumerlebnis.

La residencia Venturi es un excelente ejemplo de la exclusiva serie E-signature de VictorEric, que lleva el galardonado diseño de VictorEric al más alto nivel de artesanía, calidad de diseño y atención al detalle. La Residencia Venturi satisface la necesidad de los clientes de contar con un alto nivel de automatización, seguridad y, sobre todo, expresión creativa. Los clientes querían alejarse del diseño encajonado que predomina en la mayoría de la arquitectura moderna y querían un diseño que incorporara líneas fluidas. Esta expresión de diseño fluido se traslada sin problemas al paisaje y a los interiores. Se complementa con características tecnológicas avanzadas y acabados de lujo, como paredes de hormigón conformado, encimeras termoformadas y exquisitas superficies de mármol. Se ha creado un impresionante vestíbulo de entrada de doble altura con formas onduladas y una escalera escultórica para lograr un gran impacto visual y una rica experiencia espacial.

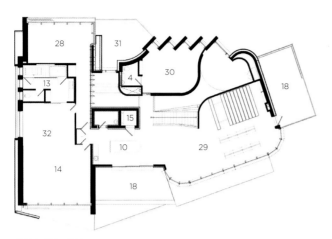

Upper floor plan

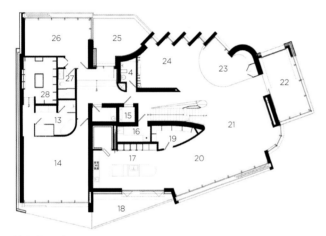

Main floor plan

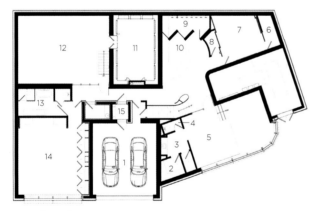

Lower floor plan

1. Two-car garage	12. Shooting gallery	23. Genkan foyer
2. Sauna	13. Ensuite	24. Entertainment
3. Changing area	14. Bedroom	25. Pet deck
4. Toilet room	15. Elevator	26. Pet room
5. Gymnasium	16. Laundry room	37. Pet ensuite
6. AV closet	17. Kitchen	28. Walk-in closet
7. Theater	18. Balcony	29. Collectibles
8. Storage	19. Pantry	30. Arcade loft
9. Wine cellar	20. Dining area	31. Pet deck below
10. Bar	21. Great room	32. Computer room
11. Library	22. Display garage	

WILTSHIRE RESIDENCE

Vancouver, British Columbia, Canada // Lot area: 6,741 sq f t; building area: 4,332 sq ft

The Wiltshire Residence is another E-signature project that takes the clients' vision from architecture, interior design, and landscape design to a wonderfully executed construction. The level of detail in this house required a hands-on approach from beginning to end. From the ground up, a French Country structure, with its luxurious yet effortless styling, is the base for a series of interventions to achieve a contemporary look.

La résidence Wiltshire est un autre projet E-signature qui concrétise la vision du client en matière d'architecture, de décoration intérieure et d'aménagement paysager pour aboutir à une construction magnifiquement exécutée. Le niveau de détail de cette maison a nécessité une approche pratique du début à la fin. Dès le départ, une structure de style français, luxueuse mais sans excès, sert de base à une série d'interventions pour obtenir un look contemporain.

Die Wiltshire Residence ist ein weiteres Projekt von E-Signature, bei dem die Visionen der Kunden von der Architektur über die Inneneinrichtung und die Landschaftsgestaltung bis hin zum Bau umgesetzt werden. Der Detailreichtum dieses Hauses erforderte von Anfang bis Ende eine praktische Vorgehensweise. Von Anfang an bildet eine luxuriöse, aber nicht übertriebene Struktur im französischen Stil die Grundlage für eine Reihe von Eingriffen, um ein zeitgenössisches Aussehen zu erreichen. Weiß gekalkte Zi.

La residencia Wiltshire es otro proyecto de E-signature que lleva la visión de los clientes desde la arquitectura, el diseño de interiores y el diseño del paisaje hasta una construcción maravillosamente ejecutada. El nivel de detalle de esta casa requirió un enfoque práctico de principio a fin. Desde el principio, una estructura de estilo francés, lujosa pero sin excesos, es la base de una serie de intervenciones para lograr un aspecto contemporáneo.

Lower floor plan

Main floor plan

Upper floor plan

1. Theater/bar	10. Covered porch	19. Mud room
2. Powder room	11. Hot tub	20. Kitchen
3. Rec room	12. Family room	21. Balcony
4. Utility room	13. Dining area	22. Bedroom
5. Laundry room	14. Music room	23. Ensuite
6. Flex room	15. Porch	24. Walk-in closet
7. Guest suite	16. Foyer	25. Master walk-in closet
8. Bathroom	17. Guest room	26. Master ensuite
9. Guest room	18. Nook	27. Master bedroom

TRIUMPH RESIDENCE

Vancouver, British Columbia, Canada // Lot area: 4,026 sq ft; building area: 2,879 sq ft

Triumph Residence is a good example of the integration of landscape design with the overall architecture. This home is on a beautiful property lot that takes in the city and the mountain views from three sides. A Japanese rock garden complements the house's modern industrial style, while a colorful lychee—carefully positioned to be enjoyed from all levels of the home—and native West Coast planting harmonize with the landscape beyond. The house makes the most of the standard size lot in Vancouver, providing generous spaces open to the light and views while maintaining privacy.

Triumph Residence est un bel exemple d'intégration de la conception paysagère à l'architecture globale. Cette maison est située sur un beau terrain qui offre une vue sur la ville et les montagnes depuis trois côtés. Un jardin de rocaille japonais complète le style industriel moderne de la maison, tandis qu'un litchi vivement coloré, soigneusement placée pour être appréciée depuis tous les niveaux de la maison, et des plantes indigènes de la côte ouest s'harmonisent avec le paysage au-delà. La maison tire pleinement parti de la parcelle standard à Vancouver, offrant des espaces généreux ouverts à la lumière et aux vues, tout en préservant l'intimité.

Triumph Residence ist ein gutes Beispiel für die Integration der Landschaftsgestaltung in die Gesamtarchitektur. Dieses Haus steht auf einem wunderschönen Grundstück, das von drei Seiten Stadt- und Bergblick bietet. Ein japanischer Steingarten ergänzt den modernen Industriestil des Hauses, während eine farbenfrohe Litschi – sorgfältig platziert, um von allen Ebenen des Hauses genossen zu werden – und einheimische Westküstenpflanzen mit der Landschaft dahinter harmonieren. Das Haus nutzt die Vorteile des Standardgrundstücks in Vancouver voll aus und bietet großzügige Räume, die offen für Licht und Ausblicke sind und dennoch die Privatsphäre wahren.

Triumph Residence es un buen ejemplo de la integración del diseño del paisaje con la arquitectura general. Esta casa se encuentra en una hermosa parcela que tiene vistas a la ciudad y a la montaña desde tres lados. Un jardín de rocas japonés complementa el moderno estilo industrial de la casa, mientras que un colorido litchi, cuidadosamente colocado para disfrutarlo desde todos los niveles de la casa, y plantas autóctonas de la costa oeste armonizan con el paisaje circundante. La casa aprovecha al máximo la parcela estándar en Vancouver, proporcionando generosos espacios abiertos a la luz y a las vistas, pero manteniendo la privacidad.

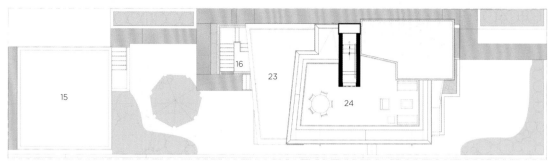

Roof plan

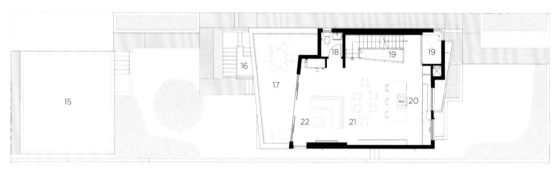

Upper floor plan

Main floor plan

Lower floor plan

1. Sunken courtyard
2. Guest suite
3. Bedroom
4. Wine cellar
5. Mechanical room
6. Bathroom
7. Two-car garage
8. Lawn
9. Den
10. Entry foyer
11. Studio/laundry room
12. Walk-in closet
13. Master ensuite
14. Master bedroom
15. Garage roof
16. Sunken courtyard below
17. Deck
18. Powder room
19. Open to below
20. Kitchen
21. Dining area
22. Living area
23. Deck below
24. Roof deck

DEMETRIOU
ARCHITECTS

DIAGRID HOUSE

Architecture and Interior Design:
Demetriou Architects
Structural Engineer:
Swenson Say Faget
General Contractor:
Bender Custom Construction
Landscape Architect:
Ken Philip/Kenneth Philip
Landscape Architects
Photographer:
© Mike Jensen

SAN JUAN RETREAT

Architecture and Interior Design:
Demetriou Architects
Structural Engineer:
Swenson Say Faget
Landscape Architect:
Steve Schramm/Island Gardens
General Contractor:
Dan Lowe/Lowe Construction
Photographer:
© Mike Jensen

GLASS BOX

Architecture and Interior Design:
Demetriou Architects
Structural Engineer:
Swenson Say Faget
General Contractor:
Jess Rathburn/Pacific Craftsmen, Inc
Photographer:
© Jay Goodrich

🌐 www.demetriouarchitects.com

Relationships and continuity describe Demetriou Architects' philosophy. From human and spatial relationships, the indoor-outdoor connection, and the interconnectedness of all parts of a project to how the firm develops every design, the studio strives to achieve continuity of vision and purpose. Led by Vassos M. Demetriou and Michelle Demetriou Cozza, the firm values long-lasting design over temporal style. Demetriou Architects was among the first to introduce International Style architecture to the Seattle/Eastside area. Though the style was new to the region, the focus on clean lines, open interiors, and large glass expanses—opening spaces to views and light and connecting indoors to out—complemented the Northwest's trees, water, and quality of light. Today these tenets continue to embody Demetriou Architects' design vision. Through close client relationships often leading to multi-year, multi-project partnerships, Demetriou Architects designs buildings that are at once specific to their clients' wants and needs and are universally functional and timeless.

Beziehungen und Kontinuität beschreiben die philosophie von Demetriou Architects. Ob es sich um menschliche und räumliche Beziehungen, die Verbindung zwischen Innen und Außen, die Verbindung aller Teile eines Projekts oder die Art und Weise handelt, wie das Unternehmen jedes Projekt entwickelt, das Studio strebt danach, die Kontinuität von Vision und Zweck sicherzustellen. Unter der Leitung von Vassos M. Demetriou und Michelle Demetriou Cozza bevorzugt das Studio nachhaltiges Design gegenüber temporärem Stil. Demetriou Architects war einer der ersten, der Architektur im internationalen Stil in die Gegend von Seattle/Eastside brachte. Obwohl der Stil für die Region neu war, ergänzte der Fokus auf klare Linien, offene Innenräume und große Glasflächen – die Räume für Ausblicke und Licht öffnen und Innenräume mit Außenräumen verbinden – die Bäume, das Wasser und die Lichtqualität des Nordwestens. Heute verkörpern diese Prinzipien weiterhin die Designvision von Demetriou Architects. Durch enge Beziehungen zu seinen Kunden, die oft zu Partnerschaften und mehrjährigen Projekten führen, entwirft Demetriou Architects Gebäude, die speziell auf die Wünsche und Bedürfnisse seiner Kunden zugeschnitten sind und universell funktional und zeitlos sind.

Les relations et la continuité décrivent la philosophie de Demetriou Architects. Qu'il s'agisse des relations humaines et spatiales, du lien entre l'intérieur et l'extérieur, de l'interconnexion de toutes les parties d'un projet ou de la manière dont le cabinet développe chaque projet, le studio assure la continuité de la vision. Dirigé par Vassos M. Demetriou et Michelle Demetriou Cozza, le studio privilégie le design durable au style temporaire. Le cabinet Demetriou Architects a été l'un des premiers à introduire l'architecture de style international dans la région de Seattle/Eastside. Bien que ce style soit nouveau dans la région, l'accent mis sur les lignes épurées, les intérieurs ouverts et les grandes surfaces vitrées qui ouvrent les espaces aux vues et à la lumière et qui relient l'intérieur à l'extérieur complétait les arbres, l'eau et la qualité de la lumière du Nord-Ouest. Aujourd'hui, ces principes continuent d'incarner la vision du design de Demetriou Architects. Grâce à des relations étroites avec ses clients, qui débouchent souvent sur des partenariats et des projets pluriannuels, Demetriou Architects conçoit des bâtiments qui sont spécifiques aux souhaits de ses clients, fonctionnels et intemporels.

Las relaciones y la continuidad describen la filosofía de Demetriou Architects. Desde las relaciones humanas y espaciales, la conexión entre el interior y el exterior y la interconexión de todas las partes de un proyecto hasta la forma en que la empresa desarrolla cada diseño, el estudio se esfuerza por lograr la continuidad de la visión. Dirigido por Vassos M. Demetriou y Michelle Demetriou Cozza, el estudio valora el diseño duradero por encima del estilo temporal. Demetriou Architects fue uno de los primeros en introducir la arquitectura de estilo internacional en la zona de Seattle/Eastside. Aunque el estilo era nuevo en la región, el enfoque en las líneas limpias, los interiores abiertos y las grandes ventanales que abren los espacios a las vistas y la luz y conectan el interior con el exterior, complementaban los árboles, el agua y la calidad de la luz del noroeste. En la actualidad, estos principios siguen encarnando la visión de diseño de Demetriou Architects. A través de una estrecha relación con el cliente, que a menudo conduce a asociaciones de varios años y proyectos, Demetriou Architects diseña edificios que son a la vez específicos para los deseos de sus clientes y son funcionales y atemporales.

DIAGRID HOUSE

Washington, United States // Lot area: 1.4 acres; building area: 25,083 sq ft

The concept for this waterfront island home was to create a "village" for family, extended family, and guests. The various zones are connected horizontally by glazed circulation "streets," which provide both physical and visual connection of spaces within the home and to the site and views. On the other hand, the vertical circulation is expressed by the diagrid structure of the stair tower volumes. Large expanses of glazing bring in natural light and blur the distinction between interior and exterior spaces. The house is designed for entertaining and as a showcase for art within a spatial composition that is novel, yet inviting, a work of art itself. Rooms are defined not by enclosure but by the use of materials, casework, and changes in the treatment of the ceiling plane.

Le concept de cette maison au bord de l'eau était de créer un « village » pour la famille, la famille et les invités. Les différentes zones sont reliées horizontalement par des rues de circulation vitrées, qui assurent une connexion physique et visuelle des espaces à l'intérieur de la maison et avec le site et les vues. D'autre part, la circulation verticale est exprimée par la structure diagonale des volumes de la tour d'escalier. De grandes étendues de verre apportent la lumière naturelle et effacent la distinction entre les espaces intérieurs et extérieurs. La maison est conçue pour le divertissement et comme une vitrine pour l'art dans une composition spatiale à la fois nouvelle et accueillante, une œuvre d'art en soi. Les pièces ne sont pas définies par les clôtures, mais par l'utilisation des matériaux, des menuiseries et des changements dans le traitement du plan du plafond.

Das Konzept dieses Hauses am Wasser war es, ein „Dorf" für die Familie, die Familie und die Gäste zu schaffen. Die verschiedenen Zonen sind horizontal durch verglaste Erschließungsstraßen verbunden, die eine physische und visuelle Verbindung der Räume innerhalb des Hauses und mit dem Gelände und den Ausblicken herstellen. Andererseits wird die vertikale Zirkulation durch die diagonale Struktur der Treppenturmvolumen zum Ausdruck gebracht. Große Glasflächen lassen natürliches Licht herein und verwischen den Unterschied zwischen Innen- und Außenbereich. Das Haus dient der Unterhaltung und der Präsentation von Kunst in einer neuartigen und einladenden Raumkomposition, die ein Kunstwerk für sich ist. Die Räume werden nicht durch die Umhüllungen definiert, sondern durch die Verwendung von Materialien, Tischlerarbeiten und Veränderungen in der Behandlung der Deckenebene.

El concepto de esta casa frente al mar era crear un «pueblo» para la familia, la familia e invitados. Las distintas zonas están conectadas horizontalmente por calles de circulación acristaladas, que proporcionan una conexión física y visual de los espacios dentro de la casa y con el lugar y las vistas. Por otro lado, la circulación vertical se expresa mediante la estructura en diagonal de los volúmenes de la torre de la escalera. Las grandes extensiones de cristal aportan luz natural y difuminan la distinción entre los espacios interiores y exteriores. La casa está diseñada para el entretenimiento y como escaparate del arte dentro de una composición espacial que es novedosa y a la vez acogedora, una obra de arte en sí misma. Las estancias no se definen por los cerramientos, sino por el uso de los materiales, la carpintería y los cambios en el tratamiento del plano del techo.

SAN JUAN RETREAT

San Juan Island, Washington, United States // Lot area: .88 acres; building area: 4,813 sq ft

The design of this contemporary Northwest island retreat was approached with respect for the environment and natural character of the site, heavily wooded and in proximity to the waterfront. The house responds to its unparalleled location through the use of large windows maximizing light during drizzly grey Northwest days, the desire to bring the outdoors in, and the use of indigenous, regional materials that are low maintenance and will patina naturally over time. Clean lines and finishes express individual volumes and visually organize the structure. Within the home, spaces are defined with minimum enclosure using structural members and architectural elements rather than walls.

La conception de ce refuge contemporain situé au nord-ouest de l'île a été abordée dans le respect de l'environnement et du caractère naturel du site, fortement boisé et proche de la côte. La maison répond à son emplacement idéal par l'utilisation de grandes fenêtres qui maximisent la lumière pendant les jours gris du nord-ouest, le désir d'amener l'extérieur à l'intérieur et l'utilisation de matériaux indigènes et régionaux nécessitant peu d'entretien et qui résisteront naturellement au temps. Les lignes et les finitions épurées expriment les volumes individuels et organisent visuellement la structure. À l'intérieur de la maison, les espaces sont définis avec un minimum d'enceinte, en utilisant des éléments structurels et architecturaux au lieu de murs.

Bei der Gestaltung dieses modernen Refugiums im Nordwesten der Insel wurde auf die Umwelt und den natürlichen Charakter des stark bewaldeten und küstennahen Geländes Rücksicht genommen. Das Haus reagiert auf seine unschlagbare Lage mit großen Fenstern, die das Licht während der grauen Tage im Nordwesten maximieren, mit dem Wunsch, die Natur ins Haus zu holen, und mit der Verwendung von pflegeleichten, einheimischen und regionalen Materialien, die im Laufe der Zeit natürlich verwittern werden. Klare Linien und Oberflächen bringen die einzelnen Volumen zum Ausdruck und gliedern die Struktur visuell. Im Inneren des Hauses sind die Räume mit minimalen Umschließungen definiert, wobei anstelle von Wänden Strukturelemente und architektonische Elemente verwendet werden.

El diseño de este refugio contemporáneo en el noroeste de la isla se planteó respetando el entorno y el carácter natural del lugar, muy arbolado y próximo a la costa. La casa responde a su inmejorable ubicación mediante el uso de grandes ventanales que maximizan la luz durante los días grises del noroeste, el deseo de llevar el aire libre al interior y el uso de materiales autóctonos y regionales de bajo mantenimiento que se patinarán de forma natural con el tiempo. Las líneas limpias y los acabados expresan los volúmenes individuales y organizan visualmente la estructura. Dentro de la casa, los espacios se definen con el mínimo cerramiento, utilizando miembros estructurales y elementos arquitectónicos en lugar de paredes.

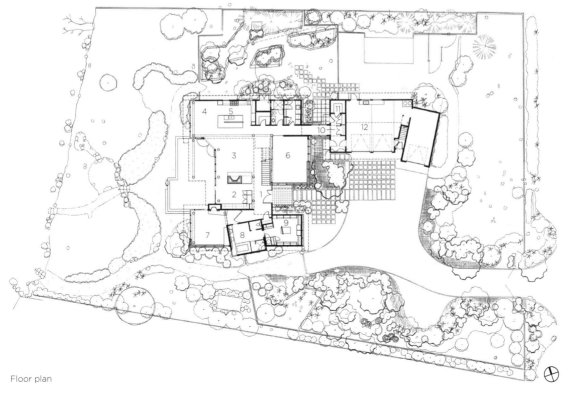

Floor plan

1. Entry
2. Office
3. Living room
4. Dining room
5. Kitchen
6. Media room
7. Master bedroom
8. Master bathroom
9. Master closet
10. Mud room
11. Wine room
12. Garage

GLASS BOX

San Juan Island, Washington, United States // Lot area: 2.6 acres; building area: 2,744 sq ft

This home atop a rocky promontory on the shore of San Juan Island is conceived as a jewel on the rock. The condition of the existing house on the site did not lend itself to renovation, and current codes prohibited new construction in this extraordinary location. Consequently, the decision was made to reuse the existing foundations, which led to an environmentally friendly approach in the design of the new home. The Glass Box sits on concrete piers floating above the rock while making the most of the light and views across the San Juan Channel. The juxtaposition of man-made and natural forms reinforce each other, preserving the rock's formation and emphasizing the architectural configuration of the house above. To the west, the house and guest house are nestled among the trees, offering a striking contrast with the open, expansive water view to the east.

Cette maison située au sommet d'un promontoire rocheux sur la côte de l'île de San Juan est conçue comme un bijou dans la roche. L'état de la maison existante ne se prêtait pas à une rénovation, et les codes en vigueur interdisaient toute nouvelle construction sur ce site extraordinaire. Il a donc été décidé de réutiliser les fondations existantes, ce qui a conduit à une approche écologique de la conception de la nouvelle maison. La Glass Box repose sur des piliers en béton qui flottent sur la roche, profitant pleinement de la lumière et des vues sur le canal de San Juan. La juxtaposition de formes artificielles et naturelles se renforcent mutuellement, préservant la formation rocheuse et soulignant la configuration architecturale de la maison sur le plan supérieur. À l'ouest, la maison et la maison d'hôtes sont nichées parmi les arbres, offrant un contraste saisissant avec la vue ouverte et étendue sur l'eau à l'est.

Dieses Haus auf einer felsigen Landzunge an der Küste von San Juan Island ist wie ein Juwel in den Felsen konzipiert. Der Zustand des bestehenden Hauses eignete sich nicht für eine Renovierung, und die geltenden Vorschriften untersagten einen Neubau an diesem außergewöhnlichen Ort. Daher wurde beschlossen, die vorhandenen Fundamente wieder zu verwenden, was zu einem ökologischen Ansatz bei der Planung des neuen Hauses führte. Die Glass Box ruht auf Betonsäulen, die auf dem Felsen schwimmen und das Licht und die Aussicht auf den San Juan Channel voll ausnutzen. Das Nebeneinander von künstlichen und natürlichen Formen verstärkt sich gegenseitig, bewahrt die Felsformation und hebt die architektonische Konfiguration des Hauses auf der oberen Ebene hervor. Im Westen liegen das Haus und das Gästehaus inmitten von Bäumen und bilden einen auffälligen Kontrast zum offenen und weiten Blick auf das Wasser im Osten.

Esta casa en lo alto de un promontorio rocoso en la costa de la isla de San Juan está concebida como una joya en las rocas. El estado de la casa existente no se prestaba a una renovación, y los códigos vigentes prohibían una nueva construcción en este extraordinario lugar. En consecuencia, se decidió reutilizar los cimientos existentes, lo que condujo a un enfoque ecológico en el diseño de la nueva casa. La Glass Box se asienta sobre pilares de hormigón que flotan sobre la roca, aprovechando al máximo la luz y las vistas del Canal de San Juan. La yuxtaposición de formas artificiales y naturales se refuerzan mutuamente, preservando la formación de la roca y destacando la configuración arquitectónica de la casa del plano superior. Al oeste, la casa y la de invitados están enclavadas entre los árboles, lo que ofrece un llamativo contraste con la vista abierta y amplia del agua al este.

Second floor plan

Third floor plan

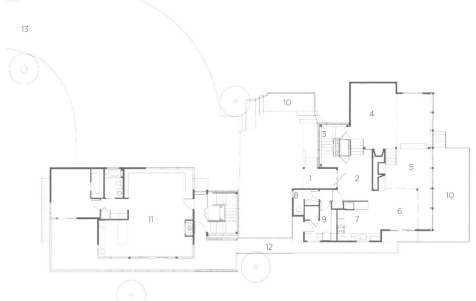

Ground floor plan

1. Covered porch
2. Entry
3. Staircase tower
4. Living room
5. Dining room
6. Sitting room
7. Kitchen
8. Powder room
9. Laundry room
10. Deck
11. Garage and guest house
12. Connecting bridge
13. Driveway
14. Study
15. Master bedroom
16. Sitting area
17. Master bathroom
18. Master closet
19. Open to below
20. Bedroom
21. Bathroom

babienko
ARCHITECTS

OC

Architecture Design Team:
babienko ARCHITECTS
General Contractor:
Merola Construction
Photographer:
© Ema Peter

PS REDUX

Architecture Team:
Babienko ARCHITECTS
Metalwork:
Keith Northrup
Casework:
Interior Environments
General Contractor:
LZL Construction
Photographer:
© Moris Moreno Photography

RT

Architecture Team:
babienko ARCHITECTS
Structural Engineer:
Harriot Valentine Engineers
Geotechnical Engineer:
Geotech Consultants
General Contractor:
SBE Construction
Photographer:
© Moris Moreno Photography

Awards:
AIA Honor Award

Founded in 2010 and located in Seattle, Washington, babienko is an inventive architecture firm whose approach to architecture is grounded in solid construction techniques and practices. babienko is comprised of a multi-disciplinary team that applies an artistic, thoughtful, and innovative approach to design and provides inspirational solutions to our clients. The team is committed to employing sustainable building practices combined with meticulous execution of detail and craftsmanship. babienko brings together the client's vision with the particulars of the site to create a livable architecture that celebrates durability and ecological integrity. babienko's collaborative and interdisciplinary approach of integrating art and science yields innovative, efficient, and inspirational designs for our clients throughout the Pacific Northwest, the United States, and Canada.

babienko wurde 2010 gegründet und hat seinen Sitz in Seattle, Washington. babienko ist ein erfinderisches Architekturbüro, dessen Architekturansatz auf soliden Bautechniken und -praktiken basiert. babienko besteht aus einem multidisziplinären Team, das einen künstlerischen, durchdachten und innovativen Designansatz verfolgt und unseren Kunden inspirierende Lösungen bietet. Das Team hat sich der Anwendung nachhaltiger Baupraktiken in Kombination mit einer sorgfältigen Ausführung von Details und Handwerkskunst verschrieben. babienko verbindet die Vision des Kunden mit den Besonderheiten des Ortes, um eine lebenswerte Architektur zu schaffen, die Langlebigkeit und ökologische Integrität zelebriert. babienkos kollaborativer, interdisziplinärer Ansatz zur Integration von Kunst und Wissenschaft führt zu innovativen, effizienten und inspirierenden Entwürfen für unsere Kunden im gesamten pazifischen Nordwesten, den Vereinigten Staaten und Kanada.

Fondé en 2010 et situé à Seattle, dans l'État de Washington, babienko est un cabinet d'architecture inventif dont l'approche de l'architecture repose sur des techniques et des pratiques de construction solides. babienko est composé d'une équipe multidisciplinaire qui applique une approche artistique, réfléchie et innovante de la conception et fournit des solutions inspirantes à ses clients. L'équipe s'engage à utiliser des pratiques de construction durables combinées à une exécution méticuleuse des détails et de l'artisanat. babienko associe la vision du client aux particularités du site pour créer une architecture habitable qui célèbre la durabilité et l'intégrité écologique. L'approche collaborative et interdisciplinaire de babienko pour intégrer l'art et la science produit des conceptions innovatrices, efficaces et inspirantes pour nos clients à travers le Pacifique Nord-Ouest, les États-Unis et le Canada.

Fundado en 2010 y situado en Seattle, Washington, babienko es un estudio de arquitectura inventivo cuyo enfoque de la arquitectura se basa en técnicas y prácticas de construcción sólidas. babienko está compuesto por un equipo multidisciplinar que aplica un enfoque artístico, reflexivo e innovador al diseño y proporciona soluciones inspiradoras a nuestros clientes. El equipo se compromete a emplear prácticas de construcción sostenibles combinadas con una ejecución meticulosa de los detalles y la artesanía. babienko reúne la visión del cliente con las particularidades del lugar para crear una arquitectura habitable que celebra la durabilidad y la integridad ecológica. El enfoque colaborativo e interdisciplinario de babienko de integrar el arte y la ciencia produce diseños innovadores, eficientes e inspiradores para nuestros clientes en todo el noroeste del Pacífico, los Estados Unidos y Canadá.

OC

Located adjacent to Stanley Park and English Bay, this condo was designed to take in the west view "corridors" framed by the existing concrete columns. The removal of the interior walls brings more natural daylight into the suite, creating a simple, comfortable living space showcasing the client's art collection. The quiet yet rich interior was achieved by juxtaposing contrasts: the vertical concrete columns against smooth-surfaced soft white cabinets; or the dark concrete floor against painted gypsum wallboard. The reclaimed wood timber stack grounds the "back" of the living spaces and conceals a cyclist training space while also establishing a spatial delineation between public and private spaces. Hidden doors and passageways throughout allow the suite to adapt to the family's need for different living arrangements, open feel, and multiple circulation routes.

Situé à côté du parc Stanley et de la baie English, ce condominium a été conçu pour tirer parti des « couloirs » orientés vers l'ouest et encadrés par les colonnes de béton existantes. La suppression des murs intérieurs apporte plus de lumière naturelle dans la suite, créant un espace de vie simple et confortable qui met en valeur la collection d'art du client. L'intérieur à la fois calme et riche a été obtenu en juxtaposant les contrastes : les colonnes verticales en béton contre les armoires blanches à surface lisse, ou le sol en béton foncé contre les cloisons sèches peintes. Le tas de bois récupéré sous-tend l'« arrière » des espaces de vie et dissimule un espace d'entraînement pour les cyclistes, tout en établissant une démarcation spatiale entre les espaces publics et privés. Des portes et des couloirs dissimulés permettent à la suite de s'adapter aux besoins de la famille en termes d'organisation de l'habitat, de sentiment d'ouverture et de voies de circulation multiples.

Die an den Stanley Park und die English Bay angrenzende Eigentumswohnung wurde so konzipiert, dass die nach Westen ausgerichteten „Korridore", die von den vorhandenen Betonsäulen eingerahmt werden, genutzt werden. Die Entfernung der Innenwände bringt mehr natürliches Licht in die Suite und schafft einen einfachen und komfortablen Wohnraum, in dem die Kunstsammlung des Kunden zur Geltung kommt. Das ruhige und doch reiche Interieur wurde durch das Nebeneinanderstellen von Kontrasten erreicht: die vertikalen Betonsäulen im Gegensatz zu den weißen Schränken mit glatter Oberfläche oder der dunkle Betonboden im Gegensatz zur gestrichenen Trockenbauwand. Der Holzstapel liegt unter der Rückseite der Wohnräume und verbirgt einen Trainingsraum für Radfahrer, während er gleichzeitig eine räumliche Abgrenzung zwischen öffentlichen und privaten Räumen schafft. Verdeckte Türen und Flure ermöglichen es, die Suite an die Bedürfnisse der Familie in Bezug auf unterschiedliche Wohnformen, ein Gefühl von Offenheit und mehrere Verkehrswege anzupassen.

Situado junto al parque Stanley y la bahía Inglesa, este condominio se diseñó para aprovechar los «pasillos» con vistas al oeste enmarcados por las columnas de hormigón existentes. La eliminación de las paredes interiores aporta más luz natural a la suite, creando un espacio de vida sencillo y confortable que muestra la colección de arte del cliente. El interior, tranquilo pero rico, se consiguió mediante la yuxtaposición de contrastes: las columnas verticales de hormigón frente a los armarios blancos de superficie lisa; o el suelo de hormigón oscuro frente a los paneles de yeso pintados. La pila de madera recuperada sirve de base a la «parte trasera» de los espacios habitables y oculta un espacio de entrenamiento para ciclistas, al tiempo que establece una delimitación espacial entre los espacios públicos y privados. Las puertas y pasillos ocultos permiten que la *suite* se adapte a las necesidades de la familia en cuanto a diferentes disposiciones de vivienda, sensación de apertura y múltiples rutas de circulación.

Floor plan

1. Entry
2. Storage
3. Kitchen
4. Dining area
5. Living area
6. Hall
7. Training room
8. Master bedroom
9. Bathroom
10. Bedroom
11. Deck
12. Master bathroom
13. Sitting room

PS REDUX

Belleview, Washington, United States // Lot area: 2.64 acres; building area: 3,200 sq ft

Jeff Babienko revisited and renovated a project with which he was intimately familiar, having been the project architect fifteen years earlier. The focus of the PS Redux was aimed at brightening the kitchen and refining the color palette of the main living and dining spaces. The evolved design refined and enhanced the original scheme while capturing the needs and lifestyle of the growing family. The exterior building envelope, constructed from a unique concrete block (ICF) made of wood chip fibers covered in a cementitious coating, is weather-resistant but vapor permeable. Jeff Babienko monitored the energy usage of the home and calculated an energy use intensity (EUI) in the mid-20s kbtu/sq ft. This achievement exceeded the guidelines of the AIA 2030 challenge for high-performance buildings for a single-family residence.

Jeff Babienko a revisité et rénové un projet avec lequel il était intimement familier, ayant été l'architecte du projet quinze ans plus tôt. L'objectif de PS Redux était d'éclaircir la cuisine et d'affiner la palette de couleurs des principaux espaces de vie et de repas. Babienko a conçu une nouvelle disposition des armoires de cuisine, agrandi l'îlot de cuisine, ajouté des étagères et amélioré l'éclairage. L'évolution de la conception a permis de raffiner et d'améliorer la disposition originale, tout en répondant aux besoins et au style de vie de la famille grandissante. Le revêtement extérieur du bâtiment, constitué d'un bloc de béton unique (ICF) fait de fibres de copeaux de bois recouvertes d'un revêtement en ciment, est résistant aux intempéries mais perméable à la vapeur. Jeff Babienko a contrôlé la consommation d'énergie de la maison et a calculé une intensité de consommation d'énergie (ICE) d'environ 20 kbtu/pied carré. Cette réalisation a dépassé les directives du défi 2030 de l'AIA concernant les bâtiments à haute performance pour une résidence unifamiliale.

Jeff Babienko hat ein Projekt, mit dem er bestens vertraut war, wieder aufgegriffen und renoviert, da er fünfzehn Jahre zuvor der Architekt des Projekts war. Das Ziel von PS Redux war es, die Küche aufzuhellen und die Farbpalette des Wohn- und Essbereichs zu verfeinern. Babienko entwickelte ein neues Layout für die Küchenschränke, vergrößerte die Kücheninsel, fügte Regale hinzu und verbesserte die Beleuchtung. Das weiterentwickelte Design verfeinerte und verbesserte den ursprünglichen Grundriss und trug gleichzeitig den Bedürfnissen und dem Lebensstil der wachsenden Familie Rechnung. Die Außenverkleidung des Gebäudes, die aus einem einzigartigen Betonblock (ICF) aus Holzspanfasern mit einer Zementbeschichtung besteht, ist witterungsbeständig, aber dampfdurchlässig. Jeff Babienko überwachte den Energieverbrauch des Hauses und berechnete eine Energienutzungsintensität (EUI) von etwa 20 kbtu/qm. Diese Leistung übertraf die AIA-Richtlinien 2030 für Hochleistungsgebäude für ein Einfamilienhaus.

Jeff Babienko revisó y renovó un proyecto con el que estaba íntimamente familiarizado, ya que había sido el arquitecto del proyecto quince años antes. El objetivo de PS Redux era iluminar la cocina y refinar la paleta de colores de los espacios principales del salón y el comedor. Babienko desarrolló una nueva disposición de los armarios de la cocina, amplió la isla de la cocina, añadió estanterías y mejoró la iluminación. El diseño evolucionado refinó y mejoró el esquema original, a la vez que captaba las necesidades y el estilo de vida de la creciente familia. El revestimiento exterior del edificio, construido con un bloque de hormigón único (ICF) fabricado con fibras de virutas de madera cubiertas con un revestimiento de cemento, es resistente a la intemperie pero permeable al vapor. Jeff Babienko supervisó el uso de energía de la casa y calculó una intensidad de uso de energía (EUI) de unos 20 kbtu/pie cuadrado. Este logro superó las directrices del reto AIA 2030 para edificios de alto rendimiento para una residencia unifamiliar.

This award-winning renovation of a 1952 mid-century modern home with views of the Puget Sound and the Olympic Mountains connects the kitchen and living room to the west elevation. The need to create workspaces for both owners while still reserving enough space for their three children to visit home simultaneously drove the design. During demolition, a steel I-beam was discovered, allowing for the removal of interior partitions without structural impact. The beam was left exposed as a new feature. A minimalist interior showcases First Nation artwork, while subtle interventions and a Zen materials palette combine with existing features such as the terrazzo floors and the fireplaces. The home's thermal envelope was improved with a new roof and the addition of shades across the entire west elevation, achieving energy efficiency.

Cette rénovation primée d'une maison moderne du milieu du XXᵉ siècle offrant une vue imprenable sur le Puget Sound et les Montagnes Olympiques relie la cuisine et le salon à l'élévation ouest. La nécessité de créer des espaces de travail pour les deux propriétaires tout en réservant suffisamment d'espace pour que leurs trois enfants puissent visiter la maison simultanément a motivé la conception. Lors de la démolition, on a découvert une poutre en acier en forme de I, une caractéristique inhabituelle dans une maison des années 1950, qui a permis d'enlever les cloisons intérieures sans affecter la structure. La poutre a été laissée exposée comme un nouvel élément. L'intérieur minimaliste présente des œuvres d'art des Premières nations, tandis que des interventions subtiles et une palette de matériaux zen se combinent avec des éléments existants tels que des sols en terrazzo et des cheminées. L'enveloppe thermique de la maison a été améliorée grâce à un nouveau toit et à l'ajout de persiennes sur toute la façade ouest, ce qui a permis d'atteindre l'efficacité énergétique souhaitée.

Diese preisgekrönte Renovierung eines modernen Hauses aus der Mitte des 20. Jahrhunderts mit weitem Blick nach Westen auf den Puget Sound und die Olympic Mountains verbindet die Küche und das Wohnzimmer mit der Westfassade. Die Notwendigkeit, Arbeitsbereiche für die beiden Hausbesitzer zu schaffen und gleichzeitig genug Platz für ihre drei Kinder zu haben, die das Haus besuchen können, war ausschlaggebend für den Entwurf. Beim Abriss wurde ein I-förmiger Stahlträger entdeckt, ein ungewöhnliches Merkmal in einem Haus aus den 1950er Jahren, das es ermöglichte, die Innentrennwände zu entfernen, ohne die Struktur zu beeinträchtigen. Der Balken wurde als neues Element belassen. In der minimalistischen Inneneinrichtung sind Kunstwerke der First Nation zu sehen, während subtile Eingriffe und eine elegante Materialpalette mit vorhandenen Elementen wie Terrazzoböden und Kaminen kombiniert werden. Die thermische Hülle des Hauses wurde durch ein neues Dach und die Anbringung von Jalousien an der gesamten Westfassade verbessert, wodurch die gewünschte Energieeffizienz erreicht wurde.

Esta galardonada renovación de una casa moderna de mediados del siglo XX con amplias vistas al oeste del estrecho de Puget y las Montañas Olímpicas conecta la cocina y el salón con el alzado oeste. La necesidad de crear espacios de trabajo para los dos propietarios y, al mismo tiempo, reservar suficiente espacio para que sus tres hijos pudieran visitar la casa simultáneamente, impulsó el diseño. Durante la demolición, se descubrió una viga de acero en forma de I, un elemento poco común en una casa de los años 50, que permitió eliminar los tabiques interiores sin que ello afectara a la estructura. La viga se dejó expuesta como un nuevo elemento. El interior minimalista presenta obras de arte de la Primera Nación, mientras que las sutiles intervenciones y la paleta de materiales zen se combinan con elementos existentes como los suelos de terrazo y las chimeneas. La envoltura térmica de la casa se mejoró con un nuevo tejado y la adición de persianas en todo el alzado oeste, logrando así la eficiencia energética deseada.

Section

Upper floor plan

Lower floor plan

1. Hallway
2. Bathroom
3. Laundry room
4. Bedroom
5. Rec room
6. Storage
7. Porch
8. Entry
9. Living area
10. Dining area
11. Kitchen
12. Master bathroom
13. Office
14. Master bedroom
15. Deck
16. Staircase

lumen
design

H HOUSE

Architecture Design Team: Petra Sattler-Smith
Landscape Designer: Intrinsic Landscapes
Structural Engineer: Arete
General Contractor: RP Construction
Photographer:
© Kevin G Smith Photography

Lumen design is a women-owned architectural practice based in Anchorage, Alaska. Projects range from commercial to multi-family and single-family residential, developing sustainable, responsible buildings for the north. The practice is committed to projects that connect the Alaskan environment to the people it supports. This results in architecture that has a strong presence and offers distinct spatial experiences,—in the spirit of Alaska—open and bold. Designs are based on a deep understanding of the socio-economic contexts of clients and rooted in a careful collaboration between them, consultants, and craftspeople. Petra Sattler-Smith holds a Master in Architecture from the Technical University in Darmstadt, Germany. Her work combines functionality with innovative contemporary design through the exploration and use of natural materials in response to the unique and extreme climatic conditions of the last frontier.

Lumen Design ist ein von Frauen geführtes Architekturbüro mit Sitz in Anchorage, Alaska. Die Projekte reichen von kommerziellen bis hin zu Wohngebäuden, sowohl für Mehr- als auch für Einfamilienhäuser, wobei nachhaltige und verantwortungsvolle Gebäude entwickelt werden. Das Studio engagiert sich für Projekte, die die Umwelt Alaskas mit den Menschen, die dort leben, verbinden. Das Ergebnis ist eine Architektur, die eine starke Präsenz hat und klare, offene und kühne Raumerfahrungen im Geiste Alaskas bietet. Die Entwürfe beruhen auf einem tiefen Verständnis des sozioökonomischen Kontextes der Kunden und einer sorgfältigen Zusammenarbeit zwischen ihnen, den Beratern und den Handwerkern. Petra Sattler-Smith hat einen Abschluss in Architektur von der Technischen Universität Darmstadt (Deutschland). Ihre Arbeit verbindet Funktionalität mit innovativem zeitgenössischem Design durch die Erforschung und Verwendung natürlicher Materialien als Antwort auf die einzigartigen und extremen klimatischen Bedingungen Alaskas.

Lumen Design est un cabinet d'architecture appartenant à des femmes et situé à Anchorage, en Alaska. Les projets vont des espaces commerciaux aux espaces résidentiels, tant multi familiaux qu'individuels, en développant des bâtiments durables et responsables. Le studio s'engage à réaliser des projets qui relient l'environnement de l'Alaska aux personnes qui y vivent. Le résultat est une architecture qui a une forte présence et offre des expériences spatiales distinctes, ouvertes et audacieuses dans l'esprit de l'Alaska. Les conceptions sont fondées sur une compréhension approfondie des contextes socio-économiques des clients et sur une collaboration étroite entre ces derniers, les consultants et les artisans. Petra Sattler-Smith est diplômée en architecture de l'Université technique de Darmstadt (Allemagne). Son travail associe la fonctionnalité à un design contemporain innovant par l'exploration et l'utilisation de matériaux naturels en réponse aux conditions climatiques uniques et extrêmes de la dernière frontière.

Lumen Design es un estudio de arquitectura propiedad de mujeres con sede en Anchorage (Alaska). Los proyectos van desde los espacios comerciales hasta los residenciales, tanto multi familiares como uni familiares, desarrollando edificios sostenibles y responsables. El estudio está comprometido con proyectos que conectan el medio ambiente de Alaska con las personas que lo habitan. El resultado es una arquitectura que tiene una fuerte presencia y ofrece experiencias espaciales distintas, abiertas y audaces, siguiendo el espíritu de Alaska. Los diseños se basan en un profundo conocimiento de los contextos socioeconómicos de los clientes y en una cuidadosa colaboración entre ellos, los consultores y los artesanos. Petra Sattler-Smith es licenciada en Arquitectura por la Universidad Técnica de Darmstadt (Alemania). Su trabajo combina la funcionalidad con un diseño contemporáneo innovador mediante la exploración y el uso de materiales naturales en respuesta a las condiciones climáticas únicas y extremas de la última frontera.

H HOUSE

Anchorage, Alaska, United States // Lot area: 31,156 sq ft; building area: 6,118 sq ft

This entry addition and master suite remodel originated with the clients' desire to incorporate three Buddha statues into their 1980's modernist home. The design quietly resolves challenges of the original home while emphasizing old and new axes with light and art. New geometry takes cues from the original form but is softened by vegetation, artwork, and playful lighting. The abrupt original entry is slowed to a procession, descending to a sunken court, traversing a pond on floating granite blocks, and turning to face a Buddha before finding the entry door. Inside, the dappled light, the sound of the pond, and the second statue enshrined in the warm wood set a meditative tone. Teak slats around the entry appear opaque outside, but from the lower light within, the transparency between slats is more obvious. This screened enclosure provides privacy while allowing views out and sun in.

Cette annexe d'entrée et la rénovation de la suite principale sont nées du désir des clients d'intégrer trois statues de Bouddha dans leur maison moderniste des années 1980. La conception résout tranquillement les défis de la maison d'origine, tout en soulignant les axes anciens et nouveaux avec la lumière et l'art. La nouvelle géométrie s'inspire de la forme originale, mais adoucie par de la verdure, les œuvres d'art et un éclairage ludique. L'entrée abrupte d'origine se transforme en une procession, descendant vers une cour creusée, traversant un étang sur des blocs de granit flottants et se tournant pour faire face à un Bouddha avant de rencontrer le portail d'entrée. À l'intérieur, la lumière diffuse, le bruit de l'étang et la deuxième statue enchâssée dans le bois chaleureux créent un ton méditatif. Les lattes de teck qui entourent l'entrée semblent opaques de l'extérieur, mais la lumière plus faible de l'intérieur fait ressortir la transparence entre les lattes. Cette enceinte grillagée offre une certaine intimité tout en permettant aux regards de sortir et aux rayons du soleil d'entrer.

Die Neugestaltung des Eingangsbereichs und des Hauptschlafzimmers geht auf den Wunsch der Kunden zurück, drei Buddha-Statuen in ihr modernistisches Haus aus den 1980er Jahren einzubauen. Das Design löst leise die Herausforderungen des ursprünglichen Zuhauses und betont gleichzeitig alte und neue Achsen mit Licht und Kunst. Die neue Geometrie ist von der ursprünglichen Form inspiriert, wird aber durch Begrünung, Kunstwerke und spielerische Beleuchtung aufgelockert. Der ursprüngliche abrupte Eingang wird zu einer Prozession, die in einen versunkenen Innenhof hinabsteigt, einen Teich auf schwimmenden Granitblöcken überquert und sich vor dem Eingangstor einem Buddha zuwendet. Im Inneren schaffen das diffuse Licht, das Rauschen des Teiches und die zweite Statue, die in das warme Holz eingelassen ist, eine meditative Stimmung. Die Teakholzlamellen, die den Eingang umgeben, scheinen von außen undurchsichtig zu sein, aber bei geringerem Licht im Inneren ist die Transparenz zwischen den Lamellen deutlicher zu erkennen. Diese Netzüberdachung bietet Privatsphäre und lässt gleichzeitig den Blick nach draußen und die Sonne hinein.

Este anexo a la entrada y remodelación de la suite principal se originó con el deseo de los clientes de incorporar tres estatuas de Buda en su casa modernista de los años 80. El diseño resuelve discretamente los desafíos de la casa original a la vez que enfatiza los ejes antiguos y nuevos con luz y arte. La nueva geometría se inspira en la forma original, pero se suaviza con vegetación, obras de arte y una iluminación acogedora. La entrada abrupta se convierte en una procesión. Se desciende a un patio hundido para atravesar un estanque sobre bloques de granito y luego girar hacia un Buda antes de encontrar la puerta de entrada. En el interior, la luz difuminada, el sonido del estanque y la segunda estatua realzada por cálida madera crean un tono meditativo. Los listones de teca que rodean la entrada crean opacidad desde el exterior, pero con la luz del interior, la transparencia entre los listones es más evidente. Este recinto protegido proporciona privacidad a la vez que deja entrar luz y se abre a las vistas.

Floor plan

View of the existing house

1. Garage (existing)
2. Guest parking
3. Kitchen (existing)
4. Dining area (existing)
5. Living area
6. Water closet
7. Entry
8. Family room (existing)
9. Walk-in closet
10. Master bedroom
11. Vanity
12. Bathroom
13. Alcove with Buddha (existing)
14. Wine cellar
15. Tree (existing)
16. Art Wall
17. Exercise room

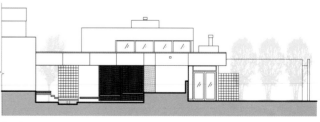

Section

CASCADIA
ARCHITECTS

1001 BLANSHARD

Architecture Design Team:
Cascadia Architects
Developer:
Fort Properties Ltd
Landscape Architect:
LADR Landscape Architects
Structural Engineer:
RJC Engineers
Civil Engineer:
J.E. Anderson & Associates
Electrical Engineer:
AES Engineering
Mechanical Engineer:
Avalon Mechanical
General Contractor:
Gorter Construction Ltd
Photographer:
© Sama Jim Canzian

CA. 10

Architecture Design Team and
Passive House Consultant:
Cascadia Architects
Structural Engineer:
Hoel Engineering Group
General Contractor:
NZ Builders Ltd
Photographer:
© Sama Jim Canzian

TALL TREE MATTICK'S FARM

Architecture Design Team:
Cascadia Architects
Landscape Architect:
Murdoch DeGreeff Inc
Arborist:
Talbot Mackenzie & Associates
Structural and Civil Engineer:
Herold Engineering Ltd
Electrical Engineer:
AES Engineering
Mechanical Engineer:
WSP
General Contractor:
Pentech
Photographer:
© Sama Jim Canzian

Based in Victoria, Canada, Cascadia was founded in 2012 by Principals Peter Johannknecht and Gregory Damant, who lead a team of skilled architects, technologists, and designers in creating a range of award-winning projects, including large-scale residential and commercial developments, private custom homes, interior design, educational, healthcare, and cultural spaces. Building performance is an integral element of the studio's design criteria, and creating projects that use sustainable design and construction methods is paramount in their process. The team uses PassiveHouse and LEED methodologies and collaborates across professions to create solutions that are right for each project within its context and location. Working within the Pacific Northwest, the studio is inspired by the environment and culture of this unique location, using innovative construction methods, natural materials, and contemporary design to create functional, sustainable spaces that elevate daily life, connect to the natural world, and raise the spirit.

Das in Victoria, Kanada, ansässige Unternehmen Cascadia wurde 2012 von den Geschäftsführern Peter Johannknecht und Gregory Damant gegründet. Sie leiten ein Team aus erfahrenen Architekten, Technologen und Designern, das eine Reihe preisgekrönter Projekte realisiert hat, darunter große Wohn- und Gewerbeprojekte, maßgeschneiderte Privathäuser, Innenarchitektur, Bildungs-, Gesundheits- und Kulturräume. Die Leistungsfähigkeit von Gebäuden ist ein integraler Bestandteil der Designkriterien des Studios, und die Schaffung von Projekten, die nachhaltige Design- und Konstruktionsmethoden nutzen, ist von größter Bedeutung für ihren Prozess. Das Team wendet PassiveHouse- und LEED-Methoden an und arbeitet mit allen Berufsgruppen zusammen, um für jedes Projekt im jeweiligen Kontext und am jeweiligen Standort geeignete Lösungen zu entwickeln. Bei seiner Arbeit im pazifischen Nordwesten lässt sich das Studio von der Umwelt und der Kultur dieses einzigartigen Ortes inspirieren und nutzt innovative Konstruktionsmethoden, natürliche Materialien und zeitgenössisches Design, um funktionale und nachhaltige Räume zu schaffen, die das tägliche Leben bereichern, eine Verbindung zur natürlichen Welt herstellen und den Geist erheben.

Basée à Victoria, au Canada, Cascadia a été fondée en 2012 par les directeurs Peter Johannknecht et Gregory Damant, qui dirigent une équipe d'architectes, de technologues et de designers qualifiés dans la création d'une gamme de projets primés, notamment des développements résidentiels et commerciaux à grande échelle, des maisons privées, des aménagements intérieurs, des espaces éducatifs, sanitaires et culturels. La performance des bâtiments fait partie intégrante des critères de conception du studio, et la création de projets faisant appel à des méthodes de conception et de construction durables est au cœur de son processus. L'équipe utilise les méthodologies PassiveHouse et LEED, et collabore avec toutes les professions pour créer des solutions appropriées pour chaque projet dans son contexte et son emplacement. Travaillant dans le nord-ouest du Pacifique, le studio s'inspire de l'environnement et de la culture de ce lieu unique, utilisant des méthodes de construction innovantes, des matériaux naturels et un design contemporain pour créer des espaces fonctionnels et durables qui élèvent la vie quotidienne, se connectent au monde naturel et élèvent l'esprit.

Con sede en Victoria, Canadá, Cascadia fue fundada en 2012 por los directores Peter Johannknecht y Gregory Damant, que dirigen un equipo de arquitectos, tecnólogos y diseñadores cualificados en la creación de una serie de proyectos galardonados, entre los que se incluyen desarrollos residenciales y comerciales a gran escala, casas privadas a medida, diseño de interiores, espacios educativos, sanitarios y culturales. El rendimiento de los edificios es un elemento integral de los criterios de diseño del estudio, y la creación de proyectos que utilizan métodos de diseño y construcción sostenibles es primordial en su proceso. El equipo utiliza las metodologías PassiveHouse y LEED, y colabora con todas las profesiones para crear soluciones adecuadas para cada proyecto dentro de su contexto y ubicación. Trabajando en el noroeste del Pacífico, el estudio se inspira en el entorno y la cultura de este lugar único, utilizando métodos de construcción innovadores, materiales naturales y diseño contemporáneo para crear espacios funcionales y sostenibles que eleven la vida cotidiana, conecten con el mundo natural y eleven el espíritu.

1001 BLANSHARD

Victoria, British Columbia, Canada // Lot area: 12,443 sq ft; building area: 8,234 sq ft

In 2012 Cascadia Architects began working with Fort Properties to develop a comprehensive plan for its properties at the corner of Blanshard and Fort Street. This improvement plan is based on Fort Property's Triple Bottom Line approach, encompassing people, planet, and prosperity. The plan's primary objective is to create a pedestrian-friendly environment that fosters a healthy commercial setting and contributes to the diversity of the urban fabric of Victoria's downtown community. The existing structure underwent an extensive renovation, including seismic upgrades, rain gardens to manage stormwater, and innovative energy efficiency measures. The result is a building that has been transformed into a focal point in the city, creating spaces for local businesses and anchoring the Fort-Blanshard retail and restaurant district as an important element in the fabric of the City of Victoria.

En 2012, Cascadia Architects a commencé à travailler avec Fort Properties pour développer un plan global pour leurs propriétés à l'angle de Blanshard et Fort Street. Ce plan d'amélioration est basé sur l'approche du triple bilan de Fort Properties, qui englobe les personnes, la planète et la prospérité. L'objectif principal du plan est de créer un environnement convivial pour les piétons qui favorise un environnement commercial sain et contribue au tissu urbain diversifié du centre-ville de Victoria. La structure existante a fait l'objet d'importantes rénovations, notamment des mises à niveau sismiques, des jardins de pluie pour gérer les eaux pluviales et des mesures innovantes en matière d'efficacité énergétique. Le résultat est un bâtiment qui a été transformé en un point focal pour la ville, créant des espaces pour les entreprises locales et ancrant le quartier commercial et gastronomique du Fort-Blanshard comme un élément important du tissu de la ville de Victoria.

2012 begann Cascadia Architects die Zusammenarbeit mit Fort Properties, um einen umfassenden Plan für deren Grundstücke an der Ecke Blanshard und Fort Street zu entwickeln. Dieser Verbesserungsplan basiert auf dem Triple-Bottom-Line-Ansatz von Fort Properties, der die Menschen, den Planeten und den Wohlstand mit einbezieht. Das Hauptziel des Plans ist die Schaffung eines fußgängerfreundlichen Umfelds, das ein gesundes kommerzielles Umfeld fördert und zum vielfältigen städtischen Gefüge in der Innenstadt von Victoria beiträgt. Das bestehende Gebäude wurde umfassend renoviert, einschließlich seismischer Verbesserungen, Regengärten zur Regenwasserbewirtschaftung und innovativer Energieeffizienzmaßnahmen. Das Ergebnis ist ein Gebäude, das zu einem zentralen Punkt der Stadt geworden ist, der Platz für lokale Unternehmen bietet und das Einkaufs- und Gastronomieviertel Fort-Blanshard als wichtiges Element im Stadtgefüge von Victoria verankert.

En 2012 Cascadia Architects comenzó a trabajar con Fort Properties para desarrollar un plan integral para sus propiedades en la esquina de Blanshard y Fort Street. Este plan de mejora se basa en el enfoque del triple equilibrio de Fort Properties, que abarca a las personas, el planeta y la prosperidad. El objetivo principal del plan es crear un entorno agradable para los peatones que fomente un entorno comercial saludable y contribuya a la diversidad del tejido urbano del centro de Victoria. La estructura existente fue objeto de una amplia renovación, que incluyó mejoras sísmicas, jardines de lluvia para gestionar las aguas pluviales e innovadoras medidas de eficiencia energética. El resultado es un edificio que se ha transformado en un punto focal de la ciudad, creando espacios para los negocios locales y anclando el distrito de tiendas y restaurantes de Fort-Blanshard como un elemento importante en el tejido de la ciudad de Victoria.

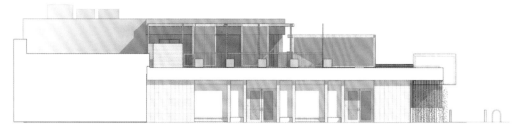

West elevation

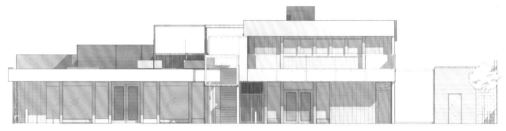

South elevation

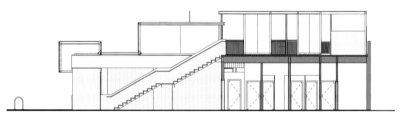

Section through staircase

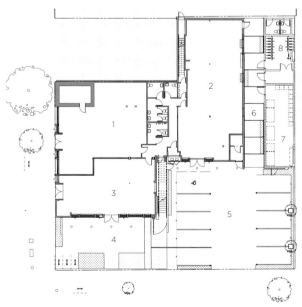

Ground floor plan

Second floor plan

1. Commercial unit (butcher)
2. Commercial unit (office)
3. Commercial unit (cafe)
4. Patio (cafe)
5. Parking

6. Pedestrian alleyway
7. Garbage/recycling
8. Bike parking
9. Outdoor seating area
10. Entryway

11. Outdoor kitchen
12. Restaurant seating area
13. Bar
14. Kitchen

This modern and elemental single-family home was the first home in the Oak Bay neighborhood designed to meet the International Passive House standard, ensuring that the energy demand is reduced by up to 90% compared to a standard house. It stands out amongst the many cottage-style homes along the street and is grounded by the surrounding mature Garry oaks and landscaping native to the Pacific Northwest. The interiors feature triple-paned Austrian windows, allowing generous natural lighting while retaining the tight insulation that is so important to Passive House Buildings. Bright whites, smooth surfaces, and touches of natural walnut contribute to the calming, clean feel.

Cette maison unifamiliale moderne et élémentaire a été la première maison du quartier d'Oak Bay conçue pour répondre à la norme internationale de « maison passive », qui garantit une réduction de la demande d'énergie allant jusqu'à 90 % par rapport à une maison standard. Il se distingue des nombreuses maisons de style cottage de la rue et est soutenu par les chênes Garry matures environnants et le paysage indigène du nord-ouest du Pacifique. Les intérieurs sont dotés de fenêtres autrichiennes à triple vitrage, qui laissent passer une lumière naturelle généreuse tout en conservant l'isolation étanche à l'air si importante pour les bâtiments de type maison passive. Les blancs éclatants, les surfaces lisses et les touches de noyer naturel contribuent à l'impression de calme et de propreté.

Dieses moderne, elementare Einfamilienhaus war das erste Haus in der Nachbarschaft von Oak Bay, das nach dem internationalen „Passivhaus"-Standard entworfen wurde, der eine Reduzierung des Energiebedarfs um bis zu 90 % im Vergleich zu einem Standardhaus garantiert. Es hebt sich von den vielen Häusern im Landhausstil in der Straße ab und wird von den umliegenden alten Garry-Eichen und der ursprünglichen Landschaft des Pazifischen Nordwestens unterstützt. Die Innenräume verfügen über dreifach verglaste österreichische Fenster, die viel natürliches Licht hereinlassen und gleichzeitig die für Passivhäuser so wichtige luftdichte Isolierung gewährleisten. Helles Weiß, glatte Oberflächen und ein Hauch von natürlichem Nussbaum tragen zu einem Gefühl der Ruhe und Sauberkeit bei.

Esta moderna y elemental vivienda unifamiliar fue la primera casa del barrio de Oak Bay diseñada para cumplir el estándar internacional de «casa pasiva», lo que garantiza una reducción de la demanda energética de hasta el 90% en comparación con una casa estándar. Destaca entre las numerosas casas de estilo cottage que hay en la calle y se apoya en los robles Garry maduros que la rodean y en el paisaje autóctono del noroeste del Pacífico. Los interiores cuentan con ventanas austriacas de triple cristal, que permiten una generosa iluminación natural al tiempo que conservan el aislamiento hermético que es tan importante para los edificios de casas pasivas. Los blancos brillantes, las superficies lisas y los toques de nogal natural contribuyen a la sensación de calma y limpieza.

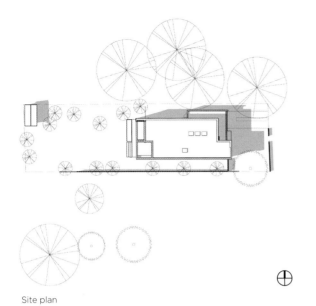

Site plan

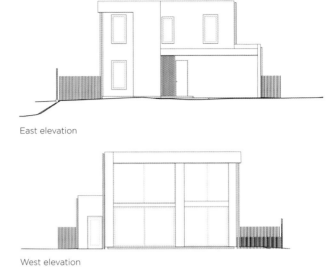

East elevation

West elevation

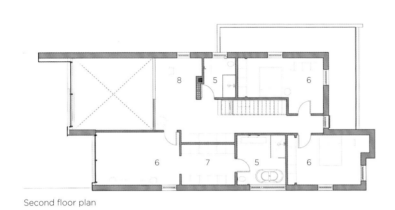

Second floor plan

Main floor plan

1. Living room
2. Dining room
3. Kitchen
4. Laundry room
5. Bathroom
6. Bedroom
7. Closet
8. Mezzanine
9. Garage
10. Hallway
11. Deck

TALL TREE MATTICK'S FARM

Saanich Peninsula, British Columbia, Canada // Lot area: 4.9 acres; building area: 4,962 sq ft

The team at Tall Trees Integrated Health Centre needed a building that would support the holistic health of their patients and foster learning, innovation, and expertise in healthcare. The brief was clear; to create a space for healing within the unique forested site. This project celebrates simplicity in form and structure, focusing on forming a relationship between the architecture and the natural world to support therapeutic treatment. Bringing the environment into the space, both visually and physically, was a clear direction at the outset of the design process. The building's form and materiality respond to the environment and root the project into its location, while full-height glazing wraps around the curved interior spaces, creating organic forms that immerse the occupants into the forest.

L'équipe du Tall Trees Integrated Health Centre avait besoin d'un bâtiment qui soutienne la santé holistique de ses patients et encourage l'apprentissage, l'innovation et l'expertise en matière de soins de santé. Le cahier des charges était clair : créer un espace de guérison dans un cadre boisé unique. Ce projet célèbre la simplicité de la forme et de la structure, en se concentrant sur la création d'une relation entre l'architecture et le monde naturel pour soutenir le traitement thérapeutique. L'intégration de l'environnement dans l'espace, tant sur le plan visuel que physique, était une orientation claire dès le début du processus de conception. La forme et la matérialité du bâtiment répondent à l'environnement et enracinent le projet dans son emplacement, tandis que des vitrages pleine hauteur enveloppent les espaces intérieurs courbes, créant des formes organiques qui immergent les occupants dans la forêt.

Das Team des Tall Trees Integrated Health Centre benötigte ein Gebäude, das die ganzheitliche Gesundheit seiner Patienten unterstützt und Lernen, Innovation und Fachwissen im Gesundheitswesen fördert. Der Auftrag war klar: einen Raum für Heilung in einer einzigartigen Waldumgebung zu schaffen. Dieses Projekt zelebriert die Einfachheit von Form und Struktur und konzentriert sich darauf, eine Beziehung zwischen der Architektur und der natürlichen Welt herzustellen, um die therapeutische Behandlung zu unterstützen. Die Einbeziehung der Umwelt in den Raum, sowohl visuell als auch physisch, war von Beginn des Designprozesses an eine klare Vorgabe. Form und Materialität des Gebäudes reagieren auf die Umgebung und verankern das Projekt an seinem Standort, während die Verglasung in voller Höhe die gekrümmten Innenräume umhüllt und organische Formen schafft, die die Bewohner in den Wald eintauchen lassen.

El equipo del Centro de Salud Integrado Tall Trees necesitaba un edificio que apoyara la salud integral de sus pacientes y fomentara el aprendizaje, la innovación y la experiencia en la atención sanitaria. Las instrucciones eran claras: crear un espacio para la curación en un lugar boscoso único. Este proyecto celebra la simplicidad en la forma y la estructura, centrándose en la formación de una relación entre la arquitectura y el mundo natural para apoyar el tratamiento terapéutico. Incorporar el entorno al espacio, tanto visual como físicamente, fue una orientación clara desde el principio del proceso de diseño. La forma y la materialidad del edificio responden al entorno y arraigan el proyecto en su ubicación, mientras que el acristalamiento a toda altura envuelve los espacios interiores curvos, creando formas orgánicas que sumergen a los ocupantes en el bosque.

1. CLT roof structure
2. Concealed drainage system
3. Aluminum-clad wood window
4. TJI wood joist above crawl space
5. Rain garden
6. Exposed aggreagate concrete patio
7. Rock cladding (granite from site)

Sectional diagram

North elevation

East elevation

South elevation

West elevation

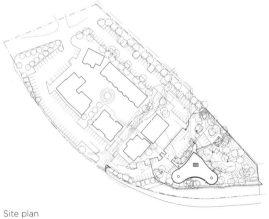

Site plan

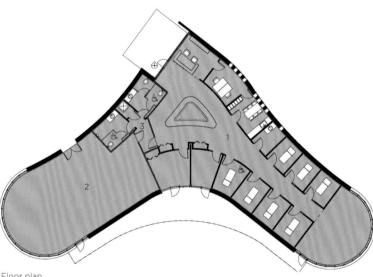

Floor plan

1. Suite A
2. Suite B
3. Common area

Lanefab
Design/Build

Design and Construction:
Lanefab Design/Build
Structural Engineer:
Deerlake Design
Window and Door Fabrication:
Builders Door & Window
Prefab. Structural Insulated Panels (SIPs):
Insulspan
Photographer:
© Latreille Architectural Photography

Design and Construction:
Lanefab Design/Build
Structural Engineer:
Deerlake Design
Window and Door Fabrication:
Cascadia Windows & Doors
Prefab. Structural Insulated Panels (SIPs):
Insulspan
Photographer:
© Colin Perry

Design and Construction:
Lanefab Design/Build
Structural Engineer:
Deerlake Design
Window and Door Fabrication:
Vetta Building Technologies Inc
Prefab. Structural Insulated Panels (SIPs):
Insulspan
Heat Pump Hot Water:
Sanden
Heat Recovery Ventilator:
Zehnder Group
Photographer:
© Brett Ryan Studios

Lanefab's integrated design/build team crafts custom high-performance homes in the Vancouver region, British Columbia, Canada, and beyond. The firm's approach blends the design ethos of Mid Century, Scandinavian and Japanese modernism with the environmental ethos of walkable urban infill and Passivhaus construction. Designer Bryn Davidson and builder Mat Turner founded the company in 2009 in response to the City of Vancouver's push to allow "laneway houses" (backyard accessory dwellings) throughout the city. In the ensuing years, the firm has completed over 100 lane houses and a range of full-size custom homes, duplexes, character homes, and certified Passive Houses. The team's work has garnered a range of accolades, including the Arthur Erickson Memorial Award for an emerging practice and the Scotiabank EcoLiving Prize, along with features in Dwell and various books about prefab and small homes.

Das integrierte Design-/Bauteam von Lanefab entwirft in der Region Vancouver in British Columbia, Kanada, und an vielen anderen Orten leistungsstarke Häuser nach Maß. Der Ansatz des Unternehmens verbindet das Designethos der Mitte des Jahrhunderts, der skandinavischen und japanischen Moderne mit dem Umweltethos der begehbaren Stadtfüllung und des Passivhausbaus. Der Designer Bryn Davidson und der Bauunternehmer Mat Turner gründeten das Unternehmen 2009 als Reaktion auf den Vorstoß der Stadt Vancouver, in der ganzen Stadt „laneway houses" (Hinterhofwohnungen) zuzulassen. In den vergangenen Jahren hat das Unternehmen mehr als 100 Häuser dieser Art und eine Reihe von Massivhäusern, Doppelhäusern, Häusern mit Charakter und zertifizierten Passivhäusern fertiggestellt. Die Arbeit des Teams wurde mehrfach ausgezeichnet, unter anderem mit dem Arthur Erickson Memorial Award for an emerging practice und dem Scotiabank EcoLiving Prize, sowie mit Artikeln in Dwell und mehreren Büchern über Fertighäuser und Tiny Houses.

L'équipe intégrée de conception/construction de Lanefab conçoit des maisons personnalisées à haute performance dans la région de Vancouver, en Colombie-Britannique (Canada), et ailleurs. L'approche de l'entreprise combine l'éthique du design du milieu du siècle, du modernisme scandinave et japonais avec l'éthique environnementale de l'aménagement urbain piétonnier et de la construction Passivhaus. Le designer Bryn Davidson et le constructeur Mat Turner ont fondé l'entreprise en 2009 en réponse à l'initiative de la ville de Vancouver d'autoriser les « laneway houses » (logements accessoires dans les cours) dans toute la ville. Au cours des années qui ont suivi, la société a réalisé plus de 100 maisons de ce type et un certain nombre de maisons sur mesure de taille normale, de duplex, de maisons de caractère et de maisons passives certifiées. Le travail de l'équipe a été récompensé par plusieurs prix, dont le Arthur Erickson Memorial Award pour une pratique émergente et le Scotiabank EcoLiving Prize, ainsi que par des articles dans Dwell et plusieurs livres sur les maisons préfabriquées et minuscules.

El equipo de diseño/construcción de Lanefab diseña casas personalizadas de alto rendimiento en la región de Vancouver, Columbia Británica, Canadá, y más allá. El enfoque de diseño/construcción de la empresa combina el espíritu de diseño del modernismo de mediados de siglo, escandinavo y japonés con el espíritu medioambiental del relleno urbano transitable y la construcción Passivhaus. El diseñador Bryn Davidson y el constructor Mat Turner fundaron la empresa en 2009 en respuesta al impulso de la ciudad de Vancouver para permitir las «laneway houses» (viviendas accesorias en el patio trasero) en toda la ciudad. En los años siguientes, la empresa ha completado más de 100 casas de esta tipología y una serie de casas personalizadas de tamaño completo, dúplex, casas de carácter y casas pasivas certificadas. El trabajo del equipo ha recibido diversos reconocimientos, como el premio Arthur Erickson Memorial Award para una práctica emergente y el Scotiabank EcoLiving Prize, además de artículos en Dwell y varios libros sobre casas prefabricadas y pequeñas.

MITCHELL HOUSE RENOVATION/ADDITION

Vancouver, British Columbia, Canada // Lot area: 7,340 sq ft; existing house: 1,500 sq ft; new addition: 1,040 sq ft; new garage: 300 sq ft

This project consists of the renovation of and addition to the Mitchell House, a 1965 mid-century modern house by Canadian architect Arthur Erickson. The house stands out for its peculiar "wedge" shape—half an A-frame—which the owners wanted to preserve rather than tear it down to build a larger new house. The primary intent was to create a new dining area and kitchen, but mainly to give the home a proper entry sequence that preserved views of the iconic timber frame structure. The entrance walkway was done as an elevated boardwalk reminiscent of the forest trails that meander through the local North Vancouver forests. The project received a heritage award from the district of North Vancouver and is emblematic of the need to consider mid-century architecture as part of our built heritage.

Ce projet consiste en la rénovation et l'extension de la Mitchell House, une maison moderne construite en 1965 par l'architecte canadien Arthur Erickson. La maison se distingue par sa forme en « coin » en forme de A, que les propriétaires ont voulu conserver plutôt que de la démolir pour construire une nouvelle maison plus grande. L'intention était de créer une nouvelle salle à manger et une cuisine, mais surtout de donner à la maison une séquence d'entrée appropriée qui préserverait les vues sur la structure en bois emblématique. La route d'accès, sous la forme d'une passerelle surélevée, rappelle les sentiers forestiers qui serpentent dans les forêts locales de North Vancouver. Le projet a reçu un North Vancouver District Heritage Award et est emblématique de la nécessité de considérer l'architecture du milieu du siècle comme faisant partie du patrimoine bâti.

Bei diesem Projekt handelt es sich um die Renovierung und Erweiterung des Mitchell House, eines modernen Hauses des kanadischen Architekten Arthur Erickson aus dem Jahr 1965. Das Haus zeichnet sich durch seine charakteristische „Keilform" aus, einen halben A-Rahmen, den die Eigentümer lieber beibehalten wollten, als ihn abzureißen und ein neues, größeres Haus zu bauen. Ziel war es, einen neuen Ess- und Küchenbereich zu schaffen, aber vor allem, dem Haus eine angemessene Eingangssequenz zu geben, die den Blick auf die ikonische Holzstruktur bewahrt. Die Zufahrtsstraße in Form eines erhöhten Gehwegs erinnert an die Waldwege, die sich durch die Wälder von North Vancouver schlängeln. Das Projekt wurde mit dem North Vancouver District Heritage Award ausgezeichnet und steht sinnbildlich für die Notwendigkeit, die Architektur der Jahrhundertmitte als Teil des baulichen Erbes zu betrachten.

Este proyecto consiste en la renovación y ampliación de la Mitchell House, una casa moderna de de 1965, obra del arquitecto canadiense Arthur Erickson. La casa destaca por su peculiar forma de «cuña», de medio armazón en forma de A, que los propietarios querían conservar en lugar de derribarla para construir una nueva casa más grande. La intención era crear una nueva zona de comedor y cocina, pero sobre todo dar a la casa una secuencia de entrada adecuada que preservara las vistas de la icónica estructura de madera. El camino de acceso, a modo de paseo elevado, recuerda a los senderos forestales que serpentean por los bosques locales de North Vancouver. El proyecto recibió un premio al patrimonio del distrito de North Vancouver y es emblema de la necesidad de considerar la arquitectura de mediados de siglo como parte del patrimonio construido.

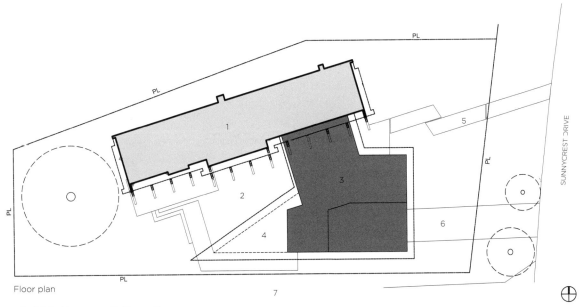

Floor plan

1. Original house
2. Patio
3. New addition
4. New veranda
5. New path
6. New driveway
   and parking pad
7. Path

POON-LI HOUSE

Vancouver, British Columbia, Canada // Lot area: 4,026 sq ft; building area: 2,800 sq ft

The two-story home with a secondary suite in the basement. The upper floor primary bedroom and living room are both oriented with views to the northwest, overlooking Douglas Park and Vancouver's North Shore mountains. Its exterior is clad in board-formed concrete, flat-panel steel cladding, and vertical cedar. The interiors feature "Bole Floor" hardwood on the main floor, a unique hardwood product where every plank is custom cut to follow the grain of the wood. The hardwood is set into a surrounding concrete floor. The house was designed around feng shui principles. Its primary bedroom balcony includes a river rock floor feature used to massage feet. The curved concrete lower floor and curved wood exterior walls on the upper floor are juxtaposed against the boxy form of the main living space.

Maison à deux étages avec une suite secondaire au sous-sol. La chambre principale et le salon de l'étage sont orientés avec des vues vers le nord-ouest, le parc Douglas et les montagnes de la côte nord de Vancouver. Les intérieurs sont revêtus de bois dur « Bole Floor » au rez-de-chaussée, un produit en bois unique dans lequel chaque planche est coupée sur mesure pour maintenir le grain. Le bois est intégré dans un sol en béton qui l'entoure. La maison a été conçue selon les principes du feng shui. Le balcon de la chambre principale comprend un sol en pierre de rivière pour masser les pieds. Le sol en béton incurvé en bas et les murs extérieurs en bois incurvés de l'étage supérieur sont juxtaposés à la forme carrée de la salle de séjour principale.

Zweistöckiges Haus mit einer zweiten Suite im Untergeschoss. Das Hauptschlafzimmer und das Wohnzimmer im Obergeschoss sind nach Nordwesten ausgerichtet und bieten einen Blick auf den Douglas Park und die Berge von Vancouvers North Shore. Die Innenräume sind im Hauptgeschoss mit „Bole Floor"-Hartholz verkleidet, einem einzigartigen Holzprodukt, bei dem jede Diele individuell zugeschnitten wird, um die Maserung fortzusetzen. Das Holz ist in einen umlaufenden Betonboden integriert. Das Haus wurde nach Feng-Shui-Prinzipien entworfen. Der Balkon des Hauptschlafzimmers ist mit einem Flusssteinboden ausgestattet, der die Füße massiert. Der geschwungene Betonboden im Untergeschoss und die geschwungenen hölzernen Außenwände des Obergeschosses stehen im Gegensatz zu der quadratischen Form des Hauptwohnzimmers.

Casa de dos pisos con una *suite* secundaria en el sótano. El dormitorio principal de la planta superior y el salón están orientados con vistas al noroeste, al parque Douglas y a las montañas de la costa norte de Vancouver. Los interiores están revestidos de madera dura «Bole Floor» en la planta principal, un producto único de madera en el que cada tabla se corta a medida para continuar la veta. La madera se integra en un suelo de hormigón circundante. La casa se diseñó según los principios del feng shui. El balcón del dormitorio principal incluye un suelo de roca de río que sirve para masajear los pies. El suelo inferior de hormigón curvado y las paredes exteriores de madera curvada de la planta superior se yuxtaponen a la forma cuadrada del salón principal.

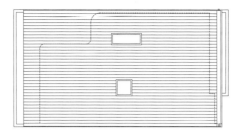

Roof plan

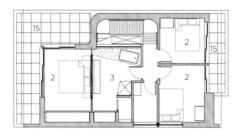

Upper floor plan

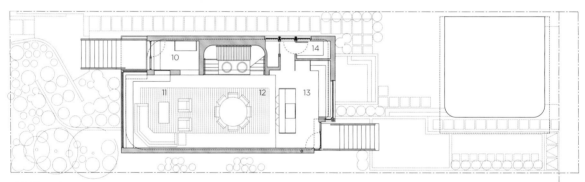

Main floor plan

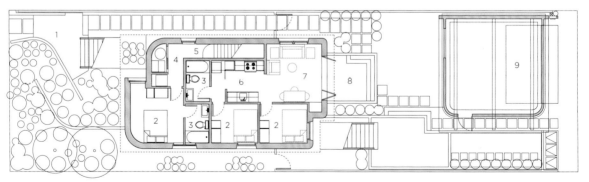

Basement floor plan

1. Front yad
2. Bedroom
3. Bathroom
4. Laundry closet
5. Stairs to main floor
6. Kitchen
7. Living/dining area
8. Rear patio
9. Garage
10. Entry to
    main floor
11. Living area
12. Dining area
13. Kitchen
14. Pantry
15. Balcony

E. 37TH PASSIVE HOUSE

Vancouver, British Columbia, Canada // Lot area: 4,026 sq ft; building area: 2,800 sq ft

The home was designed for a couple with young children who wanted to redevelop their existing 1915 house to make it larger, greener, and more comfortable. The home captures sunlight from the south via large windows and doors, with vertical and horizontal shading features that block the hot summer sunlight while letting in the low winter sun. The roof deck provides an urban retreat with a view while also allowing warm air to rise and escape in the summer. The home includes seventeen-inch-thick walls and European triple-glazed windows. Hot water is provided by a heat pump.

Cette maison a été conçue pour un couple avec de jeunes enfants qui souhaitait rénover leur maison de 1915 pour la rendre plus grande, plus verte et plus confortable. La maison capte la lumière du sud par de grandes fenêtres et portes, avec des éléments d'ombrage verticaux et horizontaux qui bloquent la lumière chaude de l'été tout en laissant entrer le soleil bas de l'hiver. La terrasse sur le toit offre une retraite urbaine avec des vues, tout en permettant à l'air chaud de monter et de s'échapper en été. La maison comprend des murs de 43 cm d'épaisseur et des fenêtres européennes à triple couche. L'eau chaude est fournie par une pompe à chaleur.

Dieses Haus wurde für ein Paar mit kleinen Kindern entworfen, das sein Haus aus dem Jahr 1915 renovieren wollte, um es größer, grüner und komfortabler zu machen. Das Haus fängt das Sonnenlicht des Südens durch große Fenster und Türen ein und verfügt über vertikale und horizontale Beschattungselemente, die die heiße Sommersonne abhalten und die tiefstehende Wintersonne hereinlassen. Die Dachterrasse bietet einen urbanen Rückzugsort mit Aussicht, während im Sommer die heiße Luft aufsteigen und entweichen kann. Das Haus hat 43 cm dicke Wände und dreifach verglaste europäische Fenster. Die Warmwasserversorgung erfolgt über eine Wärmepumpe.

Esta casa se diseñó para una pareja con hijos pequeños que quería reformar su casa de 1915 para hacerla más grande, más ecológica y más cómoda. La casa capta la luz solar del sur a través de grandes ventanas y puertas, con elementos de sombreado verticales y horizontales que bloquean la calurosa luz del sol en verano mientras dejan entrar el sol bajo de invierno. La cubierta de la azotea ofrece un refugio urbano con vistas, al tiempo que permite que el aire caliente suba y se escape en verano. La casa incluye paredes de 43 centímetros de grosor y ventanas europeas de triple capa. El agua caliente es suministrada por medio de una bomba de calor.

CAROLYNN WILSON
ARCHITECT

WINDSOR ROAD HOUSE

Architecture Design Team: Carolynn Wilson
Interior Designer: Jodi Foster and Carly Neal/
Jodi Foster Design + Planning
Structural Engineer: SPAR Consultants
Structural Engineers
Contractor and Developer: Maximilian Huxley
Construction Ltd.
Photographer:
© Tony Colangelo Photography

OPHIR TOWNHOUSES

Architecture Design Team: Carolynn Wilson
Landscape Architect: Murdoch de Greeff Inc.
Civil Engineer: JE Anderson
Developer: Formwell Homes
Renderings:
© Bobak Studio, Formwell Homes

THE RESIDENCES ON SOOKE HARBOUR

Architecture Design Team: Carolynn Wilson
Interior Designer: Carolynn Wilson, JC Scott
Eco Design Associates Inc., and
Fitzpatrick Enterprises
Landscape Architect: Lombard Group North
Structural Enginner: Read Johns
Christoffersen Ltd.
Mechanical Engineer: Avalon Mechanical
Consultants Ltd.
Electrical Engineer: PBX Engineering Ltd.
Building Envelope Consultant: WSP
Civil Engineer: Herold Engineering
Geotechnical Engineer: Ryzuk Geotechnical
Environmental Consultant: Aqua-Tex
Developer: Fitzpatrick Enterprises
General Contractor:
Homewood Constructors Ltd.
Photographers: © Lee Miliken (interiors)
and Mike Pepperdine (exteriors)
Renderings: © Neilson Digital

⊕ www.carolynnwilsonarchitect.com

Carolynn Wilson Architect Ltd. established her firm in 2017 in Victoria, British Columbia, as a full-service architecture practice. The firm focuses on providing quality, unique, and holistic design solutions that enhance how we live in our buildings, each project site, and its context. Carolynn Wilson, Principal Architect, offers twenty-six years of architectural experience, having practiced architecture in Victoria and Vancouver Island for fourteen years and in the Canadian prairies, Western Australia, and San Diego, California. She brings a creative vision and artistic approach to designing spaces and buildings that emphasize the beauty of the space through form, details, the experience of the space, materiality, and a connection to the exterior while working collaboratively with the client and team. Carolynn specializes in sustainable design and brings fifteen years of experience delivering several LEED Platinum, Gold, and Net Zero projects.

Carolynn Wilson Architect Ltd. gründete ihr Büro 2017 in Victoria, British Columbia, als Full-Service-Architekturbüro. Das Unternehmen konzentriert sich darauf, qualitativ hochwertige, einzigartige und ganzheitliche Designlösungen anzubieten, die die Art und Weise, wie wir in unseren Gebäuden leben, sowie jeden Projektstandort und seinen Kontext verbessern. Carolynn Wilson, leitende Architektin, verfügt über sechsundzwanzig Jahre Erfahrung als Architektin. Sie hat vierzehn Jahre lang in Victoria und Vancouver Island sowie in der kanadischen Prärie, in Westaustralien und in San Diego, Kalifornien, als Architektin gearbeitet. Sie bringt eine kreative Vision und einen künstlerischen Ansatz in die Gestaltung von Räumen und Gebäuden ein, die die Schönheit des Raums durch Form, Details, Raumerfahrung, Materialität und Verbindung zur Natur betonen, während sie mit dem Kunden und dem Team zusammenarbeitet. Carolynn ist auf nachhaltiges Design spezialisiert und verfügt über fünfzehn Jahre Erfahrung in der Durchführung mehrerer LEED-Platin-, Gold- und Net-Zero-Projekte.

Carolynn Wilson Architect Ltd a créé son cabinet en 2017 à Victoria, en Colombie-Britannique, en tant que cabinet d'architecture à service complet. Le cabinet s'attache à fournir des solutions de conception de qualité, uniques et holistiques, qui améliorent la façon dont nous vivons dans nos bâtiments, sur le site de chaque projet et dans son contexte. Carolynn Wilson, architecte principale, a vingt-six ans d'expérience dans le domaine de l'architecture, ayant exercé pendant quatorze ans à Victoria et sur l'île de Vancouver, ainsi que dans les prairies canadiennes, en Australie occidentale et à San Diego, en Californie. Elle apporte une vision créative et une approche artistique à la conception d'espaces et de bâtiments qui mettent en valeur la beauté de l'espace par la forme, le détail, l'expérience de l'espace, la matérialité et la connexion avec l'extérieur, tout en travaillant en collaboration avec le client et l'équipe. Carolynn est spécialisée dans la conception durable et apporte quinze ans d'expérience dans la réalisation de plusieurs projets LEED Platine, Or et Net Zero.

Carolynn Wilson Architect Ltd. estableció su firma en 2017 en Victoria, Columbia Británica, como una práctica de arquitectura de servicio completo. La firma se centra en proporcionar soluciones de diseño de calidad, únicas y holísticas que mejoran la forma en que vivimos en nuestros edificios, cada terreno del proyecto y su contexto. Carolynn Wilson, arquitecta principal, cuenta con veintiséis años de experiencia arquitectónica, habiendo ejercido la arquitectura en Victoria y la isla de Vancouver durante catorce años y en las praderas canadienses, Australia Occidental y San Diego, California. Aporta una visión creativa y un enfoque artístico al diseño de espacios y edificios que enfatizan la belleza del espacio a través de la forma, los detalles, la experiencia del espacio, la materialidad y la conexión con el exterior, mientras trabaja en colaboración con el cliente y el equipo. Carolynn está especializada en el diseño sostenible y aporta quince años de experiencia en la realización de varios proyectos LEED Platinum, Gold y Net Zero.

WINDSOR ROAD HOUSE

Victoria, British Columbia, Canada // Lot area: 6,006 sq ft; building area: 1,755 sq ft

Windsor Road House sits on a small corner lot on an oak-lined street. The traditional design elements of the surrounding neighborhood inspired the architect to design a home with a contemporary form, clarity and alignment of spaces, and definition of form and character. Two-story black gridded windows in the gables and the central recessed entrance are essential to the character and experience of the spaces. They allow abundant daylight throughout the home and visual connection with the outdoors. Despite the local restrictions, which limited the home's allowable area and building height, the design offers a large main floor footprint with a one-story, vaulted living room. To increase the sense of space, the architect created a sunken patio off of the living room connecting with the outdoors and designed the upper bedrooms to have vaulted ceilings.

La Windsor Road House se trouve sur un petit terrain d'angle dans une rue bordée de chênes. Les éléments de conception traditionnels du quartier environnant ont inspiré l'architecte pour concevoir une maison à la forme contemporaine, à la clarté et à l'alignement des espaces, et à la définition de la forme et du caractère. Les fenêtres à treillis noires de deux étages dans les pignons et l'entrée centrale en retrait sont essentielles au caractère et à l'expérience des espaces. Elles permettent une abondance de lumière naturelle dans toute la maison et une connexion visuelle avec l'extérieur. Malgré les restrictions locales, qui limitent la surface et la hauteur autorisées de la maison, la conception offre une grande surface au sol au rez-de-chaussée avec un salon voûté de plain-pied. Pour accroître l'impression d'espace, l'architecte a créé une cour en creux à côté du salon qui donne sur l'extérieur et a conçu les chambres supérieures avec des plafonds voûtés.

Das Windsor Road House befindet sich auf einem kleinen Eckgrundstück an einer von Eichen gesäumten Straße. Die traditionellen Gestaltungselemente der Umgebung inspirierten den Architekten, ein Haus mit einer zeitgemäßen Form, einer klaren Raumaufteilung und einer klaren Definition von Form und Charakter zu entwerfen. Die zweigeschossigen schwarzen Gitterfenster in den Giebeln und der zurückgesetzte zentrale Eingang sind für den Charakter und die Erfahrung der Räume von wesentlicher Bedeutung. Sie sorgen für reichlich natürliches Licht im ganzen Haus und eine visuelle Verbindung zur Natur. Trotz der örtlichen Beschränkungen, die die zulässige Grundfläche und Höhe des Hauses begrenzen, bietet der Entwurf eine große Grundfläche im Hauptgeschoss mit einem eingeschossigen, gewölbten Wohnzimmer. Um das Raumgefühl zu verbessern, schuf der Architekt einen versenkten Innenhof neben dem Wohnzimmer, der eine Verbindung zum Außenbereich herstellt, und gestaltete die oberen Schlafzimmer mit gewölbten Decken.

Windsor Road House se encuentra en un pequeño terreno de esquina en una calle bordeada de robles. Los elementos de diseño tradicionales del vecindario circundante inspiraron a la arquitecta a diseñar una casa con una forma contemporánea, claridad y alineación de espacios, y definición de forma y carácter. Las ventanas negras de rejilla de dos pisos en los hastiales y la entrada central empotrada son esenciales para el carácter y la experiencia de los espacios. Permiten una abundante luz natural en toda la casa y una conexión visual con el exterior. A pesar de las restricciones locales, que limitan la superficie y la altura permitidas de la casa, el diseño ofrece una gran huella en la planta principal con un salón abovedado de una sola planta. Para aumentar la sensación de espacio, el arquitecto creó un patio hundido junto al salón que conecta con el exterior y diseñó los dormitorios superiores con techos abovedados.

West elevation

South elevation

East elevation

North elevation

North-south section

Entry foyer section

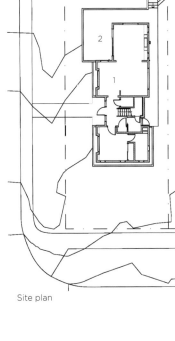

Site plan

Main floor plan

Second floor plan

1. Entry foyer
2. Dining area
3. Kitchen
4. Living area
5. Patio
6. Garage
7. Powder room
8. Bedroom
9. Bathroom
10. Laundry room
11. Walk-in closet

OPHIR TOWNHOUSES

Saanich, British Columbia, Canada // Lot area: 27,007 sq ft; building size area: 30,430 sq ft

This previously developed residential site is in a mixed density neighborhood, close to a village core. The architect worked with the developer, Formwell Homes, to create a mid-density, 14-unit townhouse development that would fit into the community context. This was achieved by breaking down the massing of the townhouses into blocks of three. The site's sloping topography led to stepping the elevations within Blocks A and C while nestling Block B into the topography with a two-story elevation facing the rear pedestrian corridor. This provided an internal street while the green spaces and townhouse patios face outward towards the neighboring properties.

Ce site résidentiel précédemment développé est situé dans un quartier à densité mixte, à proximité du noyau urbain. L'architecte a travaillé avec le promoteur, Formwell Homes, pour créer un projet de 14 unités de densité moyenne qui s'intégrerait dans le contexte de la communauté. Cela a été réalisé en divisant la masse des maisons de ville en blocs de trois. La topographie en pente du site a conduit à étager les élévations des blocs A et C, tandis que le bloc B a été placé dans la topographie avec une élévation de deux étages faisant face au couloir piétonnier arrière. De cette façon, une rue intérieure a été créée, tandis que les espaces verts et les cours des maisons de ville sont orientés vers les propriétés voisines.

Dieses bereits erschlossene Wohngebiet liegt in einem gemischten Viertel in der Nähe des Stadtkerns. Der Architekt arbeitete mit dem Bauträger, Formwell Homes, zusammen, um ein Projekt mit 14 Wohneinheiten mittlerer Dichte zu entwerfen, das sich in den Kontext der Gemeinde einfügen sollte. Dies wurde erreicht, indem die Masse der Stadthäuser in Dreierblöcke aufgeteilt wurde. Die abfallende Topographie des Geländes führte dazu, dass die Erhebungen in den Blöcken A und C abgestuft wurden, während Block B mit einer zweistöckigen Erhebung in die Topographie eingebettet wurde, die dem hinteren Fußgängerkorridor zugewandt war. Auf diese Weise wurde eine interne Straße geschaffen, während die Grünflächen und Höfe der Stadthäuser auf die Nachbargrundstücke ausgerichtet sind.

Este solar residencial previamente urbanizado se encuentra en un barrio de densidad mixta, cerca del núcleo urbano. La arquitecta trabajó con el promotor, Formwell Homes, para crear una urbanización de 14 unidades de densidad media que encajara en el contexto de la comunidad. Esto se consiguió dividiendo la masa de las casas adosadas en bloques de tres. La topografía inclinada del terreno condujo a escalonar los alzados de los bloques A y C, mientras que el bloque B se encajó en la topografía con una altura de dos pisos que daba al corredor peatonal trasero. De este modo, se creó una calle interior, mientras que los espacios verdes y los patios de las casas adosadas se orientan hacia las propiedades vecinas.

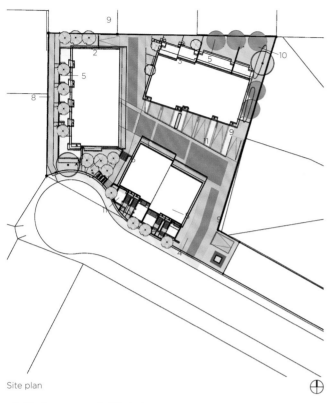

Site plan

1. Block a
2. Block b
3. Block c
4. Entry driveway
5. Patio
6. Pathway
7. Bike lock-up area
8. Public pedestrian pathway
9. Parking
10. Raingarden
11. Porous pavers

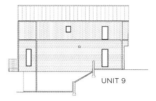

Block B - North elevation

Block B - South elevation

Block B - East elevation

Block B - West elevation

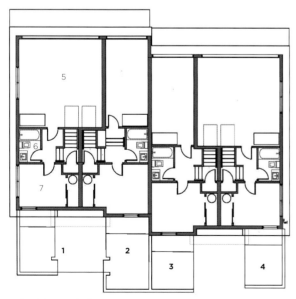

Block A – Level 1 floor plan

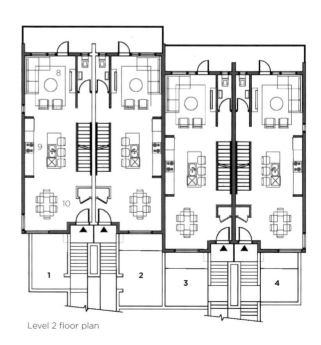

Level 2 floor plan

Louise Place Street elevation

Block A – North elevation

4   3   1   2

Block A – East elevation

4

Block A – West elevation

1

Block A – South elevation

1   2   3   4

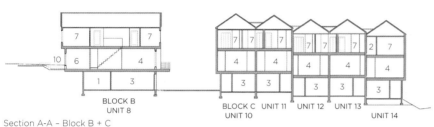

Section A-A – Block B + C

BLOCK B
UNIT 8

BLOCK C   UNIT 11   UNIT 12   UNIT 13
UNIT 10

UNIT 14

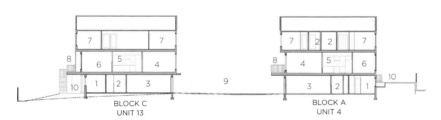

Section B-B – Block C + A

BLOCK C
UNIT 13

BLOCK A
UNIT 4

1. Den
2. Washroom
3. Garage
4. Living room
5. Kitchen
6. Dining room
7. Bedroom
8. Balcony
9. Internal street
10. Patio

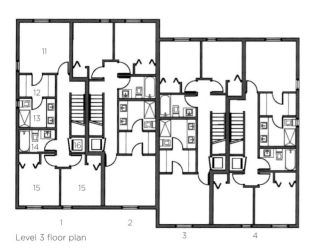

Level 3 floor plan

Conceptual sketch

1. Unit 1
2. Unit 2
3. Unit 3
4. Unit 4
5. Garage
6. Bathroom
7. Bedroom
8. Living room
9. Kitchen
10. Dining room
11. Powder room
12. Master bedroom
13. Walk-in closet
14. Master bathroom
15. Laundry room

THE RESIDENCES ON SOOKE HARBOUR

Sooke, British Columbia, Canada // Lot area: 19,623 sq ft; building area: 53,755 sq ft

Located in the threshold between the ocean, the natural west coast forest, and town, Carolynn Wilson designed the Residences on Sooke Harbour to reflect its setting through harmonizing cladding materials, shifting cantilevering forms and stepped massing created within the boundaries of the dramatically sloped site. Built into the twenty-three-feet slope, the building is conveniently connected to the wharf and the beach via multi-leveled pedestrian, vehicle, bike, and kayak paths. Specifically designed to exceed the norm in condo living and encourage downsizing from single-family homes, the spacious interiors offer generous storage and spacious suites with long private balconies that provide uninterrupted views and abundant daylight.

Situées au seuil de l'océan, de la forêt naturelle de la côte ouest et de la ville, Carolynn Wilson a conçu les Résidences du port de Sooke pour qu'elles reflètent leur environnement en harmonisant les matériaux de revêtement, les formes changeantes en porte-à-faux et la masse en gradins créée dans les limites du site en pente dramatique. Construit sur une pente de 6 mètres, le bâtiment est relié à la jetée et à la plage par des passerelles à plusieurs niveaux pour les piétons, les véhicules, les vélos et les kayaks. Conçus spécifiquement pour dépasser la norme en matière de vie en copropriété et encourager la réduction de la taille des maisons individuelles, les intérieurs spacieux offrent des rangements généreux et des suites spacieuses avec de longs balcons privés offrant des vues ininterrompues et une lumière naturelle abondante.

An der Schwelle zwischen dem Ozean, dem natürlichen Wald der Westküste und der Stadt gelegen, hat Carolynn Wilson die Residences at Sooke Harbour so entworfen, dass sie die Umgebung widerspiegeln, indem sie die Verkleidungsmaterialien, die sich verschiebenden, auskragenden Formen und die abgestufte Masse innerhalb der dramatisch abfallenden Grundstücksgrenzen aufeinander abstimmen. Das in den 6 m hohen Hang gebaute Gebäude ist über mehrstufige Wege für Fußgänger, Fahrzeuge, Fahrräder und Kajaks bequem mit dem Pier und dem Strand verbunden. Die geräumigen Innenräume bieten viel Stauraum und großzügige Suiten mit langen privaten Balkonen, die einen ungehinderten Blick und viel natürliches Licht bieten. Sie wurden speziell entworfen, um die Norm für Eigentumswohnungen zu übertreffen und das Downsizing von Einfamilienhäusern zu fördern.

Situado en el umbral entre el océano, el bosque natural de la costa oeste y la ciudad, Carolynn Wilson diseñó las Residencias en el Puerto de Sooke para reflejar su entorno mediante la armonización de los materiales de revestimiento, las formas cambiantes en voladizo y la masa escalonada creada dentro de los límites del sitio dramáticamente inclinado. Construido en la pendiente de 6 metros, el edificio está convenientemente conectado con el muelle y la playa a través de senderos de varios niveles para peatones, vehículos, bicicletas y kayaks. Diseñado específicamente para superar la norma en la vida de los condominios y fomentar la reducción de las viviendas unifamiliares, los amplios interiores ofrecen un generoso almacenamiento y amplias suites con largos balcones privados que proporcionan vistas ininterrumpidas y abundante luz natural.

East elevation

South elevation

Sooke Basin

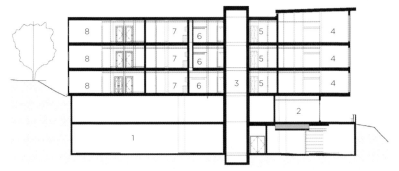

Building section

1. Underground
   parking
2. Health club
3. Elevator
4. Unit b
5. Unit c
6. Unit d
7. Unit e
8. Unit f

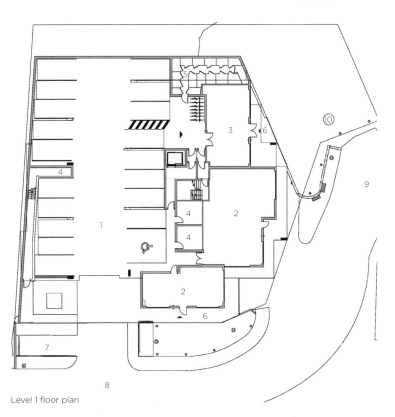

Level 1 floor plan

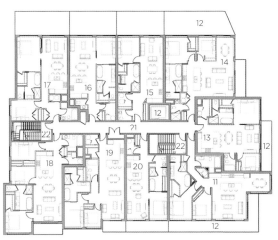

Typical floor plan, levels 2, 3, and 4

1. Parking garage
2. Commercial space
3. Health club
4. Service space
5. Storage
6. Commercial
   balcony
7. Commercial
   loading
8. Maple Ave. south
9. Wharf
10. Storm vertical
    seepage pit
11. Unit a
12. Balcony
13. Unit b
14. Unit c
15. Unit d
16. Unit e
17. Unit f
18. Unit g
19. Unit h
20. Unit i
21. Hallway
22. Staircase

BLUE SKY
ARCHITECTURE

272
﹀

276
﹀

280
﹀

OAK GROVE HOUSE

Architecture Design Team:
Bo Helliwell + Kim Smith, Bettina Balcaen,
and Matt MacLeod
General Contractor:
G. Speed Construction
Photographers:
© Peter Powles, Gillian Proctor,
and Blue Sky Archives

SOLAR CREST HOUSE

Architecture Design Team:
Bo Helliwell + Kim Smith, Elena Chernyshov,
Elise Young, and Volker Ritter
General Contractor:
R. Parson Construction
Landscape Designer:
Aaron Pitt
Photographers:
© Heath Moffatt and Blue Sky Archives

RIDGE HOUSE

Architecture Design Team:
Bo Helliwell + Kim Smith, Bettina Balcaen,
and Volker Ritter
Interior Designer:
Sabina Hill
General Contractor:
G. Speed Construction
Photographers:
© Gillian Proctor, Barry Calhoun,
and Blue Sky Archives

Blue Sky Architecture is an award-winning firm founded on Hornby Island in 1975 and currently located in West Vancouver. Blue Sky was built with an optimism embodying an emotional relationship between people, structure, materials, and nature. There is an unashamed romanticism to Blue Sky's approach to design that bonds buildings to their site. Blue Sky is consistently exploring a design path that is unique, humane, and attuned to its environment. "There is a singular, sinuous line of fine houses shaped by Kim Smith and Bo Helliwell through some of North America's most dramatic landscapes. Like a woodwind solo drifting through a mountain valley, these houses play a continuous melody marked by theme and variation in cedar, stone, and timber beam. The continuities of texture, layout, and outlook between these houses are quickly evident, but more interesting are their differences, the dappled reflections, the unexpected echoes, and the layers of architectural sound drifting through the trees." (Boddy, Trevor. "Blue Sky Living." Images Publishing, 2021.)

Blue Sky Architecture ist ein preisgekröntes Büro, das 1975 auf Hornby Island gegründet wurde und jetzt in West Vancouver ansässig ist. Blue Sky wurde mit einem Optimismus gebaut, der eine emotionale Beziehung zwischen Menschen, Struktur, Materialien und Natur verkörpert. Der Gestaltungsansatz von Blue Sky ist von einer unverhohlenen Romantik geprägt, die die Gebäude mit ihrem Standort verbindet. Blue Sky verfolgt konsequent einen Designpfad, der einzigartig, human und auf seine Umgebung abgestimmt ist. „Es gibt eine einzigartige, gewundene Linie von schönen Häusern, die von Kim Smith und Bo Helliwell durch einige der dramatischsten Landschaften Nordamerikas modelliert wurden. Wie ein Holzbläsersolo, das durch ein Gebirgstal gleitet, spielen diese Häuser eine kontinuierliche Melodie, die von Thema und Variation in Zedern, Stein und Holzbalken geprägt ist. Die Kontinuität der Textur, des Grundrisses und der Perspektive zwischen diesen Häusern wird schnell deutlich, aber noch interessanter sind ihre Unterschiede, die gesprenkelten Reflexionen, unerwarteten Echos und Schichten von architektonischen Klängen, die durch die Bäume driften." (Boddy, Trevor, „Blue Sky Living", Images Publishing, 2021).

Blue Sky Architecture est un cabinet primé, fondé sur l'île Hornby en 1975 et maintenant situé à Vancouver Ouest. Blue Sky a été construit avec un optimisme qui incarne une relation émotionnelle entre les personnes, la structure, les matériaux et la nature. L'approche conceptuelle de Blue Sky est empreinte d'un romantisme non dissimulé qui lie les bâtiments à leur site. Blue Sky explore constamment une voie de conception qui est unique, humaine et en accord avec son environnement. « Il y a une ligne singulière et sinueuse de belles maisons modélisées par Kim Smith et Bo Helliwell à travers certains des paysages les plus spectaculaires d'Amérique du Nord. Comme un solo de bois dérivant dans une vallée de montagne, ces maisons jouent une mélodie continue marquée par le thème et les variations du cèdre, de la pierre et des poutres en bois. Les continuités de texture, de disposition et de perspective entre ces maisons sont rapidement apparentes, mais plus intéressantes sont leurs différences, les reflets tachetés, les échos inattendus et les couches de son architectural qui dérivent à travers les arbres. » (Boddy, Trevor, « Blue Sky Living », Images Publishing, 2021).

Blue Sky Architecture es una empresa galardonada, fundada en Hornby Island en 1975 y situada ahora en West Vancouver. Blue Sky se construyó con un optimismo que encarna una relación emocional entre las personas, la estructura, los materiales y la naturaleza. El enfoque del diseño de Blue Sky tiene un romanticismo desvergonzado que vincula los edificios a su emplazamiento. Blue Sky explora constantemente un camino de diseño que es único, humano y en sintonía con su entorno. «Hay una línea singular y sinuosa de casas finas modeladas por Kim Smith y Bo Helliwell a través de algunos de los paisajes más dramáticos de Norteamérica. Como un solo de viento de madera a la deriva a través de un valle de montaña, estas casas tocan una melodía continua marcada por el tema y la variación en cedro, piedra y vigas de madera. Las continuidades de la textura, la disposición y la perspectiva entre estas casas son rápidamente evidentes, pero más interesantes son sus diferencias, los reflejos moteados, los ecos inesperados y las capas de sonido arquitectónico a la deriva entre los árboles». (Boddy, Trevor, «Blue Sky Living», Images Publishing, 2021).

OAK GROVE HOUSE

Salt Spring Island, British Columbia, Canada // Lot area: 4.57 acres; building area: 2,500 sq ft

Oak Grove House was originally designed as a retreat for living, sitting serenely in a beautiful oak meadow facing south above the Gulf Islands. The design team and builders took great care to preserve the natural landscape throughout the original construction and the building of an extension a decade later. The house's radial plan picks up the curve established by a Garry oak grove. Its tilted and undulating roof opens up to ocean views and south light, while an assertive structural frame—including columns of round logs—imparts visual strength and warmth inside. Siding and doors include such fine details as cedar paneling inset with copper inlay. Finessed with these appointments, the house's beauty rises in response to its glorious setting.

L'Oak Grove House a été conçue à l'origine comme un lieu de retraite, situé dans une magnifique prairie de chênes, face au sud des îles du Golfe. L'équipe de conception et les constructeurs ont pris grand soin de préserver le paysage naturel tout au long du volume original et de la construction d'une annexe dix ans plus tard. Le plan radial de la maison reprend la courbe établie par un bosquet de chênes de Garry. Son toit incliné et ondulé s'ouvre sur la vue sur l'océan et la lumière du sud, tandis qu'un cadre structurel affirmé, comprenant des colonnes en rondins ronds, apporte force visuelle et chaleur à l'intérieur. Les lambris et les portes comportent des détails raffinés tels que des panneaux de cèdre avec incrustation de cuivre. Grâce à ces détails, la beauté de la maison est rehaussée en réponse à son environnement glorieux.

Oak Grove House wurde ursprünglich als Wohnhaus konzipiert, das ruhig in einer wunderschönen Eichenwiese mit Blick nach Süden über die Golfinseln liegt. Das Planungsteam und die Bauherren legten großen Wert darauf, die natürliche Landschaft während des gesamten ursprünglichen Bauvorhabens und beim Bau eines Zusatzes ein Jahrzehnt später zu erhalten. Der radiale Grundriss des Hauses nimmt die Kurve auf, die durch einen Eichenhain in Garry entsteht. Das schräge, gewellte Dach gibt den Blick auf den Ozean und das Licht des Südens frei, während das durchsetzungsfähige Tragwerk mit seinen Rundholzsäulen dem Innenraum optische Stärke und Wärme verleiht. Vertäfelungen und Türen enthalten feine Details wie Zedernholzverkleidungen mit Kupfereinlagen. Mit diesen Details wird die Schönheit des Hauses im Einklang mit seiner herrlichen Umgebung hervorgehoben.

La Oak Grove House se diseñó originalmente como un refugio para vivir, asentada serenamente en una hermosa pradera de robles orientada al sur sobre las Islas del Golfo. El equipo de diseño y los constructores tuvieron mucho cuidado en preservar el paisaje natural a lo largo del volumen original y de la construcción de una ampliación una década después. La planta radial de la casa recoge la curva establecida por un robledal de Garry. Su tejado inclinado y ondulado se abre a las vistas del océano y a la luz del sur, mientras que un marco estructural asertivo que incluye columnas de troncos redondos, aporta fuerza visual y calidez al interior. Los revestimientos y las puertas incluyen detalles finos como paneles de cedro con incrustaciones de cobre. Con estos detalles, la belleza de la casa se eleva en respuesta a su glorioso entorno.

North elevation

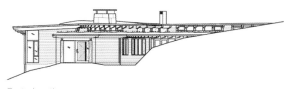

East elevation

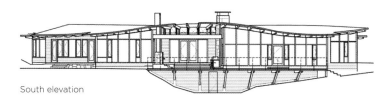

South elevation

West elevation

Section

Conceptual sketch

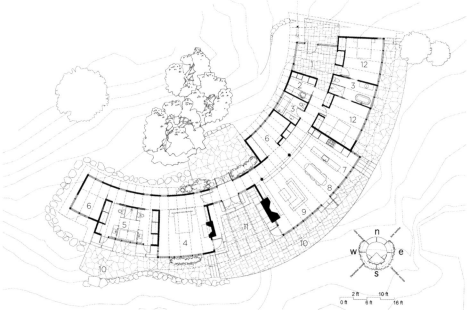

Floor plan

1. Entry
2. Utility/mud room
3. Powder room
4. Main bedroom
5. En suite
6. Den
7. Kitchen
8. Dining area
9. Living area
10. Terrace
11. Outdoor room
12. Bedroom

2 ft   10 ft
0 ft   6 ft   16 ft

SOLAR CREST HOUSE

Sidney Island, British Columbia, Canada // Lot area: 10 acres; building area: 2,800 sq ft

Solar Crest is an off-grid home and garden, embracing a rugged rocky ridge on a remote island in Juan de Fuca Strait. It combines a studied geometric formality with organic and sensuous elements that merge with its surrounding landscape of rounded glaciated granite. The plan of the house is an arc following the sun and the hill's crest opening to southern light and views across the Strait to the Olympic Mountains in Washington State. In section, the roof undulates, a living sculpture responding to the hierarchy of spatial use, the opportunities of sun, air, views, and the shape of the land itself. As with most Blue Sky buildings, wood frame was the construction choice, being relatively lightweight, easy to move, and use. Most of the fir and cedar used in the house is local, harvested and milled on nearby Vancouver Island.

Solar Crest est une maison et un jardin hors réseau, perchés sur une crête rocheuse escarpée sur une île isolée du détroit de Juan de Fuca. Il combine une formalité géométrique étudiée avec des éléments organiques et sensuels qui se fondent dans le paysage environnant de granit glaciaire arrondi. Le plan de la maison est un arc qui suit le soleil et la crête de la colline, s'ouvrant à la lumière du sud et aux vues sur le détroit jusqu'aux Olympic Mountains de l'État de Washington. En section, le toit ondule, une sculpture vivante qui répond à la hiérarchie de l'utilisation de l'espace, aux opportunités de soleil, d'air, de vues et à la forme du terrain lui-même. Comme pour la plupart des bâtiments de Blue Sky, le choix de la construction s'est porté sur une ossature en bois, car elle est relativement légère et facile à déplacer et à utiliser. La plupart des épicéas et des cèdres utilisés dans la maison sont locaux, récoltés et usinés sur l'île de Vancouver toute proche.

Solar Crest ist ein netzunabhängiges Haus mit Garten, das auf einem steilen Felsrücken auf einer abgelegenen Insel in der Strait of Juan de Fuca liegt. Es verbindet eine studierte geometrische Formalität mit organischen und sinnlichen Elementen, die sich in die umgebende Landschaft aus abgerundetem Gletschergranit einfügen. Der Grundriss des Hauses ist ein Bogen, der der Sonne und dem Kamm des Hügels folgt und sich dem südlichen Licht und dem Blick über die Meerenge bis zu den Olympic Mountains im Bundesstaat Washington öffnet. Im Schnitt ist das Dach wellenförmig, eine lebendige Skulptur, die auf die Hierarchie der Raumnutzung, die Möglichkeiten der Sonne, der Luft, der Aussicht und die Form des Geländes selbst reagiert. Wie bei den meisten Gebäuden von Blue Sky fiel die Wahl auf die Holzrahmenbauweise, da sie relativ leicht und einfach zu bewegen und zu verwenden ist. Die meisten der im Haus verwendeten Fichten und Zedern stammen aus der Region und wurden auf der nahe gelegenen Insel Vancouver Island geerntet und gefräst.

Solar Crest es una casa y un jardín sin conexión a la red eléctrica, que se alza sobre una escarpada cresta rocosa en una remota isla del estrecho de Juan de Fuca. Combina una estudiada formalidad geométrica con elementos orgánicos y sensuales que se funden con el paisaje circundante de granito glaciar redondeado. La planta de la casa es un arco que sigue al sol y a la cresta de la colina, abriéndose a la luz del sur y a las vistas sobre el Estrecho hasta las Montañas Olímpicas del Estado de Washington. En sección, el tejado se ondula, una escultura viva que responde a la jerarquía del uso del espacio, las oportunidades del sol, el aire, las vistas y la forma del propio terreno. Como en la mayoría de los edificios de Blue Sky, la estructura de madera fue la opción de construcción, ya que es relativamente ligera y fácil de mover y utilizar. La mayor parte del abeto y el cedro utilizados en la casa son locales, cosechados y molidos en la cercana isla de Vancouver.

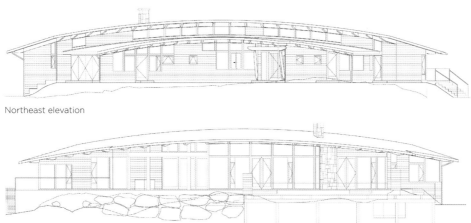

Northeast elevation

Southwest elevation

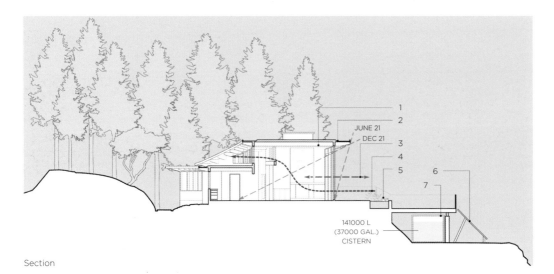

Section

JUNE 21
DEC 21

141000 L
(37000 GAL.)
CISTERN

1. Douglas fir timber frame
2. Overhangs minimize
   summer solar gain and
   maximize winter solar gain
3. Daylighting and view
4. Natural cross ventilation
5. Vegetable garden
6. Solar photovoltaic panels
7. Rainwater collection
   to cistern

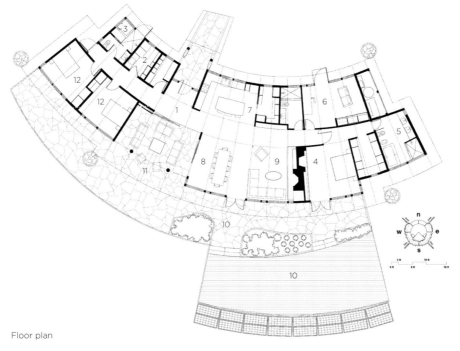

Floor plan

1. Entry
2. Utility/mudroom
3. Powder room
4. Main bedroom
5. En suite
6. Den
7. Kitchen
8. Dining area
9. Living area
10. Terrace
11. Outdoor room
12. Bedroom

RIDGE HOUSE

Salt Spring Island, British Columbia, Canada // Lot area: 9.9 acres; building area: 3,100 sq ft

The house is the embodiment of its owners' retirement dreams. Having owned and camped out at this heavily treed, steep hillside site for several years, they had time to formulate their ideas for living here. The couple had identified a narrow rocky ridge running approximately east-west through a grove of small twisted arbutus trees as their preferred building site. The Ridge House's linear plan and section are determined by this topography. The rhythm of the roof inflects the spatial moods of rooms below as it shifts from the entrance's enclosed and protective forms to open and expansive spaces for the living and dining rooms. Simple details and careful craftsmanship aggregate to form a sophisticated design that perches dramatically on its rocky forest ridge.

La maison est l'incarnation des rêves de retraite de ses propriétaires. Ayant été propriétaires et campeurs sur cette colline escarpée et fortement boisée pendant plusieurs années, ils ont eu le temps de formuler leurs idées pour vivre ici. Le couple avait identifié comme site de construction privilégié une étroite crête rocheuse traversant d'est en ouest un bosquet de petits arbousiers tordus. Le plan et la section linéaire de la maison Ridge sont déterminés par cette topographie. Le rythme du toit influence les environnements spatiaux des pièces inférieures, car il passe des formes fermées et protectrices de l'entrée aux espaces ouverts et expansifs du salon et de la salle à manger. Des détails simples et un artisanat soigné s'associent pour former un design sophistiqué qui se perche de façon spectaculaire sur sa crête forestière rocheuse.

Das Haus ist die Verkörperung der Ruhestandsträume seiner Besitzer. Nachdem sie diesen steilen, stark bewaldeten Hang mehrere Jahre lang besessen und dort gezeltet hatten, hatten sie Zeit, ihre Vorstellungen vom Leben hier zu formulieren. Das Paar hatte einen schmalen felsigen Bergrücken, der etwa in Ost-West-Richtung durch einen Hain mit kleinen, verdrehten Erdbeerbäumen verläuft, als bevorzugten Bauplatz ausgemacht. Der Grundriss und der lineare Schnitt des Ridge House werden durch diese Topografie bestimmt. Der Rhythmus des Daches beeinflusst die räumlichen Umgebungen der unteren Räume, da es von den geschlossenen, schützenden Formen des Eingangs zu den offenen, weitläufigen Räumen des Wohn- und Esszimmers übergeht. Einfache Details und sorgfältige Handwerkskunst vereinen sich zu einem anspruchsvollen Design, das dramatisch auf seinem felsigen Waldrücken thront.

La casa es la encarnación de los sueños de jubilación de sus propietarios. Después de haber sido propietarios y haber acampado en esta ladera muy arbolada y empinada durante varios años, tuvieron tiempo de formular sus ideas para vivir aquí. La pareja había identificado una estrecha cresta rocosa que discurre aproximadamente de este a oeste a través de un bosquecillo de pequeños madroños retorcidos como su lugar de construcción preferido. La planta y la sección lineal de la Ridge House están determinadas por esta topografía. El ritmo del tejado influye en los ambientes espaciales de las estancias inferiores, ya que pasa de las formas cerradas y protectoras de la entrada a los espacios abiertos y amplios del salón y el comedor. Los detalles sencillos y la cuidadosa artesanía se unen para formar un diseño sofisticado que se posa dramáticamente en su cresta de bosque rocoso.

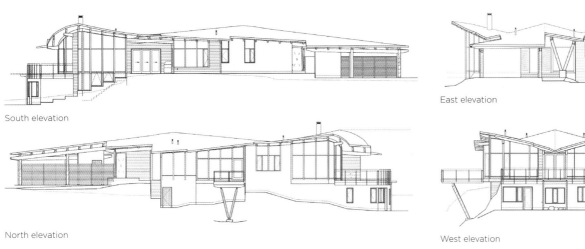

South elevation

East elevation

North elevation

West elevation

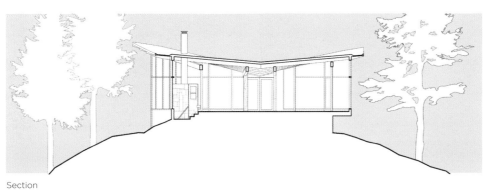

Section

Site plan

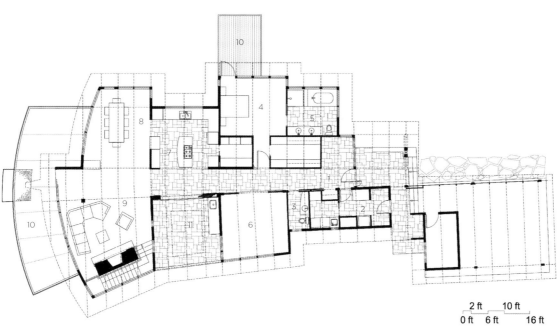

Floor plan

1. Entry
2. Utility/mudroom
3. Powder room
4. Main bedroom
5. En suite
6. Den
7. Kitchen
8. Dining area
9. Living area
10. Terrace
11. Outdoor room

workshop AD

CANYON SHELTER

Architecture Team:
workshop AD
Interior Design Team:
Lair Design
Structural Engineer:
Quantum Consulting Engineers
General Contractor:
Owner
Photographer:
© workshop AD

LIGHT BOX

Architecture and Interior Design Team:
workshop AD
Structural Engineer:
Harriot Valentine Engineers
General Contractor:
Ridgeline Northwest
Casework:
Leight Cabinets
Photographers:
© Lara Swimmer Photography, workshop AD

JANUS

Architecture and Interior Design Team:
workshop AD
Structural Engineer:
Swenson Say Fagét
General Contractor:
Loftstrom Construction
Photographer:
© Lara Swimmer Photography

🌐 www.workshopad.com   ◎ workshop_ad

Workshop AD is a Seattle-based architecture practice focused on compelling projects across a range of geographies and scales. We believe a workshop is not about a single voice but a collective effort. We also believe in a workshop's most honorable commitments to material, craft, and exploration. As leaders in this collective effort, our responsibility is not simply to design but to guide the design and construction process. Through our diverse range of work—be it a new home in the forested subarctic, a shelter in the shrub steppe, surgically interventions on a nineteenth-century loft building, or a half-block of urban housing—we gather our experience from one environment and use it to expand our thinking and influence our work in another. Our approach creates buildings informed by the needs of our clients, integrates strong building forms and environment, considers the use of materials and daylight, and defines a clear expression for the human experience of a place.

Workshop AD ist ein in Seattle ansässiges Architekturbüro, das sich auf überzeugende Projekte in den unterschiedlichsten Regionen und Größenordnungen konzentriert. Wir sind der Meinung, dass ein Workshop nicht eine einzelne Stimme ist, sondern eine kollektive Anstrengung. Wir glauben auch an das ehrbare Engagement eines Studios für Material, Handwerk und Erforschung. Als Leiter dieser kollektiven Anstrengung ist es unsere Aufgabe, nicht nur zu entwerfen, sondern auch den Prozess der Planung und des Baus zu leiten. Durch unsere vielfältige Arbeit, sei es ein neues Haus in der bewaldeten Subarktis, ein Unterstand in der Buschsteppe, chirurgische Eingriffe in einem Loft aus dem 19. Jahrhundert oder ein halber Häuserblock in der Stadt, sammeln wir unsere Erfahrungen in einer bestimmten Umgebung und nutzen sie, um unser Denken zu erweitern und unsere Arbeit in einem anderen Kontext zu beeinflussen. Unser Ansatz schafft Gebäude, die sich an den Bedürfnissen unserer Kunden orientieren, integriert starke Gebäudeformen und die Umgebung, berücksichtigt die Verwendung von Materialien und Tageslicht und definiert einen klaren Ausdruck für die menschliche Erfahrung eines bestimmten Ortes.

Workshop AD est un cabinet d'architecture basé à Seattle qui se concentre sur des projets convaincants dans un large éventail de zones géographiques et d'échelles. Nous pensons qu'un atelier n'est pas une voix unique, mais un effort collectif. Nous croyons également aux engagements honorables d'un studio envers les matériaux, l'artisanat et l'exploration. En tant que chefs de file de cet effort collectif, notre responsabilité ne consiste pas simplement à concevoir, mais à guider le processus de conception et de construction. Grâce à la diversité de nos travaux, qu'il s'agisse d'une nouvelle maison dans la forêt subarctique, d'un abri dans la steppe broussailleuse, d'interventions chirurgicales dans un loft du XIXe siècle ou d'un demi-bloc de logements urbains, nous recueillons notre expérience d'un environnement et l'utilisons pour étendre notre réflexion et influencer notre travail dans un autre contexte. Notre approche crée des bâtiments informés par les besoins de nos clients, intègre des formes de construction et un environnement forts, tient compte de l'utilisation des matériaux et de la lumière du jour, et définit une expression claire de l'expérience humaine d'un lieu donné.

Workshop AD es un estudio de arquitectura con sede en Seattle que se centra en proyectos dentro de una amplia gama de geografías y escalas. Creemos que un taller no es una sola voz, sino un esfuerzo colectivo. También creemos en los compromisos honesto de un taller con el material, la artesanía y la exploración. Como líderes de este esfuerzo colectivo, nuestra responsabilidad no es simplemente diseñar, sino guiar el proceso de diseño y construcción. A través de nuestra diversa gama de trabajos, ya sea una casa en el subártico boscoso, un refugio en la estepa arbustiva, intervenciones en un edificio de lofts del siglo XIX o una media manzana de viviendas urbanas, recogemos nuestra experiencia de un entorno y la utilizamos para ampliar nuestro razonamiento e influir en nuestro trabajo en otro contexto. Nuestro enfoque crea edificios en función de las necesidades de nuestros clientes, integra formas sólidas de construcción y entorno, considera el uso de materiales y la luz del día, y define una expresión clara para la experiencia humana de un lugar determinado.

CANYON SHELTER

Kittitas County, Washington, United States // Lot area: 12.50 acres; building area: 800 sq ft

The shelter is situated between a basalt canyon and a broad rolling ridge, creating a bridge between these two distinct landscape features. The shelter is not consumed by either, comfortably sited at the exact point where scales begin to change. It is precisely here that the inhabitants can occupy the space of the canyon while simultaneously experiencing the broad openness of the ridge. A modest weekend shelter, it is entirely off the grid. It is created from three primary components. A long wall creates a sheltered space on the exposed ridgeline; the terraces lift the outdoor activity off the rocky ground and establish a stage in the landscape; the pavilion provides visual connections with the natural environment. Through the seasons, the inhabitants experience refuge and retreat and, at the same time, exposure and connection to the western landscape.

L'abri est situé entre un canyon basaltique et une large crête ondulée, faisant le lien entre ces deux éléments distincts du paysage. Le refuge n'est consommé ni par l'un ni par l'autre, confortablement situé au point exact où la balance commence à changer. C'est précisément ici que les habitants peuvent occuper l'espace et en même temps faire l'expérience de la grande ouverture de la crête. Il s'agit d'une modeste retraite de week-end, totalement déconnectée et conçue à partir de trois éléments principaux : un long mur crée un espace abrité sur la crête du canyon ; des terrasses soulèvent les activités extérieures du sol rocheux, créant une scène dans le paysage ; et le pavillon fournit des connexions visuelles avec l'environnement naturel. Au fil des saisons, les habitants se réfugient et se retirent, tout en étant exposés et connectés au paysage occidental.

Die Schutzhütte befindet sich zwischen einer Basaltschlucht und einem breiten, hügeligen Bergrücken, der diese beiden unterschiedlichen Landschaftselemente miteinander verbindet. Das Refugium wird von beidem nicht eingenommen, sondern befindet sich genau an dem Punkt, an dem sich die Waage zu verschieben beginnt. Gerade hier können die Bewohner den Raum besetzen und gleichzeitig die Weite des Bergrückens erleben. Es handelt sich um einen bescheidenen Wochenend-Rückzugsort, der völlig losgelöst ist und aus drei Hauptkomponenten besteht: Eine lange Mauer schafft einen geschützten Raum auf dem Kamm der Schlucht; Terrassen heben die Aktivitäten im Freien vom felsigen Boden ab und bilden eine Bühne in der Landschaft; und der Pavillon schafft eine visuelle Verbindung zur natürlichen Umgebung. Im Laufe der Jahreszeiten erleben die Bewohner Zuflucht und Rückzug, gleichzeitig aber auch Ausgesetztsein und Verbundenheit mit der westlichen Landschaft.

El refugio está situado entre un cañón de basalto y una amplia cresta ondulada, creando un puente entre estas dos características paisajísticas distintas. El refugio no es consumido por ninguno de los dos, cómodamente situado en el punto exacto donde las escalas comienzan a cambiar. Es precisamente aquí donde los habitantes pueden ocupar el espacio y al mismo tiempo experimentar la amplia apertura de la cresta. Se trata de un modesto retiro de fin de semana, totalmente desconectado y concebido a partir de tres componentes principales: un largo muro crea un espacio protegido en la cresta del cañón; las terrazas levantan la actividad exterior del suelo rocoso estableciendo un escenario en el paisaje, y el pabellón, que proporciona conexiones visuales con el entorno natural. A lo largo de las estaciones, los habitantes experimentan el refugio y el retiro, pero, al mismo tiempo, la exposición y la conexión con el paisaje occidental.

BASALT

The Yakima Basalt describes a great series of flood lavas which covered the vast area between what is now the crest of the Cascade Mountains on the west and the mountains of Idaho on the east, and between the mountain of northeastern Washington on the north and the Blue Mountains of Oregon on the South. The age of the Yakima Basalt is late Miocene and early Pliocene. Today, outcroppings of basalt are revealed at fault scarps, ridges, and canyons.

WIND

Kittitas Valley is aligned between the cool, dense air over the Pacific and the less-dense warmer air of the Columbia Basin and the deserts of Southern Idaho. Westerly flows are compressed over the Cascades, then expand as they spill over the east side. The topography of the valley is nearly perfect for funneling high-speed winds.

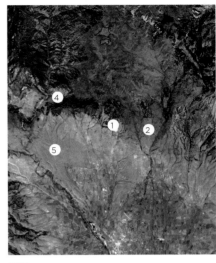

FIRE

With under nine inches of precipitation a year, the shrub-steppe and upland forests of the Kittitas Valley present an extreme fire danger every summer. In the last nine years, fires totaling more than 200,000 acres have scorched the north side of the valley.

1. Site
2. Snag canyon fire - 2014
3. Table mountain fire - 2012
4. Lauderdale fire - 2004
5. Taylor bridge fire - 2012

Environmental elements

SPRING

FALL

SUMMER

WINTER

Seasonal Change

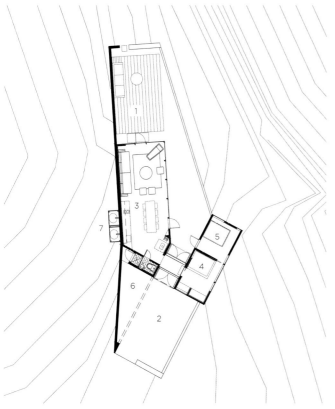

Floor plan

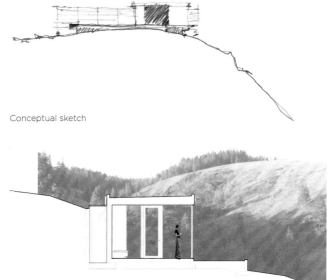

Conceptual sketch

Section

1. Canyon terrace
2. Ridge terrace
3. Pavilion
   (cooking and living)
4. Bunkroom
5. Bedroom
6. Cisterns
7. Bathroom

LIGHT BOX

Seattle, Washington, United States // Lot area: 3,060 sq ft; building area: 2,097 sq ft

Located on the edge of Seattle's Capitol Hill neighborhood, the project site is a tiny lot with an eighteen-foot height limit. With few opportunities for the home to orient spaces outward, the design turns inward and upward. Designed for an avid sailor, the house is compact and efficient like a well-crafted sailboat. It is organized around a "lightbox," which is expressed by a clerestory and light well that expand the spatial volume, engage the sky, and bring the landscape into the center of the home. As one lightbox pushes up, the other pushes down, creating a dynamic exchange of interior and exterior environments that fill the primary living spaces with daylight and intimacy. Even though the home is small in scale, it exerts a presence on the corner site. The siding is ebony-stained board-on-board cedar and creates a robust and textured façade for the muted light of the Pacific Northwest.

Situé en bordure du quartier Capitol Hill de Seattle, le site du projet est un tout petit terrain dont la hauteur est limitée à 5,5 mètres. La maison ayant peu de possibilités d'orienter les espaces vers l'extérieur, la conception se tourne vers l'intérieur et vers le haut. Conçue pour un marin passionné, la maison est compacte et efficace comme un voilier bien construit. Elle s'organise autour d'une « boîte à lumière », exprimée par une lucarne et un puits de lumière qui élargissent le volume spatial, attirent le ciel et amènent le paysage au centre de la maison. Lorsqu'un caisson lumineux se soulève, l'autre s'abaisse, créant un échange dynamique d'environnements intérieurs et extérieurs qui remplissent les principaux espaces de vie de lumière naturelle et d'intimité. Bien que la maison soit petite, elle exerce une forte présence sur le terrain d'angle. Le bardage est en cèdre teinté ébène et crée une façade robuste et texturée adaptée à la lumière tamisée du Nord-Ouest Pacifique.

Das Projekt befindet sich am Rande des Stadtteils Capitol Hill in Seattle und ist ein kleines Grundstück mit einer Höhenbegrenzung von 5,5 m. Da das Haus kaum die Möglichkeit hat, die Räume nach außen zu orientieren, wendet sich der Entwurf nach innen und nach oben. Das Haus wurde für einen begeisterten Segler entworfen und ist kompakt und effizient wie ein gut gebautes Segelboot. Es ist um einen „Lichtkasten" herum organisiert, der durch ein Oberlicht und einen Lichtschacht zum Ausdruck kommt, die das Raumvolumen erweitern, den Himmel hereinziehen und die Landschaft in das Zentrum des Hauses bringen. Wenn sich ein Leuchtkasten nach oben schiebt, schiebt sich der andere nach unten und schafft so einen dynamischen Austausch von Innen- und Außenbereichen, der die wichtigsten Wohnräume mit natürlichem Licht und Intimität erfüllt. Obwohl das Haus klein ist, übt es eine starke Präsenz auf dem Eckgrundstück aus. Die Verkleidung besteht aus ebenholzgebeizter Zeder und schafft eine robuste, strukturierte Fassade für das gedämpfte Licht des pazifischen Nordwestens.

Situado en el límite del barrio Capitol Hill de Seattle, el solar del proyecto es un terreno minúsculo con un límite de altura de 5,5 metros. Con pocas oportunidades para que la casa oriente los espacios hacia el exterior, el diseño se vuelve hacia dentro y hacia arriba. Diseñada para un ávido navegante, la casa es compacta y eficiente como un velero bien construido. Se organiza en torno a una «caja de luz», expresada por un claristorio y un pozo de luz que amplían el volumen espacial, atraen el cielo y llevan el paisaje al centro de la casa. Cuando una caja de luz empuja hacia arriba, la otra empuja hacia abajo, creando un intercambio dinámico de ambientes interiores y exteriores que llenan de luz natural e intimidad los espacios principales de la vivienda. Aunque la casa es pequeña, ejerce una gran presencia en el terreno de la esquina. El revestimiento es de cedro teñido de ébano y crea una fachada robusta y con textura para la luz apagada del noroeste del Pacífico.

Parent lot

Original lot with SFR and detached garage.

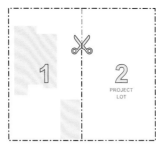

Subdivide lot

The lot size resulted to 3,073 square feet after subdivision. For a lot less than 3,200 square feet, the maximum height limit is reduced from 30 feet to 18 feet.

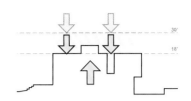

Zoning pushing in and down design pushing up

Projections such as clerestories, open rails and planters are permitted to extend four feet above the maximum height limit. The design incorporates these elements and takes advantage of zoning opportunities to create spatial variations.

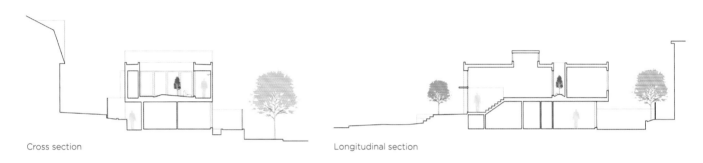

Cross section

Longitudinal section

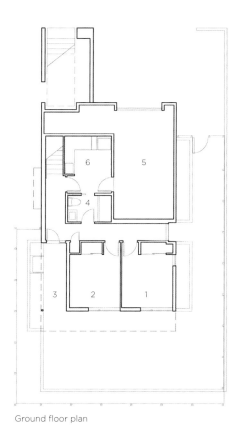

Ground floor plan

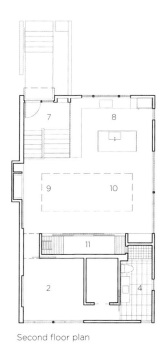

Second floor plan

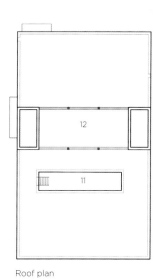

Roof plan

1. Office
2. Bedroom
3. Outdoor kitchen
4. Bathroom
5. Garage
6. Laundry room
7. Entry
8. Kitchen
9. Living area
10. Dining area
11. Lightwell
12. Clerestory

JANUS

Seattle, Washington, United States // Lot area: 5,000 sq ft; building area: 2,100 sq ft

An early twentieth-Century Tudor residence was renovated for a growing family that desired a design solution that increased the area of the living spaces without adding to the existing home. The renovation was to preserve the character-defining elements of the existing home and create crisp, modern living spaces that engaged the sweeping view to the north. The design leaves the traditional, street-facing facade untouched, concealing the dramatic change to the interior and rear wall. Given the clients' goals for cleanly detailed spaces oriented to the view, the rear wall was blown open and replaced with an aperture spanning the entire width of the structure. This new facade responds to a complete reconfiguration of the living spaces and assumes a character of its own. Like the Roman god Janus, the house now has two faces. The front looks to the past, and the rear to the future.

Une résidence Tudor du début du XXᵉ siècle a été rénovée pour une famille grandissante qui souhaitait une solution de conception permettant d'augmenter l'espace de vie sans agrandir la maison existante. La rénovation devait préserver les éléments de caractère de la maison d'origine et créer des espaces de vie modernes et nets qui profitent de la vue imprenable sur le nord. La conception laisse intacte la façade traditionnelle donnant sur la rue et dissimule le changement spectaculaire apporté à l'intérieur et au mur arrière. Étant donné que les clients souhaitaient des espaces aux détails épurés et orientés vers la vue, le mur arrière a été ouvert et remplacé par une ouverture couvrant toute la largeur de la structure. Cette nouvelle façade répond à une reconfiguration complète des espaces de vie et prend un caractère propre. Comme le dieu romain Janus, la maison a maintenant deux visages : le devant est tourné vers le passé et l'arrière vers l'avenir.

Ein Tudorhaus aus dem frühen 20. Jahrhundert wurde für eine wachsende Familie renoviert, die eine Lösung suchte, die den Wohnraum vergrößert, ohne das bestehende Haus zu vergrößern. Bei der Renovierung sollten die charakterbestimmenden Elemente des ursprünglichen Hauses erhalten und klare, moderne Wohnräume geschaffen werden, die den weiten Blick nach Norden nutzen. Der Entwurf lässt die traditionelle Fassade zur Straße hin unangetastet und verbirgt die dramatische Veränderung des Innenraums und der Rückwand. Angesichts des Ziels der Bauherren, saubere, detailreiche und aussichtsreiche Räume zu schaffen, wurde die Rückwand geöffnet und durch eine Öffnung ersetzt, die sich über die gesamte Breite des Gebäudes erstreckt. Diese neue Fassade reagiert auf eine komplette Umgestaltung der Wohnräume und erhält einen eigenen Charakter. Wie der römische Gott Janus hat das Haus nun zwei Gesichter: die Vorderseite ist der Vergangenheit und die Rückseite der Zukunft zugewandt.

Una residencia Tudor de principios del siglo XX fue renovada para una familia en crecimiento que deseaba una solución de diseño que aumentara la superficie de los espacios habitables sin ampliar la casa existente. La renovación debía preservar los elementos que definen el carácter de la casa original y crear espacios de vida modernos y nítidos que aprovecharan las amplias vistas hacia el norte. El diseño deja intacta la fachada tradicional, que da a la calle, y oculta el drástico cambio en el interior y la pared trasera. Dados los objetivos de los clientes de conseguir espacios con detalles limpios y orientados a las vistas, la pared trasera se abrió y se sustituyó por una abertura que abarcaba toda la anchura de la estructura. Esta nueva fachada responde a una re configuración completa de los espacios habitables y asume un carácter propio. Como el dios romano Jano, la casa tiene ahora dos caras; la delantera mira al pasado y la trasera al futuro.

Elevation

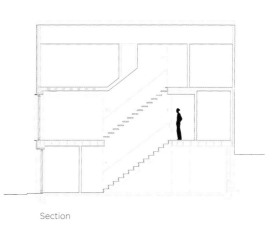

Section

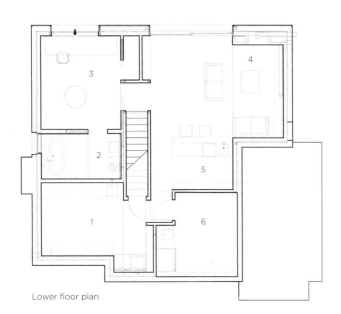

Lower floor plan

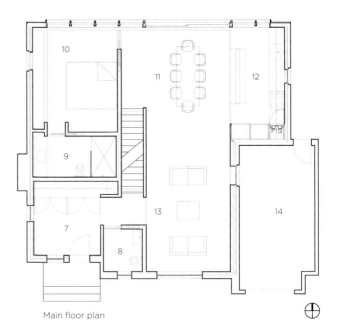

Main floor plan

1. Laundry room
2. Bathroom
3. Bedroom
4. Family room
5. Bar
6. Wine room
7. Entry foyer
8. Powder room
9. Master bathroom
10. Master bedroom
11. Dining area
12. Kitchen
13. Living area
14. Garage

HYBRID

HILL HOUSE

Architecture Design Team:
Hybrid Architecture
Construction:
Hybrid Assembly
Client:
Hybrid Development
Photographers:
© Lara Swimmer, Spencer Radford

STEEL STACKS

Architecture Design Team:
Hybrid Architecture
Construction:
Hybrid Assembly
Client:
Hybrid Development
Photographer:
© Rafael Soldi

Awards:
Best Multifamily Housing Community
2020 Golden Nugget Grand Award

THE LOOKOUT

Architecture Design Team:
Hybrid Architecture
Construction:
Hybrid Assembly
Client:
Hybrid Development
Photographer:
© Rafael Soldi

Hybrid is an architecture company with four interconnected studios—design, build, develop, and space. At Hybrid, architects are also construction managers, reinvesting the wealth of building and design information into the construction process. This design/build process allows fluidity between the construction and design process, creating a positive feedback loop. The lessons learned in the assembly of one project are incorporated into the design of the next. Avoiding the formulaic, uninspired developments that have come to signify the downside of rapid development, Hybrid projects are thoughtfully designed, site-specific, and community-focused. Housing scarcity, affordability, and gentrification are critical topics that architects can and should focus on to bring positive change to communities. As Seattle grows denser, Hybrid focuses on "growth with grace" while maintaining the sense of place and regional identity.

Hybrid ist ein Architekturbüro mit vier miteinander verbundenen Ateliers: Design, Konstruktion, Entwicklung und Raum. Bei Hybrid sind Architekten auch Baumanager, die den Reichtum an Konstruktions- und Designinformationen in den Bauprozess reinvestieren. Dieser Entwurfs- und Bauprozess ermöglicht einen fließenden Übergang zwischen den beiden Prozessen und schafft eine positive Rückkopplungsschleife. Die bei der Montage eines Projekts gewonnenen Erkenntnisse fließen in die Planung des nächsten Projekts ein. Die Hybrid-Projekte sind sorgfältig konzipiert, standortspezifisch und gemeinschaftsorientiert und vermeiden die formelhaften und uninspirierten Entwicklungen, die für die Schattenseiten der schnellen Entwicklung stehen. Wohnungsknappheit, Erschwinglichkeit und Gentrifizierung sind zentrale Themen, auf die sich Architekten konzentrieren können und sollten, um positive Veränderungen in den Gemeinden zu bewirken. Im Zuge der Verdichtung Seattles konzentriert sich Hybrid auf „Wachstum mit Anstand", wobei das Gefühl für den Ort und die regionale Identität erhalten bleiben soll.

Hybrid est un cabinet d'architecture composé de quatre studios interconnectés : conception, construction, développement et espace. Chez Hybrid, les architectes sont également des gestionnaires de la construction, réinvestissant la richesse des informations relatives à la construction et à la conception dans le processus de construction. Ce processus de conception/construction permet une fluidité entre les deux processus, créant ainsi une boucle de rétroaction positive. Les leçons apprises lors du montage d'un projet sont intégrées dans la conception du suivant. Les projets Hybrid sont soigneusement conçus, adaptés au site et axés sur la communauté, ce qui permet d'éviter les formules et le manque d'inspiration qui sont devenus les inconvénients du développement rapide. La pénurie de logements, l'accessibilité financière et l'embourgeoisement sont des questions clés sur lesquelles les architectes peuvent et doivent se concentrer pour apporter des changements positifs dans les communautés. À mesure que Seattle se densifie, Hybrid se concentre sur une « croissance avec grâce » tout en préservant le sens du lieu et l'identité régionale.

Hybrid es una empresa de arquitectura con cuatro estudios interconectados: diseño, construcción, desarrollo y espacio. En Hybrid, los arquitectos son también directores de obra, reinvirtiendo la riqueza de la información sobre la construcción y el diseño en el proceso de construcción. Este proceso de diseño/construcción permite la fluidez entre ambos procesos, creando un bucle de retroalimentación positiva. Las lecciones aprendidas en el montaje de un proyecto se incorporan al diseño del siguiente. Los proyectos de Hybrid, que evitan las fórmulas y los desarrollos poco inspirados que han llegado a significar la desventaja del desarrollo rápido, se diseñan cuidadosamente, se adaptan al lugar y se centran en la comunidad. La escasez de vivienda, la asequibilidad y el aburguesamiento son temas fundamentales en los que los arquitectos pueden y deben centrarse para lograr un cambio positivo en las comunidades. A medida que Seattle se densifica, Hybrid se centra en el «crecimiento con gracia», manteniendo el sentido del lugar y la identidad regional.

HILL HOUSE

Seattle, Washington, United States // Lot area: 8,585 sq ft; building area: 3,000 sq ft

On a steep lot that would have traditionally been deemed unbuildable, Hybrid designed, built, and developed the Hill House: an adaptable single-family home featuring a wrap-around porch and unexpected privacy for an urban dwelling. Hybrid envisioned the house as a ship with a continuous deck around the perimeter, allowing large sliding glass doors off the living room, opening the home to views of Seattle and the mountains beyond. The house further engages the outdoors with a generous patio on the lower level and a rooftop deck to take in the distant views. During the design process, the design team realized that the sloped lot would allow for an ADU with a separate entrance and private exterior space. This design strategy led the team to develop the lower level as flexible as possible for potential future homeowners.

Sur un site escarpé qui aurait traditionnellement été considéré comme inconstructible, Hybrid a conçu, construit et développé la Hill House : une maison unifamiliale adaptable avec un porche enveloppant et une intimité inattendue pour une habitation urbaine. Hybrid a conçu la maison comme un bateau avec une terrasse continue sur le périmètre qui permet d'ouvrir de grandes portes coulissantes en verre, ouvrant la maison sur des vues de Seattle et des montagnes au-delà. La maison est encore plus intégrée à l'extérieur avec un patio généreux au niveau inférieur et une terrasse sur le toit pour profiter des vues. Au cours du processus de conception, l'équipe a réalisé que le terrain en pente permettrait la construction d'une maison unifamiliale avec une entrée séparée et un espace extérieur privé. Cette stratégie de conception a conduit l'équipe à aménager le niveau inférieur de la manière la plus flexible possible pour les futurs propriétaires potentiels.

Auf einem steilen Gelände, das traditionell als unbebaubar galt, entwarf, baute und entwickelte Hybrid das Hill House: ein anpassungsfähiges Einfamilienhaus mit einer umlaufenden Veranda und Privatsphäre, die für ein Stadthaus unerwartet ist. Hybrid entwarf das Haus wie ein Boot mit einem umlaufenden Deck, das es ermöglicht, große Glasschiebetüren zu öffnen und das Haus mit Blick auf Seattle und die dahinter liegenden Berge zu öffnen. Das Haus ist nach außen hin noch stärker integriert, mit einer Terrasse auf der unteren Ebene und einer Dachterrasse, um die Aussicht zu genießen. Während des Entwurfsprozesses erkannte das Team, dass das abschüssige Gelände den Bau eines Einfamilienhauses mit separatem Eingang und privatem Außenbereich ermöglichen würde. Diese Designstrategie veranlasste das Team, die flexible untere Ebene für potenzielle zukünftige Eigentümer auszustatten.

En un terreno escarpado que tradicionalmente se habría considerado inconstruible, Hybrid diseñó, construyó y desarrolló la Hill House: una casa unifamiliar adaptable con un porche envolvente y una privacidad inesperada para una vivienda urbana. Hybrid concibió la casa como un barco con una cubierta continua alrededor del perímetro que permite abrir grandes puertas correderas de cristal desde el salón, abriendo la casa a las vistas de Seattle y las montañas más allá. La casa se integra aún más en el exterior con un generoso patio en el nivel inferior y una terraza en la azotea para disfrutar de las vistas distantes. Durante el proceso de diseño, el equipo se dio cuenta de que la parcela inclinada permitiría la construcción de una vivienda unifamiliar con entrada independiente y espacio exterior privado. Esta estrategia de diseño llevó al equipo a desarrollar el nivel inferior de la forma más flexible posible para los futuros potenciales propietarios.

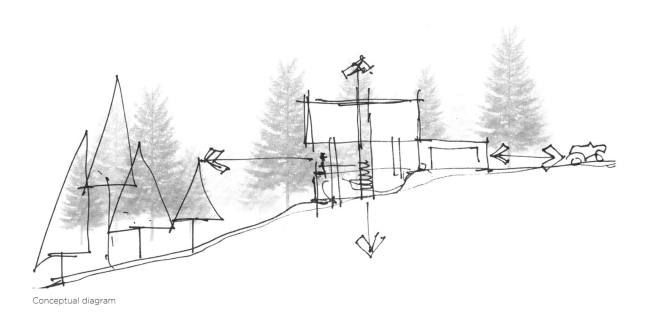

Conceptual diagram

Roof plan

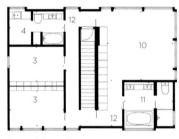

Second floor plan

Main floor plan

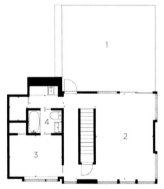

Ground floor plan

1. Patio
2. Family room
3. Bedroom
4. Bathroom
5. Deck
6. Living area
7. Kitchen
8. Dining area
9. Garage
10. Master bedroom
11. Master bathroom
12. Hall
13. Rooftop deck

STEEL STACKS

Seattle, Washington, United States // Lot area: 4,450 sq ft; building area: 6,428 sq ft (four units of 1,607 sq ft each)

Hybrid transformed an existing dilapidated one-story commercial structure into four spacious homes, providing flexible space, tall ceilings, abundant light, and a spacious, enclosed rooftop deck. Located in West Seattle, where affordable real estate is hard to come by, Steel Stacks maximizes density in a small footprint. With a striking Corten steel exterior, the homes remain deeply rooted in the commercially dense neighborhood. Hybrid takes pride in this adaptive reuse experience while contributing to historic preservation and urban densification. In this context, the ground floor flexible spaces allow the building to change over time as its occupants' needs evolve, addressing issues of density, displacement, and housing affordability.

Hybrid a transformé une structure commerciale délabreé existante d'un étage en quatre logements spacieux, offrant des espaces flexibles, de hauts plafonds, une lumière abondante et une grande terrasse fermée sur le toit. Situé à West Seattle, où il est difficile de trouver des biens immobiliers abordables, Steel Stacks maximise la densité dans un espace réduit. Avec un extérieur saisissant en acier corten, les maisons restent profondément ancrées dans le quartier commercial dense. Hybrid est fier de cette expérience de réutilisation adaptative, tout en contribuant à la préservation historique et à la densification urbaine. Dans ce contexte, les espaces flexibles du rez-de-chaussée permettent au bâtiment de se transformer au fil du temps en fonction de l'évolution des besoins de ses occupants, ce qui permet de résoudre les problèmes de densité, de déplacement et d'accessibilité au logement.

Hybrid verwandelte ein bestehendes verfallenes einstöckiges Gewerbegebäude in vier geräumige Häuser, die flexiblen Raum, hohe Decken, viel Licht und eine geräumige, geschlossene Dachterrasse bieten. Steel Stacks befindet sich in West Seattle, wo erschwingliche Immobilien schwer zu finden sind, und maximiert die Dichte auf kleinem Raum. Mit ihrem markanten Äußeren aus Cortenstahl sind die Häuser fest mit dem dichten Geschäftsviertel verwurzelt. Hybrid ist stolz auf dieses anpassungsfähige Wiederverwendungserlebnis und trägt gleichzeitig zur Denkmalpflege und städtischen Verdichtung bei. In diesem Zusammenhang ermöglichen es die flexiblen Räume im Erdgeschoss dem Gebäude, sich im Laufe der Zeit zu verändern, wenn sich die Bedürfnisse seiner Bewohner ändern, und so Fragen der Dichte, der Verdrängung und der Erschwinglichkeit von Wohnraum anzugehen.

Hybrid transformó una estructura comercial existente de un piso en ruinas en cuatro viviendas espaciosas, proporcionando espacios flexibles, techos altos, abundante luz y una amplia terraza cerrada en la azotea. Situado en West Seattle, donde es difícil encontrar vivienda asequible, Steel Stacks maximiza la densidad en un espacio reducido. Con un llamativo exterior de acero Corten, las viviendas se mantienen profundamente arraigadas en el denso barrio comercial. Hybrid se enorgullece de esta experiencia de reutilización adaptativa mientras contribuye a la preservación histórica y la densificación urbana. En este contexto, los espacios flexibles de la planta baja permiten que el edificio cambie con el tiempo a medida que evolucionan las necesidades de sus ocupantes, abordando cuestiones de densidad, desplazamiento y asequibilidad de la vivienda.

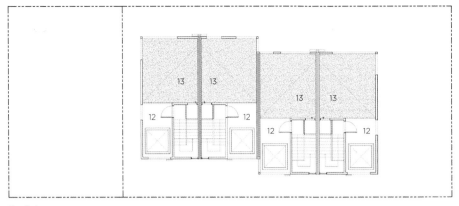

Roof plan

Third floor plan

Second floor plan

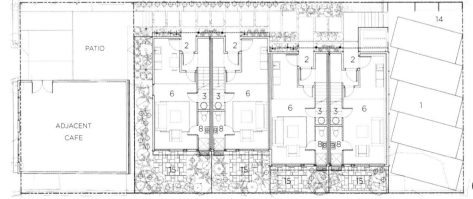

Ground floor plan

1. Parking area
2. Entry
3. Mechanical/storage
4. Courtyard
5. Deck
6. Flex space
7. Bedroom
8. Bathroom
9. Living/dining area
10. Kitchen
11. Powder room
12. Roof deck
13. Turf roof
14. Screened trash
15. Patio

THE LOOKOUT

Seattle, Washington, United States // Lot area: 1,434 sq ft; building area: 1,050 sq ft

Hybrid redeveloped a single-family lot into a set of three townhomes and The Lookout, a unique detached home elevated above the trees. This space is raised above an alley to provide parking. Its configuration inverts the typical building program, perching the living room on the top level amongst the trees and above the neighboring townhomes. Raising the unit above the alley provides visual and physical access through the ground floor. The development and site planning works around an existing large cherry tree between the front and back units. This tree provides shade, habitat, and visual interest while retaining the original homeowners' memories of the lot. The stark white siding provides an appealing contrast to the black townhomes on the site and the disjointed alley environment.

Hybrid a transformé une parcelle de terrain en un groupe de trois maisons de ville et en The Lookout, une maison unifamiliale unique surplombant les arbres. Cet espace est surélevé au-dessus d'une allée pour offrir un espace de stationnement. Sa configuration inverse le programme de construction typique, plaçant l'espace de vie au niveau supérieur, entre les arbres et au-dessus des maisons de ville voisines. L'élévation de l'unité au-dessus de la ruelle permet un accès visuel et physique par le rez-de-chaussée. L'aménagement et la planification du site s'articulent autour d'un grand cerisier situé entre les unités avant et arrière. Cet arbre fournit de l'ombre, un habitat et un intérêt visuel tout en préservant la mémoire des premiers propriétaires de la parcelle. Le bardage d'un blanc éclatant contraste avec les maisons noires du site et l'environnement de la ruelle.

Hybrid verwandelte ein Grundstück in eine Gruppe von drei Stadthäusern und The Lookout, ein einzigartiges Einfamilienhaus, das sich über die Bäume erhebt. Dieser Raum liegt erhöht über einer Gasse, um Parkmöglichkeiten zu schaffen. Seine Konfiguration kehrt das typische Bauprogramm um und platziert den Wohnbereich auf der oberen Ebene zwischen den Bäumen und über den benachbarten Stadthäusern. Die Höhe der Einheit über der Gasse ermöglicht einen visuellen und physischen Zugang durch das Erdgeschoss. Die Erschließung und Standortplanung ist um einen großen Kirschbaum zwischen den vorderen und hinteren Einheiten herum aufgebaut. Dieser Baum spendet Schatten, bietet Lebensraum und ist visuell interessant und bewahrt gleichzeitig die Erinnerung an die ursprünglichen Besitzer des Grundstücks. Die strahlend weiße Fassade steht im Kontrast zu den schwarzen Häusern auf dem Grundstück und der Alleenumgebung.

Hybrid transformó una parcela en un conjunto de tres viviendas adosadas y en The Lookout, una singular vivienda unifamiliar elevada sobre los árboles. Este espacio se eleva por encima de un callejón para proporcionar espacio de aparcamiento. Su configuración invierte el programa típico de construcción, situando el salón en el nivel superior entre los árboles y por encima de las casas adosadas vecinas. La elevación de la unidad por encima del callejón proporciona un acceso visual y físico a través de la planta baja. El desarrollo y la planificación del terreno se realizan en torno a un gran cerezo existente entre las unidades delanteras y traseras. Este árbol proporciona sombra, hábitat e interés visual, a la vez que conserva el recuerdo de los propietarios originales de la parcela. El revestimiento blanco y duro contrasta con las casas negras del solar y con el entorno del callejón.

Second floor plan

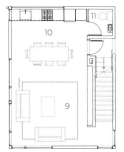

Third floor plan

Roof plan

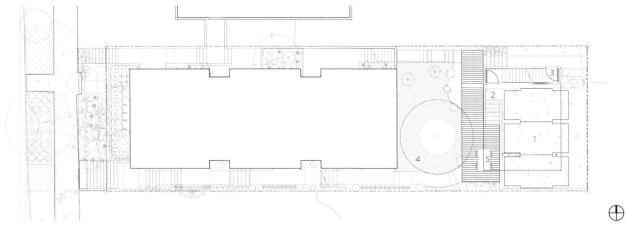

Ground floor plan

1. Parking area
2. Entry
3. Mechanical/storage
4. Courtyard
5. Deck
6. Flex space
7. Bedroom
8. Bathroom
9. Living/dining area
10. Kitchen
11. Powder room
12. Roof deck

GBL
Architects

STRATHCONA VILLAGE

Architecture Design Team: Daniel Eisenberg, Stu Lyon, Theresa Wong, Eric Stacey, Rob Forbes
Interior Designer: BYU Design
Developer: Wall Financial
Landscape Architect: PWL
Code consultant: Thorson Consulting
Structural Engineer: Glotman Simpson
Mechanical Engineer: NDY
Electrical Engineer: Nemetz (S/A) and Associates
Building Envelope: BC Building Science
Sustainability Consultant: Recollective
General Contractor: Wall Centre Construction
Photographers: © Ema Peter (exterior images), Krista Jahnke (interior images)

Awards:
- Strathcona Village was voted most Innovative Building Design and Best in Show at the Annual Urban Development Institute Awards.
- NAIOP Commercial Real Estate Awards 2020. Best Mixed Use Development.

SOMA ON CAMBIE

Architecture Design Team: Daniel Eisenberg, Jason Dong, Eric Schroeder

Interior Designer: i3 Design
Developer: SDAE
Landscape Architect: Topographics
Code consultant: Jensen Hugues
Structural Engineer: Glotman Simpson
Mechanical Engineer: Reinbold Engineering
Electrical Engineer: Nemetz (S/A) and Associates
Building Envelope: SC Engineering Ltd
Sustainability Consultant: Kane Consulting
General Contractor: Kindred Construction
Photographer: © Upper Left Photography

8X ON THE PARK

Architecture Design Team: Stu Lyon, Joey Stevens, Andrew Emmerson, Scott Restemeyer, Rod Forbes
Interior Designer: BYU Design
Developer: Brenhill
Landscape Architect: PFS Studio
Structural Enginner: Glotman Simpson
Mechanical Engineer: Integral Group
Electrical Engineer: Nemetz (S/A) & Associates
Building Envelope Consultant: Level 5 Consulting
Code Consultant: Protection Engineering
Geotechnical Engineer: GeoPacific Consultants
Sustainability Consultant: Kane Consulting
General Contractor: Ledcor Group
Photographers: © Ema Peter, Jesse Laver

Eric Schroeder Daniel Eisenberg Andrew Emmerson Amela Brudar Paul Goodwin Joey Stevens

GBL Architects is a Vancouver-based firm that started nearly 40 years ago, specializing in multi-family and social housing developments. Over the last few decades, they have grown to a staff of 75, servicing a clientele that includes both the private and public sector with wide-ranging projects from tightly constrained urban buildings to master-planned complexes. Through projects such as the LEED Platinum 2010 Olympic Athletes' Village in Vancouver and Canada's first Net Zero multi-family housing building, GBL established itself as a leader in sustainable building design. More recently, Strathcona Village and 8X on the Park have further cemented the firm's reputation for innovative design—one integrating traditionally incompatible uses and both developing unique architectural expressions that animate the communities they shape. Through this emphasis on sustainability and innovation, GBL continues to pioneer a creative design approach to increasingly complex and demanding developments.

GBL Architects ist ein in Vancouver ansässiges Büro, das vor fast 40 Jahren gegründet wurde und sich auf den Bau von Mehrfamilienhäusern und Sozialwohnungen spezialisiert hat. In den letzten Jahrzehnten ist das Unternehmen auf 75 Mitarbeiter angewachsen, die sowohl im privaten als auch im öffentlichen Sektor tätig sind, wobei die Projekte von eng begrenzten städtischen Gebäuden bis hin zu geplanten Komplexen reichen. Mit Projekten wie dem LEED-Platin-zertifizierten Olympischen Dorf der Athleten in Vancouver (2010) und Kanadas erstem Netto-Null-Mehrfamilienhaus hat sich GBL als führendes Unternehmen im Bereich der nachhaltigen Gebäudeplanung etabliert. In jüngerer Zeit haben Strathcona Village und 8X on the Park den Ruf des Unternehmens für innovatives Design weiter gefestigt – eines, das traditionell unvereinbare Nutzungen integriert und beide einzigartige architektonische Ausdrucksformen entwickelt, die die von ihnen geformten Gemeinschaften beleben. Durch diesen Schwerpunkt auf Nachhaltigkeit und Innovation leistet GBL weiterhin Pionierarbeit für einen kreativen Designansatz für immer komplexere und anspruchsvollere Entwicklungen.

GBL Architects est un cabinet basé à Vancouver qui a vu le jour il y a près de 40 ans et qui s'est spécialisé dans l'aménagement de logements multifamiliaux et sociaux. Au cours des dernières décennies, l'équipe s'est agrandie et compte aujourd'hui 75 personnes au service d'une clientèle qui comprend à la fois le secteur privé et le secteur public, avec des projets allant de bâtiments urbains aux contraintes strictes à des plans directeurs de complexes. Grâce à des projets tels que le Village olympique des athlètes de Vancouver, certifié LEED Platine en 2010, et le premier immeuble d'habitation multifamiliale à consommation nette zéro au Canada, GBL s'est imposé comme un chef de file de la conception de bâtiments durables. Plus récemment, Strathcona Village et 8X on the Park ont consolidé la réputation du cabinet en matière de conception innovante : l'un par l'intégration d'utilisations traditionnellement incompatibles et les deux par le développement d'expressions architecturales uniques qui animent les communautés qu'ils façonnent. En mettant l'accent sur la durabilité et l'innovation, GBL continue d'être le pionnier d'une approche de conception créative pour des développements de plus en plus complexes et exigeants.

GBL Architects es una empresa con sede en Vancouver que comenzó hace casi 40 años, especializándose en desarrollos de viviendas multifamiliares y sociales. En las últimas décadas, ha crecido hasta contar con una plantilla de 75 personas que atienden a una clientela que incluye tanto el sector privado como el público, con proyectos muy variados que van desde edificios urbanos con estrictas restricciones hasta planes maestros de complejos. A través de proyectos como la Villa Olímpica de los Atletas de 2010, con certificación LEED Platino, en Vancouver, y el primer edificio de viviendas multifamiliares de red cero de Canadá, GBL se estableció como líder en el diseño de edificios sostenibles. Más recientemente, Strathcona Village y 8X on the Park han cimentado aún más la reputación de la empresa en cuanto a diseño innovador: uno integrando usos tradicionalmente incompatibles y ambos desarrollando expresiones arquitectónicas únicas que animan a las comunidades a las que dan forma. Con este énfasis en la sostenibilidad y la innovación, GBL continúa siendo pionera en un enfoque de diseño creativo para desarrollos cada vez más complejos y exigentes.

STRATHCONA VILLAGE

Vancouver, British Columbia, Canada // Mixed use, market residential, non-market residential, office, industrial; 300,000 sq ft

Strathcona Village is located on the southern edge of the Port of Vancouver near the downtown core. The site, historically industrial, offers a building typology that increasingly lends to adaptation for residential use. The development is a sustainable community model, providing affordable housing while maintaining and generating light industry in the neighborhood. The building's mass is distributed across three residential towers atop a multilevel mixed-use podium. Taking cues from the neighboring infrastructure, the building volume is simple in stature while the dynamic façade is visually broken up by a loose rectangular grid, conceptually resembling stacked shipping containers mirroring the shapes and colours of the Port's ever-present railway containers and loading cranes.

Strathcona Village est situé à l'extrémité sud du port de Vancouver, à proximité du centre-ville. Ce site historiquement industriel offre une typologie de bâtiment qui se prête de plus en plus à une adaptation à un usage résidentiel. Le développement est un modèle de communauté durable, fournissant des logements abordables tout en maintenant et en générant une industrie légère dans le quartier. La masse du bâtiment est répartie en trois tours résidentielles de faible hauteur sur un podium à usage mixte à plusieurs niveaux. S'inspirant de l'infrastructure voisine, le volume du bâtiment est de taille simple tandis que la façade dynamique est visuellement interrompue par une grille rectangulaire lâche, ressemblant conceptuellement à des conteneurs d'expédition empilés reflétant les formes et les couleurs des conteneurs ferroviaires et des grues de chargement omniprésents du port.

Strathcona Village liegt am südlichen Ende des Hafens von Vancouver, nahe dem Stadtzentrum. Der historisch gewachsene Industriestandort bietet eine Gebäudetypologie, die sich zunehmend für eine Anpassung an die Wohnnutzung eignet. Die Entwicklung ist ein nachhaltiges Gemeindemodell, das erschwinglichen Wohnraum bietet und gleichzeitig die Leichtindustrie in der Nachbarschaft erhält und fördert. Die Gebäudemasse verteilt sich auf drei Wohntürme auf einem mehrstöckigen, gemischt genutzten Podium. Inspiriert von der nahe gelegenen Infrastruktur, hat das Gebäudevolumen eine einfache Größe, während die dynamische Fassade visuell durch ein lockeres rechteckiges Gitter unterbrochen wird, das konzeptionell an gestapelte Schiffscontainer erinnert und die Formen und Farben von Bahncontainern und allgegenwärtigen Ladekränen des Hafens widerspiegelt.

Strathcona Village está situado en el extremo sur del puerto de Vancouver, cerca del centro de la ciudad. El emplazamiento, históricamente industrial, ofrece una tipología de edificios que se presta cada vez más a la adaptación al uso residencial. La urbanización es un modelo de comunidad sostenible, que proporciona viviendas asequibles al tiempo que mantiene y genera una industria ligera en el barrio. La masa del edificio se distribuye en tres torres residenciales sobre un podio de uso mixto de varios niveles. Tomando como referencia la infraestructura de la zona, el volumen del edificio es de estatura simple, mientras que la fachada dinámica está dividida visualmente por una cuadrícula rectangular no rígida, que se asemeja conceptualmente a contenedores apilados que reflejan las formas y colores de los siempre presentes contenedores ferroviarios y grúas de carga del puerto.

Seventh floor plan

EAST HASTINGS STREET

LANE

RAYMUR AVE

1. Market housing
2. Amenity room
3. Common roof patio
4. Social housing

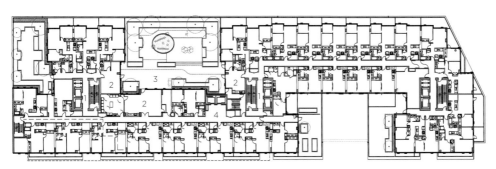

Second floor plan

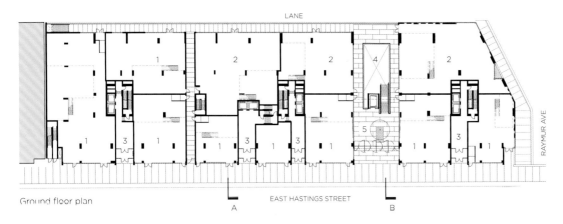

Ground floor plan

LANE

EAST HASTINGS STREET

RAYMUR AVE

1. Production, distribution, and repair (PDR)
2. Office
3. Lobby
4. Loading below
5. Plaza

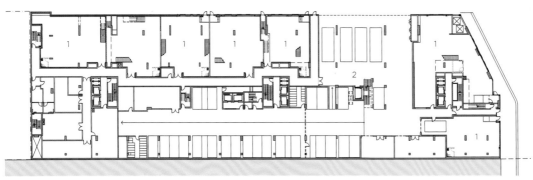

Parking level 2 plan

1. Production, distribution, and repair (PDR)
2. Loading area

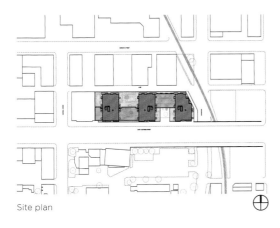

Site plan

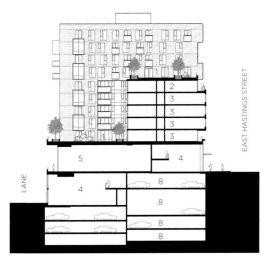

Section A-A

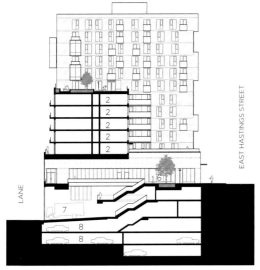

Section B-B

EAST HASTINGS STREET

LANE

1. Common roof patio
2. Market housing
3. Social housing
4. Production, distribution, and repair (PDR)
5. Office
6. Plaza
7. Loading
8. Parking

SOMA ON CAMBIE

Vancouver, British Columbia, Canada // 32-unit residential building; 28,000 sq ft

This six-story multifamily development aligns with the City of Vancouver's overarching plan for higher-density land use developments, contributing to a more sustainable and livable neighborhood along Cambie Street, one of the city's main transit corridors. While urban design guidelines typically prescribe multiple step backs on all sides, the site's size and shape allowed the building's mass to differ from its neighbors. SOMA celebrates its stereotomic nature at the southeast corner, above the public entrance, where a dramatic six-story brick elevation is expressed without a horizontal break. The other elevations follow the traditional step-backs above the third and fourth floor to reduce the building's perceived height. The extensive use of masonry cladding reinforces the monolithic expression of the building.

Ce complexe multifamilial de six étages est conforme au plan directeur de la ville de Vancouver pour l'aménagement de terrains à plus forte densité, contribuant ainsi à la création d'un quartier plus durable et plus vivable le long de Cambie Street, l'un des principaux couloirs de transport en commun de la ville. Bien que les lignes directrices en matière de design urbain prescrivent généralement plusieurs marches en arrière sur tous les côtés, la taille et la forme du site ont permis au bâtiment de se démarquer de ses voisins. SOMA célèbre sa nature stéréotomique à l'angle sud-est, au-dessus de l'entrée publique, où une spectaculaire élévation en brique de six étages s'exprime sans rupture horizontale. Les autres élévations suivent les marches traditionnelles au-dessus des troisième et quatrième étages afin de réduire la hauteur perçue du bâtiment. L'utilisation intensive du bardage en maçonnerie renforce l'expression monolithique du bâtiment.

Dieser sechsstöckige Mehrfamilienhauskomplex entspricht dem Masterplan der Stadt Vancouver für eine höhere Bebauungsdichte und trägt zu einem nachhaltigeren und lebenswerteren Viertel entlang der Cambie Street bei, einem der wichtigsten Verkehrskorridore der Stadt. Obwohl städtebauliche Richtlinien in der Regel vorschreiben, dass das Gebäude an allen Seiten mehrere Stufen zurücktreten muss, konnte es sich aufgrund der Größe und Form des Grundstücks von seinen Nachbarn abheben. Das SOMA zelebriert seine stereotomische Natur an der südöstlichen Ecke, über dem öffentlichen Eingang, wo eine dramatische sechsstöckige Backsteinfassade ohne horizontale Unterbrechung zum Ausdruck kommt. Die anderen Ansichten folgen den traditionellen Stufen über dem dritten und vierten Stockwerk, um die wahrgenommene Höhe des Gebäudes zu verringern. Die umfangreiche Verwendung von Mauerwerksverkleidungen verstärkt den monolithischen Ausdruck des Gebäudes.

Este complejo multifamiliar de seis plantas se ajusta al plan general de la ciudad de Vancouver para la construcción de terrenos de mayor densidad, contribuyendo a un barrio más sostenible y habitable a lo largo de la calle Cambie, uno de los principales corredores de tránsito de la ciudad. Aunque las directrices de diseño urbano suelen prescribir varios retranqueos en todos los lados, el tamaño y la forma del solar permitieron que el edificio se diferenciara de la de sus vecinos. SOMA celebra su naturaleza estereotómica en la esquina sureste, sobre la entrada pública, donde un espectacular alzado de ladrillo de seis pisos se expresa sin una ruptura horizontal. Las demás elevaciones siguen los tradicionales escalones por encima de la tercera y cuarta planta para reducir la altura percibida del edificio. El amplio uso de revestimientos de mampostería refuerza la expresión monolítica del edificio.

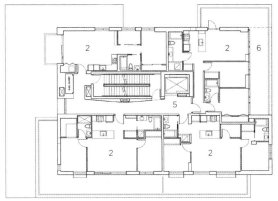

Fifth floor plan

Third floor plan

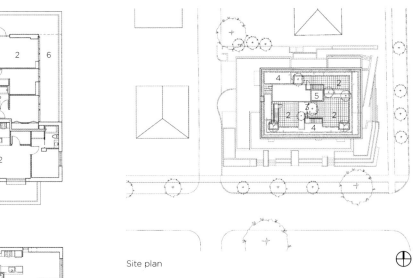

Site plan

1. Mechanical rooftop
2. Private patio
3. Access to patio
4. Green roof
5. Elevator overrun

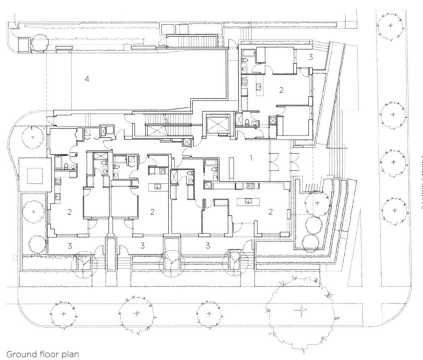

CAMBIE STREET

Ground floor plan

1. Entry lobby   4. Parking ramp
2. Apartment   5. Hallway
3. Patio   6. Private patio

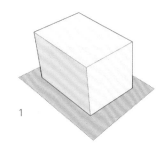

1

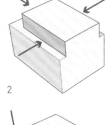

2

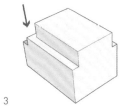

3

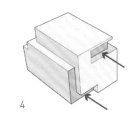

4

Form of development diagram

8X ON THE PARK

Vancouver, British Columbia, Canada // Mixed use, market residential, rental residential, retail, day care; 365,000 sq ft

Amongst the ubiquitous residential towers of downtown Vancouver, 8X On The Park stands apart for its nuanced, contextual urban gestures and rigorous commitment to detail. GBL and Brenhill deftly guided the project through a complex, decade-long planning and design process culminating in a 35-story mixed-use tower with a varied and striking presence on the Vancouver skyline. GBL approached the design with a holistic urban and architectural vision that incorporates high-quality design and materials reinforced with high-performance, sustainable initiatives. Key design considerations for height, form, articulation, and tower programming are informed by a network of visible and invisible contextual variables, resulting in a building that is highly responsive to its urban setting.

Parmi les tours résidentielles omniprésentes du centre-ville de Vancouver, 8X On The Park se distingue par ses gestes urbains nuancés et contextuels et son engagement rigoureux envers les détails. GBL et Brenhill ont habilement guidé le projet tout au long d'un processus complexe de planification et de conception qui s'est étalé sur une décennie et qui a abouti à la construction d'une tour à usage mixte de 35 étages, dont la présence dans l'horizon de Vancouver est variée et frappante. GBL a abordé la conception avec une vision urbaine et architecturale holistique qui intègre une conception et des matériaux de haute qualité renforcés par des initiatives durables à haute performance. Les principales considérations de conception relatives à la hauteur, à la forme, à l'articulation et à la programmation de la tour reposent sur un réseau de variables contextuelles visibles et invisibles, ce qui se traduit par un bâtiment très réactif à son environnement urbain.

Unter den allgegenwärtigen Wohntürmen in Downtown Vancouver sticht 8X On The Park durch seine nuancierten, kontextbezogenen urbanen Gesten und sein rigoroses Engagement für Details hervor. GBL und Brenhill leitete das Projekt geschickt durch einen komplexen, jahrzehntelangen Planungs- und Entwurfsprozess, an dessen Ende ein 35-stöckiges, gemischt genutztes Hochhaus stand, das in der Skyline von Vancouver eine abwechslungsreiche und markante Präsenz zeigt. GBL näherte sich dem Design mit einer ganzheitlichen urbanen und architektonischen Vision, die hochwertiges Design und Materialien beinhaltet, die durch leistungsstarke, nachhaltige Initiativen verstärkt werden. Die wichtigsten gestalterischen Überlegungen zur Höhe, Form, Gliederung und Programmierung des Turms basieren auf einem Netz von sichtbaren und unsichtbaren Kontextvariablen, was zu einem Gebäude führt, das in hohem Maße auf seine städtische Umgebung reagiert.

Entre las omnipresentes torres residenciales del centro de Vancouver, 8X On The Park destaca por sus gestos urbanos matizados y contextuales y por su riguroso compromiso con los detalles. GBL y Brenhill guiaron hábilmente el proyecto a través de un complejo proceso de planificación y diseño de una década de duración que ha culminado en una torre de uso mixto de 35 plantas con una presencia variada y llamativa en el perfil de Vancouver. GBL abordó el diseño con una visión urbana y arquitectónica integral que incorpora un diseño y unos materiales de alta calidad reforzados con iniciativas sostenibles de alto rendimiento. Las consideraciones clave del diseño en cuanto a la altura, la forma, la articulación y la programación de la torre se basan en una red de variables contextuales visibles e invisibles, lo que da como resultado un edificio que responde en gran medida a su entorno urbano.

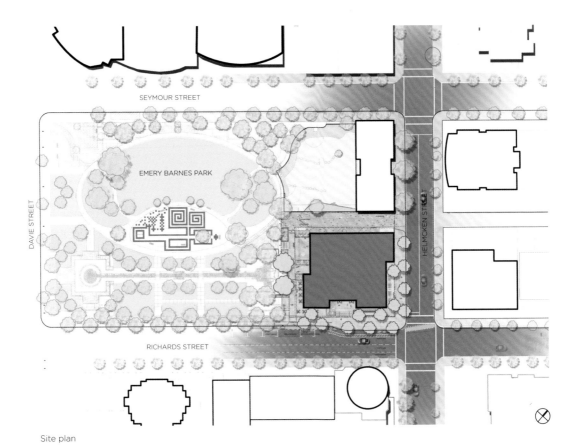

Site plan

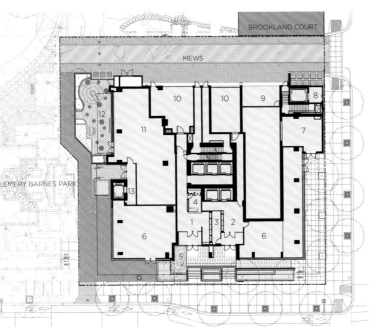

Ground floor plan

1. Market lobby
2. Rental lobby
3. Mail room
4. Concierge desk
5. Public art and water feature
6. Commercial space
7. Generator room
8. Bicycle elevator
9. Ramp to underground parking
10. Loading bay
11. Child care
12. Child care yard
13. Commercial elevator

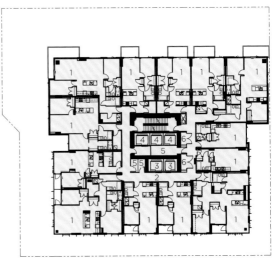

Podium level floor plan

1. Rental apartment
2. Corridor
3. Rental elevators (L2-L11)
4. Market elevators (L12-L34)
5. Storage
6. Electrical and mechanical space

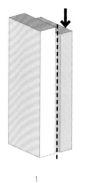
1

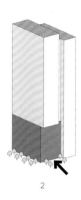
2

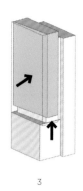
3

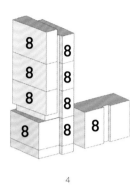
4

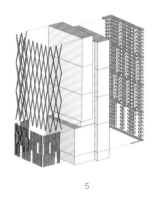
5

Concept diagram

1. The building mass is split in half to reduce the bulk. The half closest to the park is lowered two storeys in height, reducing shadow impact and allowing for a rooftop park.
2. The base is setback twelve feet from Helmcken Street to allow for a public bike share and two rows of street trees.
3. The upper tower along Richards Street is set

back and sculpted to reduce the tower size and open up views. Separating the tower above from the base allows a second rooftop park to overlook Richards Street.
4. Each building form is modulated in intervals of eight storeys to maintain a consistent scale to the neighboring eight-storey heritage Brookland Court building.

5. The park tower is wrapped in balconies to open up to the park. The urban base incorporates vertical fins for shading and a solid texture. The Yaletown Tower responds to the sun and skyline with an X fin pattern.

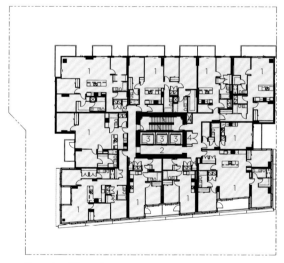

Tower level floor plan

1. Market apartment
2. Corridor
3. Market elevators (L12-L34)
4. Electrical and mechanical space

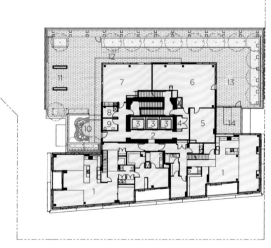

Level 34 – Penthouse floor plan

1. Penthouse apartment
2. Corridor
3. Market elevators (L12-L34)
4. Electrical and mechanical space
5. Yoga room
6. Fitness center
7. Sky lounge
8. Janitor's closet
9. Washroom
10. Children's play area
11. Outdoor lounge and fireplace
12. Outdoor kitchen
13. Dining terrace
14. Mechanical space

O.blok

THE FOUR SQUARE

Architecture Design team:
Ivan Kostic, Brian Nguy, Benjamen Prager
Illustrations:
© O.blok

Ivan Kostic   Brian Nguy   Benjamen Prager

We have been talking about it for almost a decade, finally establishing 0.blok in Seattle in 2021 as a collaborative design, strategy, and architecture collective. Over these years, we have kept coming back to the idea of democratizing our work and the practice of architecture and design. We understand this as a radical act of connecting with those who are typically underrepresented and their social, economic, and environmental ecosystem. Design and architecture do not exist in a bubble; they are not neutral and therefore cannot pick and choose what issues to take on. They are fields that literally imagine, build, and in most cases, perpetuate our collective reality. We must be all in, or not at all. Given that we have just started our practice, it feels strange to make grand statements about one's work or even our aspirations. On the other hand, we can also look at it as a way to force our hand, make our thoughts and intentions public and keep us accountable. Time will tell.

Wir hatten fast ein Jahrzehnt lang darüber gesprochen und gründeten schließlich 2021 0.blok in Seattle als kollaboratives Design-, Strategie- und Architekturkollektiv. Im Laufe der Jahre sind wir immer wieder auf die Idee zurückgekommen, unsere Arbeit und die Praxis von Architektur und Design zu demokratisieren. Wir verstehen dies als einen radikalen Akt der Verbundenheit mit denen, die unterrepräsentiert sind, und ihrem sozialen, wirtschaftlichen und ökologischen Ökosystem. Design und Architektur existieren nicht in einer Seifenblase, sie sind nicht neutral und können sich daher nicht aussuchen, welche Themen sie behandeln. Sie sind Bereiche, die unsere kollektive Realität buchstäblich erfinden, konstruieren und in den meisten Fällen aufrechterhalten. Man muss ganz dabei sein, oder gar nicht. Da wir noch ganz am Anfang stehen, ist es seltsam, große Aussagen über unsere Arbeit oder gar unsere Ziele zu machen. Andererseits können wir es auch als eine Möglichkeit sehen, unsere Gedanken und Absichten zu erzwingen und zu veröffentlichen und uns selbst zur Verantwortung zu ziehen. Die Zeit wird es zeigen.

Nous en parlions depuis près de dix ans et avons finalement créé 0.blok à Seattle en 2021 en tant que collectif de conception, de stratégie et d'architecture collaborative. Au fil des ans, nous sommes revenus sur l'idée de démocratiser notre travail et la pratique de l'architecture et du design. Nous comprenons cela comme un acte radical de connexion avec ceux qui sont présentés et leur écosystème social, économique et environnemental. Le design et l'architecture n'existent pas dans une bulle, ils ne sont pas neutres et ne peuvent donc pas choisir les questions à traiter. Ce sont des domaines qui imaginent, construisent et, dans la plupart des cas, perpétuent littéralement notre réalité collective. Il faut être dans tout ça, ou pas du tout. Étant donné que nous commençons à peine, il est étrange de faire de grandes déclarations sur notre travail ou même nos aspirations. D'autre part, nous pouvons également y voir un moyen de forcer et de rendre publiques nos pensées et nos intentions et de nous tenir responsables. Le temps nous le dira.

Llevábamos casi una década hablando de ello, y finalmente establecimos 0.blok en Seattle en 2021 como un colectivo de diseño, estrategia y arquitectura colaborativos. A lo largo de estos años, hemos vuelto a la idea de democratizar nuestro trabajo y la práctica de la arquitectura y el diseño. Entendemos esto como un acto radical de conexión con aquellos que están infra presentados y su ecosistema social, económico y medioambiental. El diseño y la arquitectura no existen en una burbuja, no son neutrales y, por lo tanto, no pueden elegir qué temas abordar. Son campos que literalmente imaginan, construyen y, en la mayoría de los casos, perpetúan nuestra realidad colectiva. Hay que estar en todo, o no estar. Dado que acabamos de empezar, resulta extraño hacer grandes declaraciones sobre nuestro trabajo o incluso nuestras aspiraciones. Por otro lado, también podemos verlo como una forma de forzar y hacer públicos nuestros pensamientos e intenciones y de hacernos responsables. El tiempo lo dirá.

THE FOUR SQUARE

Seattle, Washington, United States // Building area: Six 12-feet-square modules

The Four Square is a response to the city of Seattle's competition for a series of standardized backyard cottage (DADUs) designs. This is part of the local government's effort to combat the severe housing shortage the region is experiencing. In order to tackle such an abstract problem, where site, orientation, vegetation, etc. are unknown, we propose a strategy and a process, a further abstraction. Starting with a 12-foot square, a purposefully non-directional geometry, we develop six programmatic modules, which can be combined and configured to suit the particular characteristics of a site. Two modules form a studio, three a small one-bedroom, and four the Seattle Four Square. The massing and materiality of the house are purposefully playful.

Le Four Square est une réponse au concours lancé par la ville de Seattle pour une série de modèles standardisés de cottages d'arrière-cour (DADU). Cette mesure s'inscrit dans le cadre des efforts déployés par le gouvernement local pour lutter contre la grave pénurie de logements dans la région. Pour aborder un problème aussi abstrait, où la localisation, l'orientation, la végétation, etc. sont inconnues, nous proposons une stratégie et un processus, une abstraction supplémentaire. À partir d'un carré de 3 mètres de côté, une géométrie intentionnellement non directionnelle, nous avons développé six modules programmatiques, qui peuvent être combinés et configurés pour s'adapter aux caractéristiques particulières d'un site. Deux modules forment un studio, trois un petit dortoir et quatre le Seattle Four Square. La masse et la matérialité de la maison sont intentionnellement ludiques.

Der Four Square ist eine Antwort auf den von der Stadt Seattle ausgeschriebenen Wettbewerb für eine Reihe standardisierter Entwürfe für Hinterhofhäuser (DADU). Dies ist Teil der Bemühungen der lokalen Regierung, die große Wohnungsknappheit in der Region zu bekämpfen. Um ein solch abstraktes Problem anzugehen, bei dem Standort, Orientierung, Vegetation usw. unbekannt sind, schlagen wir eine Strategie und ein Verfahren vor, eine weitere Abstraktion. Ausgehend von einem 3-m-Quadrat, einer absichtlich ungerichteten Geometrie, haben wir sechs programmatische Module entwickelt, die je nach den besonderen Merkmalen eines Standorts kombiniert und konfiguriert werden können. Zwei Module bilden ein Studio, drei einen kleinen Schlafsaal und vier den Seattle Four Square. Die Masse und die Materialität des Hauses sind absichtlich spielerisch.

The Four Square es una respuesta al concurso de la ciudad de Seattle para una serie de diseños estandarizados de cabañas construidas en los patios traseros (DADU). Esto forma parte del esfuerzo del gobierno local por combatir la grave escasez de viviendas que sufre la región. Para abordar un problema tan abstracto, en el que se desconoce el emplazamiento, la orientación, la vegetación, etc., proponemos una estrategia y un proceso, una abstracción más. Partiendo de un cuadrado de 3 metros, una geometría intencionadamente no direccional, desarrollamos seis módulos programáticos, que pueden combinarse y configurarse para adaptarse a las características particulares de un emplazamiento. Dos módulos forman un estudio, tres un pequeño dormitorio y cuatro el Seattle Four Square. La masa y la materialidad de la casa son intencionadamente lúdicas.

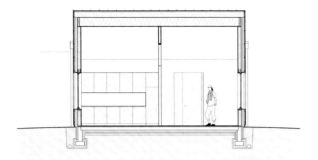

North-south section

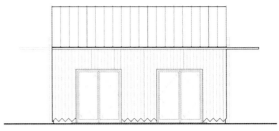

North elevation

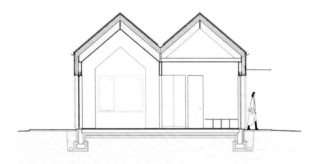

East-west section

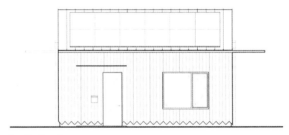

South elevation

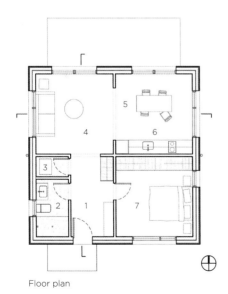

Floor plan

1. Entry
2. Bathroom
3. Laundry room
4. Living area
5. Dining area
6. Kitchen
7. Bedroom

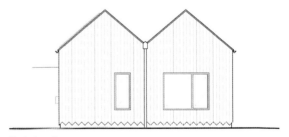

East elevation

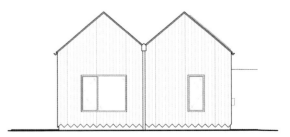

West elevation

Programmatic module diagram